KW-480-346

Sonya Mills is a former architectural
journalist who now freelances,
specialising in do-it-yourself topics,
mainly for women's magazines. She has
also edited a craft book, *The Book of
Presents*, and supplied the original
material for most of the d-i-y section in
Shirley Conran's *Superwoman 2*.

To date she has renovated three
completely different houses – a Victorian
terrace, a Tudor-style former almshouse
and a 1930's semi – and is now starting
on yet another, a 150-year-old
Oxfordshire cottage.

Handywoman

Sonya Mills

CORGI BOOKS

HANDYWOMAN

A CORGI BOOK 0 552 12543 1

First publication in Great Britain

PRINTING HISTORY
Corgi edition published 1985

Copyright © Sonya Mills 1985

Illustrations by Industrial Art Studio

This book is set in 10/11 Cheltenham

Corgi Books are published by Transworld Publishers Ltd.,
Century House, 61–63 Uxbridge Road, Ealing,
London W5 5SA, in Australia by Transworld Publishers
(Aust.) Pty. Ltd., 26 Harley Crescent, Condell Park,
NSW 2200, and in New Zealand by Transworld Publishers
(N.Z.) Ltd., Cnr. Moselle and Waipareira Avenues,
Henderson, Auckland.

Made and printed in Great Britain by
The Guernsey Press Co. Ltd,
Guernsey, Channel Islands.

Contents

Acknowledgements

My thanks to all the people and organisations who helped me to write this book, especially Stanley Tools, Jacqueline Wright, ICI Dulux, Jack Widgery, Crown Decorative Products, Tony Byers, Ernest Roth, FIDOR (Fibre Building Board Organisation), RoSPA (The Royal Society for the Prevention of Accidents), Copydex Ltd. and Arthur Cooper.

Introduction

The first shelf I ever put up fell down the next day, tearing large holes in the landlady's plaster and breaking all my best glasses.

Since then I've learned a lot, put up dozens of shelves that didn't fall down, decorated more rooms than I care to remember, and gone on to ambitious things like installing a new wash-basin, building a Welsh dresser, tiling a shower unit and wiring in light fittings.

I did all these jobs because I needed to — not because I'm crazy about do-it-yourself. I'd rather sit and read any day! And I know from my experience on women's magazines that there are thousands of women in the same position. They are girls sharing flats, married women whose husbands are too busy to do all the jobs around the house that they would like to; the many, many women, most of them divorced or separated, who are bringing up families alone; and widows with no one to call on for even the simplest repair.

A great many women are already keen do-it-yourselfers, particularly in the decorating field. Indeed, in the north of England decorating is considered woman's work. But they don't stop at decorating — lots of women can tackle routine maintenance and repair jobs like mending the window pane the kids' football broke, fitting new draught excluders or fixing dripping taps. And I know of plenty more who are much more ambitious, and have gone on to greater things like rewiring the house and installing their own central heating!

For each of these there are probably ten more who would like to tackle such jobs, but are inhibited. There's still a vague feeling around that do-it-yourself, particularly woodwork, is terribly difficult and takes enormous strength. It's all nonsense! All you need to make a start is a little basic knowledge. My shelf fell down simply because the screws fixing it to the wall were too short; once I discovered that I was away.

As for physical strength . . . it rarely comes into it. What you need much, much more is patience, which most women have more of than men. If you type, you'll have strong fingers anyway; you may find yourself a bit weak in the wrists and arms to begin with, but using them will soon develop a few muscles — nothing that shows. On top of patience you need determination not to be beaten. I have on occasion had jobs that drove me to tears of frustration, but I always found that a break for tea, a fresh approach or perhaps a different tool, eventually solved the problem.

Having the right tools is half the battle. Just as in sewing you wouldn't get far without needle and thread, pins and the like, so in do-it-yourself you must have a basic tool kit.

The secret of success is to start modestly and build up from there. If you're decorating, don't begin in the living room with an expensive hand-printed wallpaper — try out something cheap in the childrens' bedroom. If it's woodwork, practice on some scrap wood and then put up a few shelves before you start getting ideas about building your own furniture.

And remember, you've got one big advantage over the professional: you don't mind how long it takes to get the job done; within reason, of course! That's another thing you'll pick up as you go along — how to steer a middle course between impossible perfectionism and slap-dashery.

This book is designed to show you how to tackle the basic tasks that crop up in most homes at some time or another. I've done nearly all of them myself, and if I can do them I'm sure you can, given a little practice. And each one will bring you a threefold reward: money saved on paying someone else (if you can find anyone!); the pleasure of having the broken article mended or the shabby room transformed; and the satisfaction of saying, 'I did it all myself'.

Handywoman

1 Choosing and using tools

If you are starting from scratch and buying your own tools it pays to buy good ones. They are excellent value for money and should last a lifetime. But don't make the mistake of buying expensive, gimmicky things. What you need are the basic hand tools that craftsmen have been using for generations.

Go to a proper tool shop with a big selection, not the hardware shop round the corner. Make sure you know beforehand what types you want. Don't rely on advice from behind the counter. I did this when I bought my first tools and came out with a tenon saw — which caused me end-less trouble as I tried to use it for general-purpose cutting, and it's meant for fine joinery work — and a tiny tack hammer, very ladylike but far too light to knock in any serious-sized nails.

Don't buy a kit of tools. It's bound to have things in it that you will never use, some you will not want for ages. Also a kit is an expensive way of buying tools as, at the very least, you are paying extra for the con-tainer. Also avoid Taiwanese counterfeits of well-known British makes. You should not find these in a good tool shop, but they turn up regularly in discount stores and markets. Such tools are not only poor value as they don't last, but can be dangerous — a hammer badly made from poor-quality steel can fly apart in use.

If you are using someone else's tools remember that you'll have to take ten times better care of them than you would of your own. Bending a screwdriver by opening paint tins with it ruins good-neighbour relations, while putting nicks in a husband's chisel could lead to divorce.

STARTER KIT

To tackle the jobs described in this book you will need a set of at least twelve hand tools (not counting those needed for decorating). Buying this little lot is going to cost over £50. If this seems expensive just stop and think how quickly you could spend a lot more than that if you had to pay tradesmen to do the simple jobs that these tools will enable you to do yourself. Also you probably won't go out and splurge £50 all at once.

1

Most people acquire tools gradually, as and when they need them, which eases the pain.

If you don't have a single tool to your name and are about to move into your first own-home, be it bedsitter, flat or house, I suggest you start off with a steel tape, two screwdrivers, a hammer, Stanley knife, bradawl and mini hacksaw. These should cope with most of the odd jobs involved in getting settled in: measuring up for floor coverings and curtains, wiring up plugs, putting up curtain rails, removing old tacks and nails from floor boards, cutting floor coverings, hanging pictures and mirrors etc.

You may think a steel tape is a luxury to start off with, but it is the foundation of your tool kit because practically every job involves some measuring. A dressmaker's tape will do for measuring up for curtains, but little else. It is too short to tackle floor areas conveniently, and far too inaccurate for woodwork. A steel tape is much more finely calibrated, and has a hook on the end so that you can measure long pieces of wood single-handed. The cheapest ones have round cases, and are fine for general measuring — get one 3 or 3.5 metres long rather than only 2 metres. They are, however, not so good for taking inside measurements, as when putting shelves in alcoves. To get an inside measurement with a steel tape you have to add the diameter of the case on to the measurement you can read, and it is very difficult to do this accurately with a round case. A better-quality tape has a square-sided case making this much easier. It should also feature what's called a true zero hook — instead of being fixed, the end hook moves to compensate for its own thickness and to ensure that both inside and outside measurements are accurate. Even more expensive tapes offer additional refinements such as a lock to fix the tape at the measurement required (very useful when working in dark corners or inside built-in cupboards) and powered return — the tape zips back into the case under its own steam after use. All DIY tapes are marked in both metric and imperial.

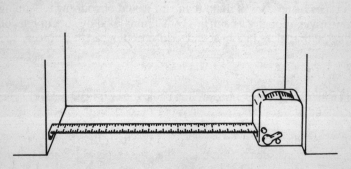

A cheap 3-metre tape will do for your starter kit, but for accuracy and ease of working it's worth getting something a little better. The one I use is a Fisco Uni-vision tape, which has yet another feature: a window in the top through which you can read off an inside measurement automatically. This was given to me after I had ruined a vast, expensive piece of mahogany-veneered chipboard shelving meant for a deep alcove by forgetting, not for the first time, to allow for the width of the tape when I measured up and cut it.

Your first screwdrivers should be a titchy one for electrical work and a medium-length one with a 6mm tip for putting in, tightening and removing average-sized slotted screws. A basic electrical screwdriver has a small tip, transparent plastic handle and is very cheap; refinements are ones with insulated handles and incorporating a wire-stripping tool. Alternatively you could buy a wallet containing a plastic handle and five or so screwdriver blades of assorted sizes and types. This is a cheap way of getting a lot of different blades, but personally I find it very irritating having to chop and change. Also, if buying a proper screwdriver you can get a very superior kind with a ratchet handle rather than plain wood or plastic. The ordinary ones have to be turned full circle to drive a screw, so that you must keep changing your grip. With the ratchet type, by flipping the ratchet knob up or down you only have to make half turns, and no change of grip is needed. This makes them much quicker and easier to use; but of course they are a bit more expensive. (Do not confuse ratchet screwdrivers with *spiral* ratchet screwdrivers, also known as Yankees. These are pump-action drivers designed for tradesmen putting in maybe hundreds of screws in a day, and are very expensive, right out of our league.)

The hammer needs careful choice. There are three basic types, and it doesn't matter much which you get. What does matter is the weight of the head. You want one light enough to swing easily, but heavy enough to knock in large nails, say when refixing loose floorboards; a 400g one is about right. All three types have metal heads, with one end designed for striking nails. It's what happens at the other end that differs. The claw hammer has a large prong for pulling out nails. The Warrington or cross pein has a tapered end for starting small nails and working in confined spaces. The ball pein or engineer's hammer has a round end for metal beating and riveting. For light woodwork and general use a Warrington is the most suitable; a claw is really a builder's hammer.

The Stanley knife is a very versatile tool, essential for all cutting jobs. It consists of a metal handle made in two halves which screw together to hold basic cutting blades, and a range of specially shaped blades for such things as cutting plastic laminate, as well as small saw blades for cutting wood and metal. A guard is supplied to shield the blade when not in use; or you can buy a version with a retractable blade.

The last two starter kit tools are mercifully cheap, but no less useful for that. The mini hacksaw is primarily for cutting curtain rails and any other metal (cutting metal with an ordinary wood saw ruins it instantly). Or you could buy a metal sawing blade for your Stanley knife. The bradawl, which is just a sharp metal point set in a handle, is for making pilot holes in wood in order to screw on things like hooks and door handles, curtain rail brackets and screw eyes for expanding curtain wire.

COMPLETE BASIC KIT

This is a misnomer as no tool kit is *ever* complete. However many tools you have you can always do with more! But the tools described so far are only about half what you need for general DIY work. For a start, you don't yet have a woodworking saw. Definitely the best type to get first is a small all-purpose panel saw with a replaceable blade. Use it for cutting wood, chipboard, plywood, hardboard and even metal. There are many other different types of saw, but whether or not you will need them depends on the type of work you get involved in, as they are all more specialised, (see woodwork chapter).

Next you need a means of drilling holes, so that you can put screws into pieces of wood to join them together, and into walls to hang things up, whether it be a modest plate rack or utility shelf, or a wall-to-wall display unit. The basic tool is a hand drill, also called a wheelbrace because it is worked by turning a wheel on the side, just like an egg beater. This holds metal drill bits, often confusingly referred to simply as drills, which make holes ranging in size from 1.5 to 6.5mm. This is one occasion where it is best to buy a set — you will need a selection of sizes in order to put in different-sized screws, and also single drills are easily mislaid or broken. A small set of seven high-speed twist drills comes in a plastic case, will drill metal as well as wood and is adequate for most DIY jobs. In addition get a countersinker, a fluted, coneshaped bit for making a recess for countersunk screw heads to sit in; and a masonry bit for drilling into walls. I find that a 6mm No. 12 size is all I need. But if your walls are very hard you will have to use it in a power drill (see page 15).

A steel tape is not sufficient for measuring a piece of wood, as it cannot guarantee that a cutting line marked across it is at a perfect right angle to the sides. To mark the line you use another tool. The simple traditional one is a try-square, a rectangular piece of steel set at right angles to a rectangular handle. But I prefer the more sophisticated combination or engineer's square because it does so many other jobs as well. In this the plain steel blade of the try-square becomes a calibrated foot rule, and the

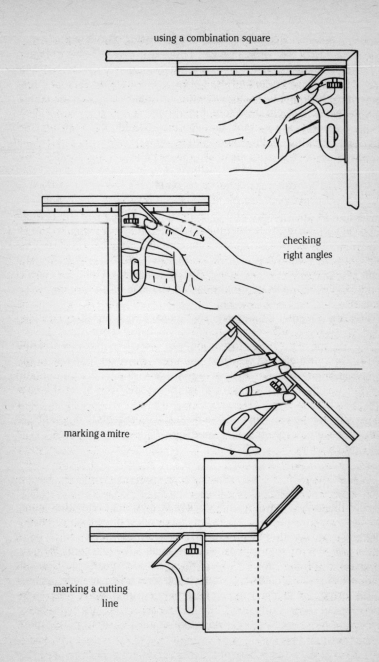

using a combination square

checking
right angles

marking a mitre

marking a cutting
line

5

handle part contains a spirit level for checking that shelves etc. are truly horizontal. This type of square can be used to mark both inside and outside right angles, also mitres (45° angles), and is also a marking gauge, depth gauge, ruler and straight edge. It is actually cheaper than a try-square of comparable size, and with a try-square you will still need a spirit level and a steel rule at sometime, so it is a very good buy indeed.

Other general-purpose tools that you are bound to need are a pair of pliers for gripping, pulling and cutting wire; pincers for pulling out unwanted or wrongly driven nails (a claw hammer only tackles nails with heads); a tack lifter to get at those deeply embedded; and a nail punch or set for driving the heads of panel pins below the surface of wood. A Surform tool of some kind is also handy. These are rasping tools used like a plane to shape wood, but need less skill and no sharpening. They can also be used on other materials, even metal. Finally, as you go along you will need extra screwdrivers. In some situations a short stubby one is the only answer to a problem; in others an extra long one. And some things you buy will have Posidriv, Supadrive or Phillips screws in them, which cannot be adjusted except with the appropriate cross-point screwdriver.

Also buy a container to keep your precious kit together. A cheap plastic carry-all from hardware stores is ideal. It also ensures that, having gone to the top of the house to do a job, you don't then instantly find that you haven't brought the very tool you need. However, don't store the combination or try square in it, as they are precision tools which should be hung up out of harm's way; or saws, unless protected by a cardboard sheath.

As you go along you will find you need still more tools to do particular jobs, especially decorating and woodwork. These are described in the relevant chapters.

ACCESSORIES

Besides the tools you will need a stock of screws, nails and other items. The best way to build this up is always to buy a few more than you need, which you usually have to anyway as in most shops screws and nails are either packeted or sold in tens. Beware small advertisements for bulk purchase of screws. I fell for one of these over ten years ago, and still have a rusting stock of the tiny, rarely-used screws which made up most of the consignment. You can buy flash plastic containers to keep these items in, but most thrifty souls like me use screw-top jars, old tobacco tins, plastic film slide boxes, cartridge film containers, or the plastic tubes they came in.

Screws The size of a screw is expressed by its length times the gauge number, which represents the diameter of the plain shank above the threaded bit. The higher the gauge number the sturdier the screw: a No. 6 is a fine screw, usually seen between 1cm to 4cm long; a No. 12 is a coarse one, from 5 to 10cm long. Screws are made in gauges ranging from 0 to 20, but for DIY work you will normally use only those in the 4 to 10 range. In practice by far the most commonly used one is a 5cm No. 8.

Screws are also made in different metals, with different finishes, and in different head styles, so the possible permutations are virtually endless. But an average DIY shop will stock only the most popular ones. Basic maid-of-all-work screws are made of mild steel; the others most commonly stocked are brass, and those with a black japanned or chrome finish. The heads are usually countersunk — for driving level with or below the surface of the work — and round or raised — for fixing hardware items with pre-drilled plain or countersunk holes. All these have slots in the top. A new type, the Pozidriv or Supadrive, has a cross-shaped slot and is put in using a special matching screwdriver which cannot jump out and scratch the work, which can happen with ordinary screws and drivers. Other types you may need occasionally are chipboard screws, threaded all the way to the head to give a firm fixing between pieces of chipboard; and domehead screws, for fixing mirrors, which have a chromed cap covering the screwhead.

Countersunk screws put into wood can be concealed with plastic wood or plastic screw caps. Any types can be made into a feature by setting them into brass or steel screw cups.

Magic formula: If you want to buy some more of a particular screw but don't know what it is, find the gauge number by measuring across the slot in sixteenths. Double this and take away 2 to find the answer. ($5/16''$ $\times$ 2 = 10 $-$ 2 = No 8 gauge.)

Nails These usually come in packets nowadays, but if you need a lot of one kind there are still a few places, such as builders' merchants, where they are sold in the old way by weight, and will be cheaper. They are commonly made of bright mild steel, or galvanised for outdoor use to prevent rusting. Nails are sized by length; the gauge will be appropriate to this, or may be indicated as fine, medium etc. There are many different types.

The common round-section wire nail with a big flat head is for coarse work, where appearance does not matter, as, although it gives a good grip, it cannot be concealed. It is often used to fasten floor boards to the joists below, although the proper nail for this is the cut floor brad, a flat section nail with a rectangular head. A slightly more refined wire nail is oval in section with a smaller head. Lost-head nails also give a strong grip, and can be punched below the surface of the wood, leaving a hole to be filled with plastic wood. For woodwork where appearance is important use panel pins, which have small heads which are easy to punch into the wood and conceal. Small, fine-gauge panel pins are indeed pin like, but the biggest are 5cm long and quite sturdy.

Other nails are more specialised. Hardboard pins, usually copper coloured, have a diamond shaped head which disappears completely into the board. Clouts are coarse nails with very big heads, usually galvanised, designed to fix sash cords and roofing felt. Masonry nails are supposedly a quick way of securing battens or skirting boards to walls, but personally I have never got on with them. It takes a great deal of effort to get them in, and hitting the second one usually causes the first one to bounce out.

Little'uns needed from time to time include tacks, for fixing furnishing fabrics and carpets to wood; brads or sprigs, for securing glass against a window frame, or a picture backing board against the frame; and chair nails, domed-head decorative ones used in upholstery.

A mooch around a big DIY store will soon show you that there are dozens more fixings of various kinds to be had. Ones I find I have got in stock include cable clips, for securing electric flex neatly and safely to walls; picture hangers, hardened steel pins supporting a brass hook, easy to hammer into walls; screw hooks of various types and small screw eyes, open and closed, for fixing expanding curtain wire.

USING TOOLS

However good the tools you buy you need to know how to use them properly to get results and avoid injury. Here are a few tips; having read them experiment on some scrap wood. As with sewing or any other craft, skill comes with practice.

Nailing Coarse nails are used for rough work like fixing down floor boards or building cupboard frames. Finer ones are used in conjunction with adhesive to hold timber components together in the desired position until it dries. Nails will not go in satisfactorily unless the work is resting on a good solid surface — over the leg of the table or work bench, or on the floor.

Avoid crushed fingers and crookedly-driven nails by giving the nail a gentle tap before the main blow to make sure your aim is right: tap-*tap*, rather than bonk, bonk, ouch! Hold the hammer towards the end of the handle, not halfway down (see diagram). Do not swing wildly, but pivot your arm straight down from the elbow, without bending the wrist. This

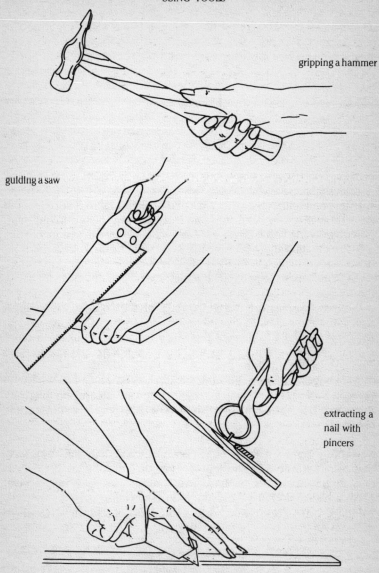

gripping a hammer

guiding a saw

extracting a
nail with
pincers

cutting against a straightedge

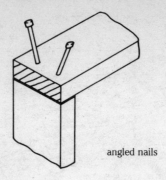

angled nails

should ensure that the hammer face strikes the nail head square on, and not at a slight angle, which leads to bruise marks on the wood. To put in very tiny nails either hold them in a pair of pliers to start them off, or put them through a strip of polythene and tear this away before driving them home. Nails grip best if driven in at a slight angle, (see diagram). But this is difficult to do without bruising the wood with the final blows until you become more experienced. If you do it, remember which way they were slanted and angle the nail punch accordingly when driving them below the surface.

If the wood splits the nail is too thick or set too close to the edge. Staggering a row of nails, if possible, instead of setting them in a straight row, will also help to prevent this. Oval nails are less likely to cause splitting, but only if put in correctly, with the long axis of the head parallel to the grain of the wood.

To remove ill-driven or unwanted nails use a claw hammer or a pair of pincers, with a piece of scrap wood or hardboard underneath to protect the wood. Use pincers in short sharp jerks; this leaves a smaller hole behind.

Screwing Screws make stronger joints in wood than nails. Normally they are used with adhesive, but this can be omitted if the item needs dismantling from time to time. They are also used to secure metal hardware such as hinges, and to fix things to walls.

Joining two pieces of wood with a countersunk screw involves three different drilling operations: (see diagram)

1 Drill *clearance hole* in top piece just big enough for screw to pass through.
2 *Countersink* this to enable screw head to sit slightly below surface.
3 Drill *pilot hole* in second piece just large enough for screw to be driven in with firm pressure.

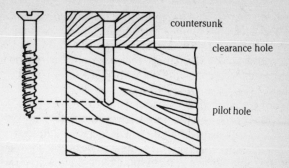

countersunk

clearance hole

pilot hole

If the screw is securing a piece of hardware, the clearance hole, which may or may not be countersunk, is already in existence. When fixing screws into walls the pilot hole becomes a full-sized one which is then filled with a plug, (see Shelving, page 120).

Although screws are unlikely to split the wood, not being driven in by brute force, they should still not be placed too close to the edges or ends. Whenever possible avoid putting them into the end grain of wood, as they do not grip well there. When this must be done, as in any shelf-and-upright construction, maximise grip by making only a minimal pilot hole, or none at all; just puncture with the bradawl. If using veneered chipboard get proper chipboard screws.

Difficulties in putting in screws are usually caused by one of the following:

1 Screw impossible to drive home: pilot hole too small; withdraw screw and enlarge it.
2 Screw fails to grip: pilot hole too large; fill with plastic wood and redrill.
3 Driver blade the wrong size — too large or too small. (Or wrong type — see page 6).
4 Screw does not sit flat when driven home: holes drilled on the slant; if possible make new ones close by.
5 Driver being turned the wrong way: it's *clockwise* for putting in; *anti-clockwise* for taking out.

To remove an old screw apply maximum effort on the very first turn, at the same time pushing as hard as you can. (If it has been painted over scrape the slot clean first.) Once it moves even a fraction it will go the rest of the way. If it resists, do not persevere too much, or the edges of the slot will be destroyed and then all is lost. This happens very easily if the driver blade is too small; it should be the same size as the slot. The problem may be rust, so squirt on some 3-in-one penetrating and easing oil, leave for a few hours and try again. Other tricks to try are striking the driver sharply with a mallet; applying heat to the screw head or turning it clockwise; any of which may break its grip. With a round head screw you may be able to deepen the slot with a hacksaw in order to give the driver a better grip.

For very large, heavily painted and rusted-in screws a more powerful screwdriver may be the only answer. Get hold of an Easydriver, which has a big ball-shaped handle which increases turning power; a Paramo ratchet handle, which fits on to their range of cruciform screwdrivers and has the same effect; a Yankee spiral ratchet screwdriver with its powerful pump action; or an impact screwdriver (available by mail order from Sarjents Tools, see page 210).

Sawing Wood is quite easy to saw *across* the grain, provided that the saw is sharp and you resist the temptation to push: let the saw do the work. Sawing *down* the grain, that is down the length of a plank, is laborious and to be avoided whenever possible; use a Surform tool, or plane if necessary, to reduce wood to the width required.

The wood must be held steady in some way while you saw, either in a bench hook, mitre box or vice, or simply by holding it down with your knee. To start the cut draw the saw backwards a few times, just outside the marked cutting line (to allow for the thickness of the saw). To keep a straight line point your index finger down the blade, stand square on to the work, and watch out that your sawing hand does not slope to either side. As when cutting bread this will produce a sloping cut. As you reach the end of the cut, support the waste piece of wood or it will break away and tear bits off the main piece.

Drilling Make sure that the drill bit is securely held in the chuck of the drill or it can get stuck in the hole. Hold the drill at right angles to the work, not sloping backwards/forwards or to either side (you may sometimes need a helper to guide you, if it is critically important). Do not move the drill bit out of position while drilling; a power tool especially could snap it. To get the bit out of the finished hole either reverse drilling direction (hand drill) or with a power tool continue drilling while withdrawing it. A masonry bit that squeaks is hopelessly blunt and due for the dustbin (or some manufacturers will sharpen them, if you can be bothered to send them away).

Cutting There is no need to be scared of sharp blades. It's the blunt ones that are more likely to cause injury, as you have to put on excessive pressure to cut through. The golden rule for keeping fingers in one piece is, whenever possible, to cut *away* from your body, not towards. When using a blade against a steel straight edge, as when cutting a vinyl tile to size, hold the straight edge down hard, with fingers well out of harm's way, but cut lightly.

Measuring It always pays to double check measurements before cutting, particularly when using expensive materials. Remember this old carpenters' saying: 'Measure once, cut twice; measure twice, cut once.'

TOOLS TO HIRE

Most towns have tool hire shops from which you can borrow expensive, rarely used tools and equipment which it would be madness to buy. Find them in the Yellow Pages under Hire Services.

Good tools to hire are steam wallpaper strippers, to take the slog out of removing a lot of old wallpaper, particularly if it is multi-layered and over-painted; floor sanders to bring old floorboards up like new; and steam carpet cleaners if you take over a house complete with fitted carpets which look sadly grubby once the former owners' furniture has been removed. Some of these are big and/or heavy — you will need transport. Should you be unlucky enough to get blocked drains, equipment for clearing the obstruction can be hired and will save a mint, if you can face doing the job, as sending for Dyno-Rod costs a minimum of £15. And when the time comes round for exterior decorating, you can hire not only ladders and scaffold towers but all sorts of other things like paint sprayers and cement mixers.

Book your equipment in advance, as some items are much in demand, especially at weekends and on bank holidays. You will have to pay a deposit, and give some proof of identity. Make sure that you are well organised beforehand so that you can use the equipment intensively, and not run over the period paid for. Don't forget to get enough accessories, such as glasspaper for a floor sander and shampoo for a carpet cleaner, to finish the job.

OLD TOOLS

If you are given or inherit a set of old tools be very fussy about what you keep. A skilled tradesman can, and usually seems to, manage with the most dreadful worn-out objects; but beginners need the best.

Measuring tools will probably be of limited use, lacking metric calibrations, but a steel rule is always useful as a straight edge, provided that it is not bent. Old folding boxwood rules are very likely inaccurate.

Screwdrivers are invariably useless, the blades having lost their sharp edge and square corners long ago. Hammers are all right if the face is still flat and unpitted, but check that the handle is secure and if necessary fit new metal wedges to keep it safely in place, or a whole new one. (Check all wooden handles for woodworm — small round holes — as one eaten away inside could break suddenly in use.) An axe is useful if you have an open fire, to split up offcuts of wood for kindling instead of wasting them. An old one is easily sharpened with a file, and a new handle can be fitted as for a hammer.

Good saws and chisels can be reset and sharpened if they are not too far gone—covered in heavy rust with broken teeth or badly nicked blades. (But a clapped-out chisel is a good tool for levering open large paint tins.) Have sharpening professionally done — look in Yellow Pages under Saw Sharpening, or the windows of the more old-fashioned kind of DIY or hardware shop for a sign. Plane blades can also be sharpened or replaced.

A try-square is useless unless it is accurate. To check, place the tool against a straight edge and draw a line down the blade. Turn it over to left or right and see whether the line is still against the blade — if it veers off the square is out of true.

With old power tools first check the wiring in the plug (see page 78). Then run the motor: excessive noise and blue flashes are both signs that all is not well. A high-quality tool may be worth having repaired, if you can find an agent for the brand in your town, but with a cheap tool made for the DIY market it is probably better to put the money towards a new one.

Note: very old tools, such as big wooden planes, or anything in ebony wood with brass fittings, are collectables.

CARE OF TOOLS

Keeping tools in good condition is mainly a matter of fighting off rust and keeping cutting edges sharp. You are supposed to lightly oil metal parts after use, but few people, including myself, have the moral fibre to do this. But it's a good idea to make the effort if you don't plan to use them for a month or two. The best possible thing you can do for your treasured set is to keep it indoors, at least in the winter (but not where children can get at it). Storage in the average cold, damp garage or shed inevitably leads to rust. If you simply have to do this, don't leave tools hanging up on a cold wall during the winter. Put them into warmly lined drawers or boxes, and wrap power tools in scraps of old woollen blanket.

If you have chisels keep them in good shape by regular sharpening on an oil stone lubricated with a few drops of oil, using a honing guide to get the correct angle. If this is not done they rapidly become useless. Have saws professionally sharpened regularly, or fit new blades. Replace Stanley knife blades frequently.

POWER TOOLS

These are by no means essential — after all people managed without them until very recently. But today six out of ten householders in Britain own an electric drill, and they do take a great deal of the the hard work out of DIY. But don't get the idea that they will endow you with skills you do not possess; they won't.

How urgently you need a power tool depends on the type of house you live in and the type of work you do. Unless you intend drilling a million holes, there is no particular advantage in having one for working in wood. But for drilling into walls a power drill is a great boon, and not only makes a hole more easily and quickly, but often more neatly as well. Walls in old houses, built of brick covered with soft plaster, can be drilled without too much effort using a hand drill and a sharp masonry bit. But in newer houses you may find this very hard going indeed, even impossible.

The second function of the power tool is to take the hard labour out of sanding wood and preparing paintwork for redecoration, by fitting various attachments into the chuck (see page 138).

A Black and Decker power drill designed for the DIY market can be had for around £25. There is no particular point in buying a more expensive tool, as these are designed for tradesmen who use them for heavy work, day in day out; your tool is only going to get intermittent use. Also a more sophisticated tool may be too heavy for you to handle comfortably. All but one of the Black and Decker range of electric drills feature optional hammer action, which is useful if you hit a hard spot when drilling into walls, or find that they are made of concrete. They take drill bits up to 10mm diameter. There are four types: basic single speed, two-speed, variable speed and one that can be put into reverse as well. A single-speed is perfectly adequate for sanding work. Having a slower speed to switch into is recommended for drilling into masonry. A variable speed enables you to start slowly; good if you are a bit nervous or for jobs like drilling into ceramic tiles. A variable speed plug reversing facility enables the drill to be used with screwdriver bits.

Some women are scared of power drills, but there is no reason to be. They are rather noisy, but no more so than a lot of kitchen appliances. (The noise of the hammer action is horrendous, and not something to use on a Sunday afternoon if you value good neighbour relations.) The main things to remember are to hold the tool firmly, using two hands and the side handle, so that you have good control of it; and to make sure that you drill at right angles to the work. To ensure the hole is drilled in exactly the right place, tap the centre of the marked spot with a nail punch to make a slight indentation. The drill bit or attachment must be set straight in the chuck, and this tightened up *hard* with the key provided. Be prepared for the fact that the drill or attachment will not stop revolving immediately the trigger is released, and allow time for this before putting it down.

Another power tool you might acquire in time is a jig saw, which is safer and easier to use than a circular saw, and excellent for making both straight and curved cuts in wood and man-made boards up to 5cm thick. Use one to reduce full-size sheets of hardboard etc. to manageable pieces (it's much cheaper to buy boards uncut); for cutting a hole in a door for a cat flap; for making fancy curves in say a spice rack. They cost from about £30.

To make maximum use of power tools you will also need an extension lead, unless your home is exceptionally well endowed with socket outlets, as their leads are only about 1.5 metres long. An extension lead also enables you to work out of doors, which is a good idea when sanding, as indoors the dust settles *everywhere*.

Safety tips Switch off at the wall socket every time you put the tool down or change bits/attachments. Do not work with long hair dangling near a power tool; tie it safely back. Ensure that the plug is correctly wired: a modern tool is double insulated and has a 2-core cable with no earth wire (green-yellow striped). But an older model may not be double insulated, and will have a 3-core cable of which the earth wire *must* be connected. Never drill above or below electric light switches or sockets — you could hit the electric cable buried in the wall and at the very least blow all the fuses.

2 Odd jobbing

Learn how to fix those little things around the house that break, go wrong or just wear out, from cracked window panes to dripping taps, and you can save a mint. If you have to call in a tradesman for jobs like these you are not paying for his skill, as they are simple tasks, but mainly for his time; and your time comes free.

Note: if you live in Australia or New Zealand the amount of plumbing repairs you are allowed to do yourself is very limited and varies from one state to another, so consult your water authority first.

IN BETWEEN DECORATING

After a few years' battering by the average family, most rooms begin to look a bit shabby and sorry for themselves. If time, budget and inclination do not allow for redecorating, what can you do to brighten things up? Quite a bit.

Start with the ceiling: a good clean will work wonders, particularly if you're a smoking household, as a layer of dirt and nicotine considerably reduces its light-reflecting powers. Or give it a quick coat of emulsion; the new solid type produced by ICI Dulux is ideal for situations like this, as it is totally non-drip and ready to use. A dingy polystyrene tile ceiling will need emulsioning as it cannot be cleaned satisfactorily. First repair any damage. Lever off badly dented tiles with a broad-bladed filling knife. Fix replacements and restick any coming adrift with some polystyrene tile adhesive, applying it all over and not in blobs. (If there is only a bit of sticking to do, use some Copydex latex adhesive.)

Give paintwork a thorough wash with sugar soap, Polywash or Flash (don't use anything abrasive or what's left of the shine on gloss paint will disappear altogether). You should work from the bottom up, which seems a funny way of going about things, but with powerful cleaners if you work from the top the dirty water runs down and leaves permanent rivulets behind.

Vinyl wallpaper (plastic surface) can be washed hard, even scrubbed; washable wallpaper (shiny surface) should be treated a little more gently.

17

Ordinary matt paper may only stand up to dusting, although you might get away with wiping with a barely damp cloth provided the colours are fast. Remove gravy stains from wallpaper with K2R spot cleaner; this may or may not shift children's scribbles done in wax crayon or ball-point pen. For large grease stains try covering with blotting paper and pressing with a hot iron. Vague unknown marks may respond to rubbing with a very soft rubber (an artist's putty rubber is ideal) or a piece of squeezed-up fresh bread.

To further revive the appearance of wallpaper stick down loose, tatty-looking joins with any adhesive you have to hand: children's glue, thinned woodworking adhesive, or Copydex. Failing any of these mix up a bit of flour and water paste (cook slowly together like a sauce). If you had the foresight to keep some unused paper you can always patch a badly stained or torn area. This is remarkably unnoticeable, particularly if the paper is patterned, although it will stand out a bit at first just because it's cleaner. Cut a piece quite a bit bigger than the damaged area, making sure the pattern or texture coincides. Tear a strip off all sides, working with the plain side facing you, to produce a feathered edge which will blend in much better than a sharply cut one when stuck down. An alternative method (use for hessian) is to cut a square patch slightly larger than the damage, tape it in place and cut through both layers with a sharp knife. Remove the waste bit from the bottom layer and stick the patch in the hole.

To patch up chipped paintwork get a tinlet of gloss to match the colour as closely as possible; you may need to do a bit of mixing. It's no good getting white; whatever the manufacturers may claim, white paint does yellow over time, and white blobs will stand out worse than the chips. Apply the paint in several layers with a very small brush (an artist's or child's paintbrush rather than a decorator's) so that it is only on the chip and not on the surrounding paint. A good way to do this is to decant the paint into an empty nail varnish bottle and use the brush that goes with it (clean bottle and brush first with white spirit). Then you have a chip repair kit ready for use whenever disaster strikes.

If you have any of the original emulsion paint left you can repair chipped corners or holes in plaster almost invisibly by patching with Polyfilla mixed with the paint instead of water. You may need to thin it a little with water first.

PATCHING CARPETS

If the worst happens and you get a burn or an ineradicable stain in a fitted carpet, it can be patched with a leftover piece, or a bit stolen from a hidden corner or under the bed. How invisible it will be depends on the type of carpet and whether it is plain or patterned. Shampooing after patching will help. Worn areas, usually in doorways or at the foot of the stairs, should also be patched, not just for aesthetic reasons but because eventually they will split, and someone catching a foot in the opening could have a nasty fall.

The following applies whether the patch is a few inches across, or several feet. Make sure to match not only any pattern, but the direction of the pile — the way it roughs up or lies down when stroked. Cut out a neat square or rectangular patch slightly larger than the damaged area. Lay it on top, pattern and pile matching, and fix temporarily with a few tacks. Take a Stanley knife fitted with a brand new blade and cut right through both patch and carpet, just inside the edges of the patch. Remove the patch and brush a band of Copydex latex adhesive along the under side edges, taking it halfway up the pile to prevent fraying. Remove and discard the cut-out damaged piece.

Cut four pieces of carpet seaming tape a little bit longer than the sides of the hole. Brush them with adhesive and lay them under the edges of the hole, sticky side up, so that half the width and the excess at each end runs underneath the carpet. Brush the back of the patch with adhesive and put it in place, matching pattern/pile, and tap around the edges with a hammer to seal the join.

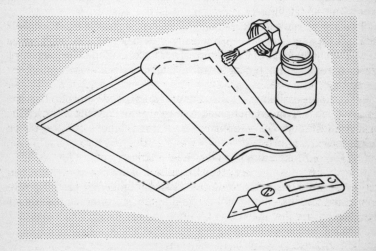

This method of repair is suitable for any carpet without a separate underlay. If there is one, if possible lift the carpet at the nearest edge and slide in a piece of hardboard to protect it during the cutting operation.

Otherwise simply proceed as above, and if the underlay does get cut through, leave it lying and fix with some sticky tape.

Patching a carpet from the back is not very satisfactory as it is difficult to get pile and pattern directions matching as you cannot see.

To patch small holes in a shaggy carpet or rug pull a few tufts from the edge, or buy some double knitting or rug wool as closely matching the colour as possible. Trim away any singed or damaged tufts with scissors. Cut wool into short pieces a little longer than the pile. Brush the bottom of the hole with Copydex adhesive (use a manicure stick or matchstick if it is very small). Bunch the tufts or several strands of wool tightly together and stand them on the adhesive. Gradually add more, working them into place with a toothpick or sharpened matchstick. Leave to dry, then trim level with the pile and brush to blend in.

TIRED TILING

Particularly in bathrooms prone to condensation, tiling can become very dingy because, although the tiles themselves have been cleaned regularly, the grouting in between has accumulated not only dirt, but black mould. So cleaning *in between* the tiles — an old nail brush is the ideal tool — can have a spectacular effect. If mould growth is present use a 1:8 mixture of bleach and water. Where this fails, or if the grout is crumbling and falling out, regrouting is the answer. It's somewhat tedious, as you have to rake out enough of the old grout to replace it with new (see Chapter 8 for details), but really does make the tiling look brand new. You might achieve even more of a transformation by using one of the coloured grouting powders now available instead of the customary white.

Yet another possibility is to use a new product called Versatile. This is a liquid which is sponged on to make old grey grout dazzling white again, or if you feel more adventurous, to stain it red, blue, green, brown or beige.

Cracked or broken tiles should also be replaced, not just for aesthetic reasons but because in wet areas they allow water to seep in, and the whole lot could begin to deteriorate. Prise the broken pieces off gently with something like an old chisel, holding the surrounding tiles down firmly to ensure that they don't lift up. If the tile is only cracked drill a hole in the centre with a masonry bit, or whack it with a hammer to break it up. Next scrape off all the old adhesive so that the new tile will lie flat. If dealing with only one or two tiles, don't bother to buy tile adhesive and grouting powder — do the whole job with Polyfilla.

Some tile designs stay around for a long time, and you may well be able to get matching replacements if you hawk bits of the old one around to enough different DIY outlets. Obviously you can always get white; also standard sanitary pottery colours, but they won't be an exact match. It may look better to lever off a few more tiles and use some deliberately contrasting tiles in such a way that it all looks intentional.

Cracked tiles can be hidden under a set of tile transfers; but don't expect them to stick on long in a very wet area.

Nasty-coloured tiles can be over-painted, but this doesn't wear very well; acceptable on fireplace surrounds, possible in a bathroom but not recommended for kitchens. Wash the tiling until spotless, leave to dry for 24 hours, (or dry with a fan heater or hairdryer) then paint with two coats of high-quality gloss paint; do not use a primer or undercoat.

BLEEDING RADIATORS

I have not resorted to swearing; this is the technical term for letting air out of radiators. Radiators are meant to be full of circulating hot water, but air gradually accumulates in the system and can result in some of them going cold at the top as the water cannot circulate properly. All you need to do the job is a radiator key, from any hardware shop. Fit the key into the air vent: this may be at either left or right top, but the key won't fit into the wrong end. Turn the key gently anti-clockwise to release air; as soon as water starts to dribble out tighten it up again. After 20 minutes or so the radiator should heat up. It's a good idea to do this routinely on all the radiators at the beginning of the heating season.

LOOSE DOOR HANDLES

The knobs on interior doors are secured to the metal bit that runs through the door by a small grub screw. These have a maddening habit of slowly undoing themselves. This gradually loosens the door handle, until one day it comes away in your hand. The screw falls to the floor, never to be seen again. You then find that no-one can sell you a new grub screw and you have to buy a whole new door handle set. So it's well worth routinely tightening up these little screws before the worst happens. Also fit them into the hole in the top of the handle, instead of underneath, so that they cannot fall out.

PROBLEM DOORS

If a door sticks do not rush to plane a bit off the edge. First inspect the hinges closely. If screws are loose or missing, the hinges sag and cause the door to tilt. If they won't tighten up, but just turn round and round, or if a new screw goes into empty space, take them out, one at a time, and plug the holes with bits of matchstick or a straight-sided plastic wall plug.

Sometimes doors fail to close properly because both door and frame have been redecorated so many times that sheer paint thickness causes binding. You may be able to improve matters by scraping some off — find out where it is sticking by putting pieces of carbon paper in between door and frame. A Surform tool is handy for removing paint and/or a little wood. If the door springs open when closed try scraping paint off the hinges.

If when the door is shut, or nearly shut, there is a sizeable gap down the handle side, and it's tight at the hinge side, take the hinges off and put a thin piece of card behind them before refitting. The opposite condition, binding at the handle side and a gap at the hinge side is rarer, but can be remedied by deepening the hinge recesses, for which you need a chisel.

When a door rattles in the wind it may be because it has shrunk so that the latch is no longer engaging tightly with the latch plate on the frame. To cure this unscrew the latch plate and move it a little further back. Use a chisel to enlarge the recess the latch sits in, and also the holes that the catch and perhaps a key go into. This won't work on some front doors with different types of combined handle and lock; try fitting some foam draught excluder to take up the slack.

Yet another problem with old-style panelled doors is sagging, caused by joints working loose so that the bottom rail drops slightly, making the door very hard to open and close. The tell-tale sign is a gap or gaps between side and bottom rails. Scrape this clean of dirt from both sides. Scrape all the paint off the bottom back edge of the door so that you can see the end of the mortice and tenon joint. Squirt woodworking adhesive into the gap. Open the door wide, drive a wedge underneath it and leave for a few hours for the adhesive to dry. (If it is an external door use a waterproof one such as Cascamite.) Inspect the mortice and tenon joint: if there are gaps at the bottom, make thin wedges to the width of the tenon and coat them with adhesive and hammer in. Let the adhesive dry before sawing the surplus bits of wedge off and sanding smooth. Prime and repaint an exterior door without delay.

All exterior doors should have a sloping weatherbar fitted across the bottom to stop rain driving underneath when the wind is in the right (wrong!) direction. If there isn't one, buy and fit either a length of weatherboard moulding, or a patent aluminium one which may come with a draught excluder as well. Fit either so that there is a slight gap on each side to allow for the door stops.

Interior doors with glass panels in them can develop an irritating rattle because the glass is usually fixed in place with timber beading, not bedded in putty, which gets loose as the timber dries out. To cure this remove the beading and bed the glass on strips of foam draught excluder before replacing it.

CREAKING STAIRS AND SQUEAKING FLOORBOARDS

When resounding creaks and piercing squeaks frustrate late-comers' and midnight snackers' efforts to creep around at night unnoticed, a few minutes with the toolkit can usually put things right. But not always; some creaks are chronic and have, like British weather, to be endured.

Stairs The tread, the bit that you step on, should be fixed to the riser and if it has worked loose that stair will creak. Cure can be simple: get that invaluable tool, the large old chisel, and prise up the tread just enough to get some wood glue underneath on a brush or bit of card. Then hammer it down with a couple of 5cm oval nails in the centre of the front edge, angled to give a good grip. If this fails, more can be done *if* the underside of the staircase is accessible and has not been panelled over.

Look underneath and you should find pairs of triangular wooden blocks in the angle between tread and riser. If these have gone missing on the offending stair, replacing them with large metal brackets should do the trick. Or you might even find the original block or blocks lying on the floor, in which case nail and glue them back in place.

Floorboards Usually the cause of squeaks is that some of the boards have been lifted and not nailed down again, or that the nails have worked loose, or that someone used nails too small for the job. Start by examining the floor carefully. Regular lines of nails show where the joists run across underneath, and these are the *only* places where nails should be put. Normally the joists are 5cm wide, so that is the width available to fix into. Knock a nail in outside these bands and at best you achieve nothing; at worst you could puncture a water pipe or electric cable. (Sometimes cable or pipes have been laid in a channel cut in the top of a joist, so it is always safest to lift the board and check before hammering in any new nails.)

When nails are present but loose, try punching them down further into the wood. If that doesn't work pull them out and put in larger ones; or put extra ones alongside the existing ones. Sometimes nails have been pulled out and replaced so often that the wood is full of gaping holes and also split at cut ends, so that there is nowhere for fresh nails to get a grip. In such cases use screws instead: a No.8 or 10, 5cm long, would be suitable. Do not drill the usual large clearance hole, but drill a pilot hole right through the floorboard and down into the joists. Countersink the top so that the screw lies flush.

When floorboards have been cut to get them up at some time in the past, the cut end has often been left loose, leading to squeaking or bouncing up and down when walked on. In such cases fix a wooden batten on to the side of the joist and then screw the board to that. Make sure the batten is at the right height for the board to lie flush with its neighbours.

Occasionally boards squeak because they have swollen and are rubbing together. Brushing talcum powder in between may effect a miracle cure, but DIY life is rarely that easy, and you will probably have to lift such a board and plane it down a fraction.

To lift a floorboard for the first time cut across it with a tenon saw about 2.5cm away from the nail line in order to miss the joist. It's as well to switch the electricity off at the mains, just in case there is electrical wiring underneath in places where it shouldn't be. Also keep the saw at a shallow angle to reduce the risk of cutting into wiring, or pipes. Gently lever the board up with our old friend the clapped-out chisel. Slide a piece of wood underneath to hold the board up as you work along. Continue as far as required and cut through in the same way at the other end, near a joist. Refit as described above.

Note some superior houses have tongued and grooved floorboards which lock together. Here you also have to saw down each side of the board to cut through the tongue.

PROBLEM WINDOWS

Windows that rattle alarmingly at night, or have to be wrestled open, should not be lived with but dealt with.

With rattling casement windows check that the furniture is all present and correct. A main window should have a stay at the bottom with a peg or pegs to hold it open in various positions, and a catch to hold it tightly closed. A small top light should have a stay and peg(s). If they do not engage, properly they have been refitted incorrectly and a little juggling about should put things right. Jamming can be caused by loose hinges — check that all the screws are present and turned fully home. Or it may be excessive paint thickness: find the sticking spots with a bit of carbon paper, then remove just enough paint to allow the window to open freely. If you get down to bare wood, prime and repaint as soon as possible. Windows often swell in wet weather and become tight, but will recover in drier times. Regular opening helps to prevent them getting 'frozen' shut.

A palliative measure for a rattling sash-window is to buy a pair of plastic wedges from a hardware shop. But check the catch that holds the upper and lower parts together — it may be loose, broken or missing altogether. The old catch may be usable, given new screws, but sometimes the two rails of the window no longer meet level — glue on a bit of wood to raise one half of the catch level with the other. But on a ground floor it's best to fit new catches, of the Brighton pattern which not only holds the sashes together more firmly, but is more burglar-proof. (A Brighton pattern catch screws open and shut, whereas the common type slides.)

Very often the cause of a rattling sash is more deep-seated: worn parting beads. To find out what these are and how to refit, see Broken Sash-Cords, page 27. Badly fitting beads, plus a broken cord, can also cause jamming. Don't try curing this by oiling the pulleys; it will do no good at all, and may damage the cords.

Any type of window will jam if the corner joints have opened up and it is out of square. This can be fixed by bracing the joint with a flat, L-shaped metal corner plate. Unscrew the hinges, or remove sash as described on page 27, and lay the window flat. Knock the joints back together, preferably with a mallet; otherwise protect the frame from hammer blows with a bit of wood. Check that the corners are square with a try-square and screw repair plates over each one. They do not look pretty, so put them on the outside where they will be less noticeable. Make sure they clear the frame and paint with metal primer before replacing the window, or they will go rusty in days.

Windows and window frames often rot where water has penetrated and allowed wet rot fungus to flourish. The wood may look quite sound but be spongy if pressed; or it may have crumbled away. A convenient way to repair such disaster areas is to cut away the worst, saturate the area with Ronseal wood hardener and then replace the missing wood with Ronseal high performance wood filler. To prevent the problem occurring again you can insert Ronseal wood preservative tablets, which dissolve if water penetrates and so protect the wood from fungal attack.

Broken and cracked window panes Fitting a new pane of glass in a normal-sized window is a perfectly straightforward operation, and there's absolutely no need to call in a glazier and pay a large bill; the cost of the glass alone will give you quite enough to groan about. Glass should also be replaced if it's only cracked, as the sharp edges can cut your hands when cleaning the window. Reglazing has to be done from outside, so if it's an upstairs window it might be easier to take the window off; but a lot depends on the state of the hinges. (Do a sash window *in situ*, unless you can combine the job with cord replacement.)

Start early in the day so that you can be sure the new glass will be in by nightfall. If this is not possible fix a sheet of polythene over the frame with drawing pins to keep out rain if not burglars.

Tools required are minimal: hammer, old chisel, pincers and steel tape. A putty knife makes shaping the putty easier, but you can make do with the chisel or an old table knife.

The first step is to locate a glass supplier — look in the Yellow Pages under Glass Merchants. Telephone your choice to find out if they will take an order over the phone for collection or delivery later, or operate a while-you-wait service. If the glass is patterned you'll have to take a piece into the shop to see if they can match it, and also to make sure that it is cut with the pattern running the right way.

Next remove the old glass, so that you can get a really accurate measurement for the new. As glass cannot be trimmed to fit, and is in no way elastic, this is crucial. Wear stout work gloves and, working from inside, gently tap and lever the broken glass away from the putty with a large hammer, little by little. Stand on a stepladder so that your face is always above your hands as they work, safe from any dropping fragments. Make sure to retrieve all the bits. Stubborn pieces round the edge may have to be levered off with the old chisel, but mind your eyes. (If nervous and not already a glasses wearer, get some safety specs.)

Use the chisel to hack away all the old bedding putty from the rebate, the ledge on which the glass rests, and brush clean. Pull out any glazing sprigs or panel pins sticking out of the frame and discard. On a metal frame, remove the metal clips from their holes and keep for re-use.

Measure up for the new glass from top to bottom and side to side of the opening, including the rebate. Then deduct 5mm from each measurement. This is essential in order to make sure that there is enough clearance between pane and frame to allow for any slight distortion, and also seasonal expansion and contraction. Buy the glass — just tell the supplier that it is for a window and he will make sure you get the right thickness for the area involved — and at the same time get a tub of putty, suitable for timber or metal as required, and a few glazing sprigs (small headless tacks) if it's timber.

Cover the face of the rebate all round the window — where the flat side of the glass edges will rest — with a thin, even bed of putty. If the wood is at all damp the putty will fall off; dry it out with a hair dryer if necessary.

Again wearing gloves, position the new glass. The vertical tolerance you allowed for when measuring must be equally distributed between top and bottom, so place a couple of bits of matchstick on the bottom frame. Rest the lower edge of the glass in position and swing it gently against the rebate. Press it home with light fingertip pressure, keeping your hands close to the edges of the glass. Don't worry about surplus putty squeezing out messily; scrape this away later.

Gently tap a couple of glazing sprigs into the frame on all four sides. Provided that you keep the hammer moving parallel with the glass, and don't hit it square on, it won't crack. On metal windows fit the clips back into their holes. (Both sprigs and clips are just to hold the glass secure during the weeks while the putty hardens.)

Mould putty into long sausages and press it into the angle between glass and frame. Shape it to a 45° angle with the putty knife, mitring the corners. (Look at neighbouring panes to see how it goes.) Dip the putty knife into warm water to help get a smooth finish. Before finishing, have a look from inside to see that the putty does not extend above the top of the rebates. It should not be visible from inside; if it is, just cut it back slightly.

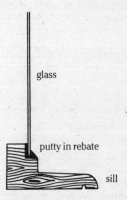

Leave for at least a couple of weeks to allow the putty to harden enough to paint; but don't forget about it — putty needs the protection of a coat of paint and without it, it will crack. Smears of putty can be wiped off the glass with white spirit, but gently. While the putty is still soft keep fingers well away from it, or very unprofessional-looking dents will appear. When painting the putty, carry the paint film fractionally on to the glass to make a waterproof seal. Clean the glass first with methylated spirits or nail varnish remover to remove any grease.

REPLACING BROKEN SASH-CORDS

This is not difficult if you set about it methodically, and the window is not giant-sized, but needs two people as the whole window has to be lifted out. It is done from inside, so there is no extra problem if the window is an upstairs one. If possible pick a fine warm day to do the job, and always start early. Also do the job *before* redecorating, as it inevitably makes a mess of the paintwork. Describing how it's done makes it sound complicated, but if you study the diagrams, and follow the instructions blindly but to the letter, as with the tricky bits of a dressmaking pattern, success should be yours.

Sash-windows consist of an upper and a lower sash which slide up and down past each other. Each hangs on a pair of cords which are attached to heavy iron weights which counterbalance the weight of the sash when it is raised. Usually only one or both the top cords break, but it pays to replace the lot as this is not a job you want to be doing again in a few months' time. (Do not leave a sash hanging on one cord only; the other one, being under extra strain, may snap at any time, and people have been trapped and hurt by falling sashes.)

Before starting, obtain a hank of sash cord and a few clout nails (stubby galvanised nails with big flat heads used to fasten the cord to the window) and some 40mm panel pins. You may need new lengths of parting and staff bead, the vertical pieces of wood which keep the two sashes in place: for instance if the old ones are in several pieces, having been broken before and replaced; or if they are worn, causing the window to rattle; or if you break them while trying to lever them off.

1) Pull the top sash down as far as it will go. Cut off all the cords a few inches above the sashes. Lever off the staff beads holding the lower sash in place (see diagram), at one side and the bottom. Use that large old chisel, and go gently, starting in the *middle* of each one. Take the bottom sash out.

2) Prise off the parting beads at each side and remove the top sash. Now you can see a rectangular pocket cut into each side of the window frame at the bottom. Prise out the covers to reveal the lower sash weights; lift them out. Reach in, past a loosely fixed bit of wood, to remove the top sash weights.

3) Remove all cord and clout nails from the sashes; brush and scrape clean. Remove old cord from sash weights.

4) Do this bit from the diagram: it looks like a cat's cradle but it works. Tie a piece of fine string to a small weight such as a short screw or a nut. This is known as a mouse and is used to feed the new sash cord into the frame. Test that it is small enough to ride over the metal pulley wheels at the top of the window. Attach the other end of the string to one end of the hank of sash cord. Feed mouse over pulley A, drop down and pull cord out through pocket B. Feed mouse over pulley C, drop down and out at pocket D. Feed mouse over pulley E, drop down and remove at pocket B. Feed mouse over last pulley, F, drop down and pull out of pocket D. Remove the string and knot that end of the cord on to one sash weight; tie firmly leaving nothing sticking out to get in the way. Put the weight into pocket D, at the back behind the wooden divider.

5) Pull the weight right up to the top and put a wedge over the pulley to hold it there. Keeping the cord taut, cut it three-quarters of the way

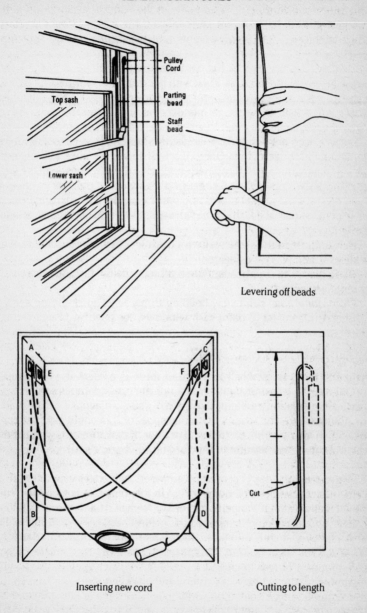

Pulley
Cord
Top sash
Parting
bead
Staff
bead
Lower sash

Levering off beads

Inserting new cord

Cutting to length

Cut

down the window opening (see diagram). Repeat this process with the cut end of the cord on the other side of the window, again putting the weight into the back pocket and wedging the pulley. Similarly attach cord to the two remaining weights and place them in the two front pockets.

6) Place the free end of the cord passing over pulley F in the right-hand groove of the top sash. Fix it with just one clout nail placed near the bottom of the groove. Remove the wedge from the pulley. Repeat on the other side: nail free end of cord passing over pulley E and remove wedge. Put the sash in place and test to see if it opens and closes properly. If by ill chance it does not you have to adjust the clout nails so as to shorten or lengthen the cords slightly. Once all is well put in two more nails on each side to secure the cords permanently, close to the first ones — do not put them in at the top or they will get in the way of the pulleys.

7) Replace the pocket pieces and parting beads. If the parting bead is new make sure that it is the same thickness as the old one and position it carefully.

8) Continue in the same way with the lower sash; the cords ride over pulleys C and A. Test as before.

9) Replace the staff beads. Punch all nails below the surface and fill with plastic wood.

Decorating note paint new beading thinly with quick-drying acrylic primer/undercoat. (To paint sash windows, see page 54.)

CONDENSATION AND DAMP

The first thing to establish is which of these is present in your house. Condensation is just unsightly and a nuisance, but damp is serious and can lead to dreadful problems like dry rot. Usually diagnosis can be made by noting where and when the trouble appears. If in doubt tape a square of kitchen foil over the affected wall or floor. If moisture drops appear on the front it's condensation; if they are on the back it's damp.

Condensation This is caused by air laden with water vapour striking cold surfaces, and can be quite severe in kitchens and bathrooms. You can actually watch it happening after you've had a bath: the air is full of water vapour, which gravitates to the coldest surfaces — exterior walls and windows — and condenses into water droplets which run down in trickles. The ever-present dampness caused by this creates ideal conditions for fungus to grow: the well-known black spots, usually high up on walls, concentrated in corners, and blackened window sills. There is no complete cure (invent one and make yourself a millionaire) and all that can be done is to improve ventilation and warm the surfaces up. Any or all of the following will help:

1) Install an extractor fan. This gets rid of the steam efficiently and quickly, but is expensive and personally I don't like the noise they make. Fitting entails cutting a hole in a window or wall.

2) Keep the room as warm as you can all the time, but not with a paraffin or flueless gas heater. These produce gallons of water as they burn and so aggravate the problem.

3) Use warm materials when redecorating: polystyrene ceiling tiles; polystyrene wall lining covered with warm-surfaced polyethylene wallpaper (Novamura); cork floor tiles. Avoid floor-to-ceiling ceramic tiles on every wall as they are intrinsically cold; also gloss paint on ceilings or walls.

4) Fit lined curtains, or blinds, and make sure they are drawn at nightfall. (Double glazing may help; but not always.)

5) If you can be bothered, run cold water into the bath first, then run the hot water in through a rubber tube reaching down into the cold. Very little steam will escape into the air.

6) In kitchens always open a window and close the door when creating unavoidable steam from slow-boiling puddings or when doing laundry. Cut down steam as much as possible: don't let saucepans or kettles boil away unnoticed, and always put lids on pans. In bathrooms always open the window and close the door after bathing.

7) Condensation can also occur in bedrooms, partly because of the remarkable fact that a sleeping person breathes out about a pint of moisture during the night. Opening the window a little will help a lot and is supposed to be good for you too.

8) Condensation can be a serious problem inside fitted wardrobes, ruining not only the decorations but spoiling clothes with mould. Ensure that they are warm and well-ventilated. If possible place them on internal rather than external walls. Louvre doors are good as they allow warm air from the room to circulate; otherwise fit ventilator grilles at top and bottom, or leave sliding doors slightly open. Leave a small gap at the back of shelves. Polystyrene wall lining should help if the unit is against an outside wall. Do not have clothes too tightly packed; leave room for air to circulate.

9) Control condensation in between double glazing panes by putting in trays of condensation killer crystals.

Before redecorating a room badly affected by mould growth it is vital to kill off every trace of the fungus, otherwise it will break through and spoil the work. Do this by washing with a 1 : 8 solution of household bleach and water. Leave it on for a few hours to get to work, then wash off with plain water. Or you can buy a proprietary fungicidal wash. Despite every precaution the dreaded fungus may still reappear; if so wash down regularly with bleach solution.

Penetrating damp This should not affect a modern house with cavity walls, but may occur in old houses with solid ones, characteristically in spots where driving rain strikes old porous bricks with decaying mortar in between. Signs are damp patches anywhere on an external wall, visibly worse after rain, and possibly moss growing outside. Brushing a proprietary silicone waterproofer such as Aquaseal on to the outside may do the trick, but if not, repointing brickwork or repairing cracked masonry will be required.

Damp patches around windows or doors often occur when the frame has shrunk away from the wall leaving gaps: fill with a flexible mastic sold for the purpose. Also check the drip groove underneath outside timber window sills; if it has been filled up with paint scrape it clean.

Penetrating damp is much rarer on upper floors but may occur on walls just below the ceiling. It is usually a sign that something is wrong with the roof and/or guttering.

Rising damp occurs when a house has no damp proof course, or one which has failed, and creeps slowly up the walls from ground level. Wallpaper peels off at the bottom and emulsion paint and paper both show wavy tidemarks where the damp has brought discolouring salts along with it. It will be worse in wet weather, may dry out in summer, but always returns. Rotten skirting boards, with criss-cross cracking and so soft you can stick a knife in them, are a sure sign.

A modern house will always have a damp course, visible on the outside as a black line, the edge of the polythene barrier, in between two rows of bricks. This should be about 15cm above ground level. If soil has been heaped up above the line remove it at once as it enables water to bridge the damp proof course and get into the walls. In older houses a primitive damp proof course may have failed, or there may never have been one. The only cure is to have one fitted. This is not a DIY job, but is not expensive bearing in mind that a damp house will always be cold and unhealthy to live in; also damp can lead to even more serious problems, e.g. dry rot, (see page 203). Nowadays this is usually done by drilling holes in the bottom of the walls and injecting a damp proofing chemical; the work should be guaranteed for 25 years (which is no use whatsoever if the company goes bust the following week — pick an established one.) Check first with your local authority: grants for part of the cost may be available if the work is part of a general improvement of the property.

If you are not able to have a DPC fitted, palliative measures can be taken to keep the damp at bay and at least stop it ruining the decorations. These may also be necessary while the walls dry out after treatment, as this takes many months. You can buy various damp repellent products to paint on, or hang a foil-backed lining paper such as Star Wall.

Having a DPC fitted will not prevent damp rising through a solid floor (concrete, flagged or tiled) if this was laid without a damp proof membrane underneath, although it may improve considerably by virtue of the drier environment, especially if central heating is installed. Unless the problem continues to be severe in 6–12 months' time, paint it with water-repellent and/or lay foil-backed building paper underneath the floor covering. Never lay vinyl floor coverings on a suspect solid floor as they are completely impervious and will trap any water that appears. Rush matting is an ideal choice as it actually enjoys being slightly damp (but turn it regularly); or rugs made from natural fibres (jute or cotton, but not wool). If contemplating fitted carpet seek advice before buying, but broadly speaking a carpet containing some natural fibre, laid on a natural-fibre or paper underlay, will be better than an all-synthetic foam-backed one, or a foam underlay.

Efflorescence This is the name given to an accumulation of salts in a wall which crystallize on the surface forming fluffy or powdery white deposits. It often occurs on brand-new brickwork, and should disappear when this dries out, but is also a sign that rising or penetrating damp is present, or has not been fully cured. It is not serious, just unsightly. It can be temporarily concealed under wallpaper or paint, but always breaks through again, when it should be brushed off, not wiped with a damp cloth. The only real cure is replastering the affected area with a waterproof render, and the paperwork that comes with a chemical DPC may specify this.

UNWANTED FIREPLACES

When a fireplace is not going to be used it should at the very least be boarded up, otherwise precious heat escapes up the chimney in winter. Removing it altogether, especially if it is a large tiled one with a raised hearth, will make a small room look unbelievably bigger. If that is beyond you, removing a raised hearth alone is surprisingly easy, and will do a lot to make a room look bigger as the floor covering can then be carried right through. But think twice before removing every single fireplace in the house. Personally I like to have one potentially usable hearth (boarded up in a temporary way), for emergency use. Central heating is great, but if either gas or electricity fails it stops dead.

Whenever a fireplace is sealed up it is advisable to have the chimney capped otherwise birds occasionally fall down and become trapped. If taking one out, have the chimney swept first, or put up with the possibility of great drifts of soot being dislodged by vibration as you work.

Boarding up   This is a good method to use for Victorian cast iron or marbled slate fireplaces, which make attractive focal points regardless of their original use. A small fireplace opening can be very simply boarded up with hardboard. There is usually a convenient ledge somewhere to rest the board against; if it happens to be timber you can screw or nail it in place. But usually it will be metal, so you will have to use an epoxy adhesive (Araldite). I have even successfully bedded a small panel in with Polyfilla.

Lacking a convenient ledge, make up a simple timber frame to fit into the opening tightly and fix the panel to that. This is often the best method with a tiled fireplace. Decorate the panel to match the wall behind.

If the opening is large use a more rigid material: chipboard, or something incombustible such as asbestos fibre board, if a gas fire or other heating appliance is to stand on the hearth.

Boarded-up fireplaces are supposed to be fitted with a plastic ventilator to allow air to circulate up the chimney. As this looks very ugly when the fire surround is left in place and the wretched thing cannot be hidden by furniture, either use perforated hardboard, or leave a small gap at the bottom of the panel.

Removing a raised hearth   The raised part of a tiled fireplace which lies on the floor is quite separate from the actual fireplace surround, and can be removed without disturbing that part. It is just bedded on to cement laid on the floor, and should leave nothing behind it except a mark. You need some husky tools to do the job: club hammer and cold chisel or bolster chisel (the wide cold chisel used by bricklayers), and a crowbar if possible; otherwise make do with a garden spade. Hammer away at the cement all round the base of the hearth to break its grip, then gradually prise the hearth up with the crowbar and/or spade.

You now have a disposal problem. Your local council should have a large refuse tip for items like this, but getting it there is up to you. Otherwise keep an eye open for hired rubbish skips in your area and negotiate a fee with the householder for feeding in your mite.

Removing a fire surround   Doing this is not as hard as it looks, because although the fire surround appears to be an integral part of the structure, it is actually just fixed on to the face of the wall by metal lugs, which are concealed under the plaster. But it is very heavy work,

34

needing at least two fairly strong people. Tiled fire surrounds, in particular, are unbelievably heavy, as they are made of solid concrete underneath the tiles, reinforced with metal bars. So you may prefer to have this part of the job done for you (which also gets you out of the disposal problem) and just tackle the making good afterwards.

Note Nobody wants 50s tiled fireplaces, but a large cast iron or marbled slate one could bring eager buyers waving pound notes if you advertise it in the columns of your local newspaper.

Start by getting the hearth out of the way, if there is one, as described above. (You will need the same tools for the whole job.) Next locate the fixing lugs: there is usually one each side near the top and bottom. Chip away plaster to expose them and unscrew or prise them off. Lever the surround gently away from the wall with a crowbar; the second person should stand ready to support it in case it begins to topple forward. If it is too heavy to move in one piece, cover it with cloth to stop debris flying and smash it up. A sledge hammer, which has a longer handle, is the best tool, but a heavy club hammer will do.

Depending on the type of fireplace, it may then be necessary to hack out some more rubble and bricks in order to leave a neat hole, especially if the opening is sizable and you want to make use of it rather than close it up level with the chimney breast. However much you remove, do not disturb the horizontal lintel; this is supporting all the weight of the masonry above the opening. It usually consists of a metal bar, sometimes with brick or timber as well.

The opening can be closed with lightweight concrete blocks, with bricks, or with a piece of chipboard. (If using the space, board off the chimney with a chipboard or plasterboard 'ceiling'.) Bricking up is quite straightforward if the opening is neat and rectangular. You then have to replaster the new brick or blockwork; but this is not such an awesome task as it used to be now that you can buy ready-mixed plaster especially designed for DIY use. It is called Polyplasta and stays workable for considerably longer than regular builders' plaster. To apply a large area of plaster like this you need a proper steel float. These are expensive; try and borrow one. The surface when dry is smooth enough to paper over, but for painting finish it with a coat of Polyskim. This is a fine-surfaced ready-mixed plaster which comes complete with a plastic spreader.

Boarding the opening up is easier and quicker, provided that you can find some chipboard or plywood of exactly the same thickness as the surrounding plaster (or fractionally less). For a perfect finish skim over the whole chimney breast with Polyskim; otherwise the edges of the board are liable to show up as hard line, even under thick textured paper. Fix the board at frequent intervals with countersunk screws.

Whichever method you use leave or cut a hole at centre bottom and fit a plastic ventilator. Or if using bricks insert a perforated air brick in the appropriate place.

BLOCKED SINK

When that awful moment comes and the dirty washing-up water fails to swirl merrily away but just sits there sulking, the first thing to do is to look underneath the sink. There you will see what plumbers call a trap, which is permanently filled with water to stop drain smells from entering the house. What has gone wrong is that it has also trapped some solids — often tea leaves or congealed fat — which are stopping the water above from flowing through. Some traps are U-shaped, others are like an antique bottle with rounded bottom. Depending on which type you see you can expect the job to be difficult, fairly easy or a walkover, (see diagrams).

Metal U-trap This is the old-fashioned type and often cannot be opened unless you have a wrench to undo the eye at the bottom, although there are some with lugs which are turned by inserting a length of wood between them. This is often near impossible with either type because the nut has been in place for so many years it has seized up solid. If it's one of these horrors that confronts you it's worth trying to clear the blockage with a rubber plunger first (cheap from hardware stores). Block the overflow hole in the sink, if there is one, with a cloth; part-fill the sink with water if this is not already the case, and pump the plunger up and down over the outlet; this creates a vacuum pressure which will, with any luck, dislodge the blockage.

If this fails place a bucket under the trap and undo the eye as shown in the diagram. Go carefully as it is surprisingly easy to damage these old traps, made of soft lead. Grip the nut firmly with the wrench and place a piece of wood inside the U. Simultaneously turn the wrench anti-clockwise to undo the eye, and counteract this turning force with the wood. Poke around inside the trap with a piece of bent coathanger wire to clear all the debris and run the tap to flush the trap clean. Replace the nut firmly. Keep the bucket in place and run the tap; there may well be a slight leakage from the eye. Do not overtighten the nut attempting to cure this; buy something called PTFE joint tape and wrap a little around the threaded bit at the bottom of the U before replacing the nut.

Plastic U-trap These can be opened by hand. Take hold of both the big lock nuts on the U bend and unscrew them so that the whole U comes off. If they are tight wrap your hands in a cloth, and/or try applying a little boiling water. Then proceed as above, applying tape to both threads if necessary.

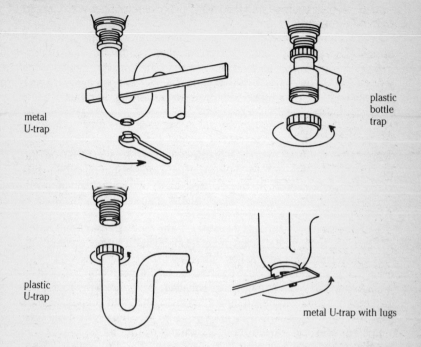

metal
U-trap

plastic
bottle
trap

plastic
U-trap

metal U-trap with lugs

Bottle-trap All you need do here is grab hold of the trap to steady it and unscrew the rounded bottom part.

Note To prevent it all happening again next week, wash tea leaves down with plenty of cold water, and if you must pour used cooking oil down the sink, dilute it with lots of very hot detergent solution.

Blocked drain If water leaves a sink slowly, with loud noises, the trouble is usually that the gully outside is blocked with leaves and kitchen waste, which can easily be cleared away; clean the lift-off grid thoroughly while you're at it. (To prevent this happening again, fit a plastic cover — from builders merchants.) Sometimes the bottom of the gully becomes blocked with the silt of ages. To clear this, bale out the water with a jam jar and sop up the last bit with an old mop or rags. Scoop out the dirt with a trowel; finally poke around with a bit of wire to feel that the outlet is clear. Flush clean, ideally with a hose pipe so that you can get the water down under pressure.

If a blockage is caused by congealed grease, a solution of caustic soda or proprietary drain cleaner should do the trick. Follow the instructions

37

exactly as it's dangerous stuff, and use it all up; don't leave it lying around for children to find.

For more deep-seated problems, revealed by lifting up the metal lid of an inspection trap and finding it full of unpleasant water, most of us, including myself, will deem it time to send for Dyno-rod. But having written the cheque I resolved that should it ever happen again I would grit my teeth, hold my nose and hire some drain-clearing rods.

TAP TROUBLES

When a tap continues to drip, drip, drip however hard you turn it off, the time has more than come for a new washer. Don't be put off if doing this job sounds complicated; it's one of those things that's hard to explain but easy to do. But you will need an adjustable spanner that opens up to at least 25mm to undo the relevant nut.

The first step is to shut off the water. If the tap is the cold one in the kitchen, no problem: this is fed direct from the main supply in the street, and the stop tap is close by, very often right there under the sink. With other cold taps you must close the stop tap or stop cock which should be fitted to the cold water storage tank, usually to be found in the roof space (remember about walking on the timber joists only, and not putting your foot through the ceiling). With hot taps close the stop cock on the pipe supplying cold water from the storage tank to the hot tank, which is usually close by. You then have to drain the hot water off so; a) remember to switch off any hot water heaters or boilers involved and b) try to do the job at a time when it is not full to the brim of expensively heated water (i.e. *after* doing laundry or having a bath).

Once you have had some experience at rewashering taps it is theoretically possible to rewasher hot taps without draining the system; but I can't claim to have tried it. What you do is turn all other hot taps full on to reduce the amount of water that will be flowing from the one being worked on; also muffle the outlet in a large piece of old towel. Then you carry out the operation described below with the dexterity and speed of a Cuban cigar roller.

With a basic pillar tap, (see diagram), the kind found in kitchens, first undo the cross head, the bit you turn it on and off by. Undo the protective shield — this should be possible by hand, but if not use the adjustable spanner on the flat-sided rim at the bottom. Slip the spanner underneath the shield and lever upwards to force off both shield and cross head. Use the spanner to unscrew the large hexagonal gland nut, holding the tap firm while turning. You can now lift out the body of the tap to expose the cause of the trouble, the jumper — a metal disc and stem carrying the washer. This may be just sitting there, or may be loosely attached.

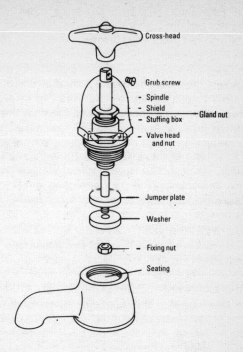

Cross-head

Grub screw

Spindle
Shield
Stuffing box — **Gland nut**
Valve head
and nut

Jumper plate

Washer

Fixing nut

Seating

Removing the old washer can be difficult as the nut securing it to the
metal disc may be corroded. If possible hold the stem in a vice while
turning the nut with the adjustable spanner. Otherwise hold the edge of
the metal disc in a pair of pliers. Remove the old washer and fit a new one
of the same size. (If the screw is impossible to undo take the whole thing
to a hardware shop and get a replacement.) Tap washers are usually
12mm across for a sink or basin tap, 19mm for a bath one, and are now
suitable for both hot and cold taps. They are cheap, so if in doubt get one
of each before starting.

Check before fitting the new washer that the metal disc is clean, with
no corroded bits of old washer sticking to it, as it must be a snug fit.
Replace the jumper inside the tap, tighten the hexagonal nut, replace the
shield and screw back the cross head. Turn on water, test and sit back
with glow of satisfaction.

Bathroom taps These often have a chunky type of pull-off head
instead of the common-or-garden cross head, and there is no fixing

screw to be seen. But it is there, lurking under the button in the top, which can be prised out with a screwdriver. The whole thing then just pulls off and you can proceed as before.

Supataps These are the skinny-looking taps which burn your fingers if the water is very hot as the tap nozzle is combined with the cross head. But they have a great advantage: washers can be renewed without cutting off the water, as a check valve inside does this automatically. Hold the nozzle firmly with one hand and loosen the large nut above it with the spanner. Then hold the nut in place and unscrew the nozzle: water will flow out at first, but will gradually stop. Stick a pencil into the nozzle outlet to push out a complicated piece called the flow straightener. The jumper is in the top of this, and is all in one piece; obtain a new one of the same size.

Mixer taps With these you can get water leaking from around the base of the swivelling outlet as well as via the actual taps. First get some replacement seals from a builders' merchant. They differ, as usual — quote the brand of tap stamped on front or back (use a mirror to read if at back). Unscrew or lever up the ring-shaped shroud at its base (no need to turn off water) and slip it off. Grip the ends of the metal clip inside with a pair of pliers and contract or expand it so that it comes out and can be slipped off. Pull off the nozzle. Remove the remains of the perished seals inside and fit the new ones.

Pillar taps — leaking When a tap leaks water at the top, just underneath the cross head, it can be fixed without turning off the water. Remove the cross head and shield as above. Then instead of undoing the gland nut, *tighten* it by one quarter turn. Replace the cross head temporarily and see if the tap turns off easily enough; if not loosen the nut off a bit. Reassemble tap as before. If this treatment fails it means that the packing inside which is meant to waterproof the tap has failed. Turn off the appropriate stop tap, disassemble the tap as above, unscrew the gland nut and pack the space around the bottom of the tap spindle with string or thick wool coated with petroleum jelly (Vaseline).

Lime scale Taps leaking in all directions will have caused a build-up of lime scale on the sink, bath or basin. On sanitary pottery and vitreous enamel this can be removed with a proprietary chemical; but this marks stainless steel, so on such a sink scrape thick deposits lightly and finish off with steel wool pads.

LOO PROBLEMS

Water tanks such as a lavatory cistern contain a simple device inside to ensure that once sufficient water has entered, the supply shuts off automatically: the ball valve. This floats on top of the water and as it rises operates a valve to shut the water off. When water is drawn off the ball sinks and the valve opens. They seldom go wrong but if they do the likely causes are mis-aligned ball, perforated ball or worn valve washer. Signs of trouble are a persistent drip from the overflow pipe projecting through the outside wall

(The water storage tank serving the whole house also has a ball valve and may suffer from the same ills.)

Lift off the cistern lid and first try bending the long arm attached to the floating ball gently but firmly *downwards*. This causes the water supply to be shut off more quickly and may be all that is needed. Second check for signs that the ball is perforated — this is more likely with an old-fashioned metal one than with a modern plastic one. To test tie up the long arm to a piece of wood placed across the cistern, to stop water flowing in. Unscrew the ball, plunge into water like a bicycle inner tube and watch for air bubbles. Repair is a matter of getting a new one and screwing it on. But as such troubles are invariably noticed on bank holiday weekends or over Christmas, here's how to make a temporary repair. Empty out the water and cover the ball in a plastic bag (not the sort with safety holes in it!) and tie on tightly round the arm. Screw it back on, remove the wood and string and the cistern can safely be used.

If water still flows when the ball is lifted up to its fullest extent a perished washer is usually the cause. Mending this entails turning off the water supply to the cistern from the storage tank by closing the stop cock. The bad news is that there are now so many different types of valve (I took a look at mine and was confronted with something quite unlike anything in my reference books — no large ball float, just a little nylon canister) that I can't possibly explain how to deal with them all; nor do I know! The good news is that washers rarely perish these days. If you do get the problem, acquire an up-to-date book on DIY plumbing and you will find that it's a straightforward job once you know what type of creature you are dealing with.

Antique cisterns If you are living with the really old-fashioned kind of lavatory cistern, one of those noisy cast-iron monsters fixed high on the wall, a modern plumbing book may not help you in case of trouble, as they don't have a ball valve, but operate in a much more primitive way. What usually goes wrong is that water continues to flow slowly down the flush pipe, and can only be stopped by pulling the chain again. This is probably happening simply because years of rust and dirt have built up in the bottom of the cistern, and a good clean out should put things right.

Flush pipe seal Modern lavatories have another weak point, which I have never seen mentioned in DIY books, but have had to repair twice, and that is the rubber seal covering the flush pipe where it enters the back of the pan. These eventually perish and a steady drip ensues. All you have to do is measure what size it is, obtain a replacement from a hardware store and fit. This should not be difficult but, as usual, you can't do the job unless you have the right tool — a large spanner or wrench with which to undo the nut at the base of the cistern. This enables you to free the short length of pipe between cistern and loo, take off the perished seal and push on the new one.

Poor flushing This can be caused because the ball valve is misaligned and is closing before the full quantity of water has flowed into the cistern. In this case bend the arm gently but firmly *upwards*.

If the loo has been neglected, the cause may be lime scale blocking the outlet holes concealed under the rim: use a mirror to see if this is the case. Use a lime-scale-removing lavatory cleaner to attack it (bleach is no good), leaving it on for plenty of time and scraping as well as brushing clean.

Note in cases of emergency such as cistern failure, or freezing up or a long break in the public water supply a lavatory can be flushed perfectly well with a household bucket full of water.

Blockage To clear this you need a special long-handled plunger with a metal plate above the rubber bit; ones designed for sinks won't do the trick. Move it up and down inside the pan vigorously to create enough suction to shift the blockage. If this fails, unless you fancy hiring some drain rods you need the plumber.

3 Decorating

Decorating is the most popular of all DIY activities. In a recent Polycell report on the DIY market, 75 per cent of women interviewed had had experience of painting and paperhanging, 65 per cent within the last twelve months. Which is not surprising given the steady increase in home ownership combined with the fact that doing your own decorating is a major way of saving money, as well as being extremely satisfying. Redecorating a room really can transform it. I once did a friend's living room while she and small children were on holiday. When they returned the little boy went into the room first and hurtled out again shouting, 'Mummy, Mummy, we've got a new room!'

Much of the popularity of DIY decorating stems from the new materials developed over the last twenty years. In the good old days gloss paint smelled vile and gave patchy results. Emulsion and non-drip paints hadn't been invented. Neither had ready-pasted vinyl wallcoverings; there was just wallpaper, which had to have its selvedges laboriously and unevenly trimmed off on a funny machine or by hand, and was hung with paste hell-bent on going lumpy and smudging the pattern. And as for trying to do the preparation work without Polyfilla, I don't think I could contemplate it.

On the whole I think women make better decorators than men because they are more patient and are prepared to take pains. Slapping on a coat of emulsion regardless may be the right thing occasionally, but usually it pays to do a thorough job which not only looks good on day one, but will endure five years of family life before it needs redoing. On the other hand you don't want to be too perfectionist or you may get fed up after doing one room. So in the pages that follow I have tried to steer a middle course between perfectionism and slapdashery, and to indicate when it may be sensible to veer towards one or the other.

BASIC EQUIPMENT

Getting equipped to do your own decorating involves a whole raft of new tools. But fortunately they are not nearly as expensive as general-purpose hand tools. Indeed some are very cheap indeed; but as usual it's best to buy good-quality ones as they will last longer and often do a better job. However I no longer apply this to paintbrushes, as I find that modern easy-brush-clean paints, marvellous though they are, have a bad effect on them, as the constant washing splays out the bristles. So now I buy cheap sets costing about £1.99 for three. The beauty of this is that if you do suffer total collapse after a gruelling session and fail to clean them you can throw them out with a clear conscience.

Unless your ceilings are exceptionally low and can be touched while standing on the floor you will need a step-ladder in addition to the equipment listed below. Never be tempted to work standing on a chair. You can't actually do it anyway if emulsion painting or washing, as there is nowhere to put the tray or bucket. But even for wallpapering it's very dangerous as you have nothing to hold on to and can easily fall. As falling off chairs or stools while trying to clean windows, do spring cleaning or reach high cupboards is a major cause of domestic accidents, in most houses you need a stepladder anyway, even if it's only small. But make sure that it is one suitable for decorating, with a platform at the top (three-in-one type ladders, although temptingly versatile, lack this essential feature).

Tools for preparation work Sanding block and abrasive papers for smoothing rough walls and keying paintwork; stripping knife for removing old wallpaper; triangular and combination shave hooks for scraping paint off flat and moulded woodwork; filling knife for applying

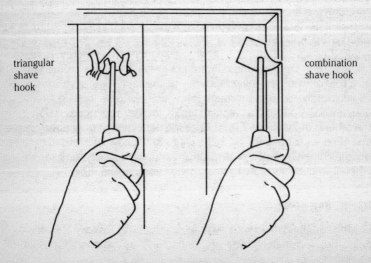

triangular
shave
hook

combination
shave hook

filler to cracks; plastic bucket and household sponge for washing down.

Tools for painting 18cm sponge roller with paint tray; set of brushes (5cm, 2.5cm, 20mm).

Tools for hanging ready-pasted wallcoverings Steel tape and Stanley knife from basic tool kit; wallpaper shears; plumb-line; water trough; sponge.

Tools for hanging conventional wallcoverings As above minus trough, plus pasting brush and smoothing brush; (Vinyl can be hung with a sponge, but a brush is better as the bristle ends are good for knocking wallcoverings into corners.) Also somewhere to paste: professionals use lightweight folding tables which are just the right width, but I have never bothered to acquire one myself, not just because of the cost, but also the attendant storage problem. Any work surface about 1.5 metres long will do; if the top is likely to object to having paste washed off it, cover with polythene first. Some people use a flush door set on trestles or placed on top of a table. A door fitted with rising butt hinges is ideal as they just lift off. Or you could always hire a regular pasting table.

EXTRA EQUIPMENT

Sometimes economy is not the first consideration; speed and getting the job done easily can be just as important. Three recently introduced tools can help here.

One is the Black and Decker Paintmate, a spray painting system powered by a soda syphon bulb. A litre can of paint fits into the plastic body of the Paintmate machine, which is not much bigger than a litre bottle of

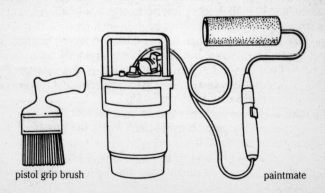

pistol grip brush   paintmate

45

wine, and has a clip to hang it on to your belt. The machine delivers a supply of paint via a plastic tube to a control handle, into which fit a roller, large paint pad or brush, as required. It is an extremely clean and convenient way to paint, and quite foolproof; provided that you clean the machine out properly after use, it won't clog up halfway through the job. Cleaning is easy too: you just fit a rubber fitment on to the kitchen tap and force water through the system until it runs clear.

The original Paintmate could only be used with special tubs of Berger paint, emulsion or gloss, which limited the colours available, but now an adaptor enables other brands of emulsion paint to be used also. Price is about £15 for the machine, £5 for an adaptor.

Another Black and Decker brainchild is an electric hot air stripper. If I had had one of these in my first house, a Victorian terrace in which every

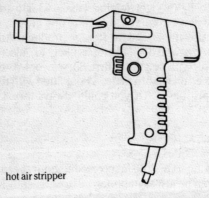

hot air stripper

last door, window and skirting was painted either black or brown, and mostly in terrible condition, I would have saved a fortune on extra coats of paint, paint-removing chemicals and payments to professional door strippers, not to mention hours of labour. *And* I would still have had the tool at the end of it all. It looks like an overgrown hairdryer, and blasts out a stream of air which is hot enough to melt paint so that it can be scraped off, but not hot enough to char the wood, which is what usually happens with a blowlamp. It is also all-but guaranteed not to crack the glass when used on window frames, another common disaster. Price is about £15. Alternatively use a gas torch or blowlamp, but be very careful with the flame (see Safety First, page 188).

The third useful aid is much cheaper than the first two — only about £4.50. This is a Ting paint brush, which has a big pistol-grip handle instead of the conventional straight one, designed to make painting large areas both quicker and easier as it is much less tiring to use.

Another time-consuming situation is a house papered throughout with unbearable wallpaper, particularly if some of it is the hard-to-strip washable kind, or has been painted over. Hiring a steam wallpaper stripper and doing the lot in one ghastly weekend can be money well spent. It doesn't matter if you don't get round to actually redecorating some of the rooms for months (in my case years). Bare plaster will come to no harm, and is infinitely preferable to cabbage roses or glittering Regency stripes. Cost is around £6 for two days, plus £20 deposit.

Note steam wallpaper strippers are also good for removing textured wall paints.

REACHING THE HEIGHTS

Decorating the stairway, particularly in an old house with high ceilings, presents problems because to reach the ceiling and upper walls you need to be floating in thin air over the stair well. It is easier to paint than hang paper because for the latter you have to be close up, whereas emulsion paint can be applied from quite a distance by using a long-handled roller and a brush tied to a stick for finishing off. Another problem with wallpaper is that the lengths towards the bottom of the stairs are extremely long and hard to handle, as they run clear up to the first floor ceiling. With ordinary wallpaper their sheer weight may cause the paper to stretch, thus making it impossible to match up any pattern, so it's best to use vinyl wallcovering which does not stretch. This also wears much better, pushing the prospect of having to do it all again well into the future.

To get good access to the top you need both a stepladder and a ladder, and a long scaffold plank. Exactly how they are arranged depends on the design of the stairs. But generally the ladder is placed towards the bottom of the stairs, leaning against the wall or banister rail above it, and the plank runs across to a stepladder on the landing. If there is no room to open it up, use it folded like a ladder, nailing a batten across the foot to prevent it from slipping. On some stairs you may need a further length of plank, lashed at right angles to the first one and supported on a strong box or Workmate bench.

Working on a stairway is more dangerous than elsewhere inside the house because you can fall so much further. When using a ladder make sure not to have it at too acute an angle to the wall, or it could tip back taking you with it. If it is used standing with its foot on a step, and pointing up the staircase, nail a batten across the step to prevent it from slipping.

If possible do painting with the stairs bare, but if a carpet has to be protected, tack the dust sheets securely into the treads.

To reach the area over a bath, instead of balancing dangerously on the bath rim, make a platform to stand on. Cut two stout planks to fit across the bath, braced with two lengths of batten screwed on underneath to fit snugly inside the bath sides. Protect the bath with bits of cloth when using the platform.

PREPARATION

Thorough preparation, we are always told, is the key to a successful decorating job that will look good and last long. But the work can become so tedious that it's tempting to ignore all that good advice and just slap on some paint regardless. What can you get away without doing, and what is essential?

Cleaning and filling Whatever else you shirk you must provide a clean surface: no paint, or wallpaper paste, will stick on properly over dirt, grease or dust. And if the old finish is flaking off it will continue to do so, taking your nice new paint with it. More of that later.

Ceilings can often just be brushed clean, but walls and woodwork are bound to have greasy fingermarks and other dirt all over, and should be washed. They call it washing *down*, but actually you are supposed to do it from the bottom up, to prevent dirty streaks from staining the wall. This is really more important if you are only spring-cleaning, as the marks are not very likely to show through paint. Sugar soap or proprietary products based on it are best for this job, but there's nothing wrong with Flash and hot water. (Other detergents make too much lather.)

Then fill all holes and cracks with cellulose filler such as Polyfilla. If left, everything except holes so small they get filled by paint will show up an ugly black in fresh light-coloured paint. (If papering, of course you don't have to be so fussy.) When old woodwork is black or brown, holes are very hard to see — fill them *after* applying a light undercoat.

To cope with dirty great holes you need to have a few tricks up your sleeve. Part-fill deep ones with crumpled newspaper, or they take forever to dry. Also use newspaper to stop filler dropping down through large gaps at tops of skirting boards. On plasterboard, squash some wire netting into the hole to trap the filler. Bashed corners: put on plenty of filler, mould with a wet rubber glove and rub down with abrasive paper on a sanding block when dry to match the angle on the undamaged part. With all large holes, brush out dust before filling, and knock away any loose material (you may have to make the damage quite a bit worse in order to make it better). Cellulose filler shrinks slightly when drying, so give all noticeably 'fallen-in' spots another layer. Don't forget to fill the little gap that often appears between ceiling and walls; it is surprisingly noticeable. A finger is good for pressing the filler into the angle.

If you have really bad luck, and removing wallpaper also removes large areas of plaster, you need something more than cartons of cellulose filler, or you will go bankrupt. Ordinary pink plaster is the cheapest stuff to use, but it dries while you're still thinking where to put it. A ready-mixed plaster, though more expensive, is much easier to use as it dries very slowly. Also you get a plastic float to put the stuff on with (steel floats are very expensive). If only the thin top layer of plaster has come away use Polyskim; for deeper holes (up to 5cm) use Polyplasta.

Note the best thing to use for mixing up filler is a square of hardboard; because it's flat you can scrape off every bit and not waste any. Mix in the water by making a well in the centre of the heap of powder, as if making Yorkshire pudding batter.

Ceilings A ceiling in an old house may have old-fashioned distemper or whitewash on it (test with a wet finger to see if it turns grey and comes off). This *must* be washed off, or the wetting action of emulsion paint will fetch it off in patches as you work and you will never get a good finish. A thick ceiling paper should take a coat of ordinary emulsion perfectly well (make sure it is still well stuck down at seams) but if you plan to use one of the new textured paints remove paper first. A gloss-painted ceiling (or wall) needs thorough sanding before being emulsion-painted or the new paint will adhere so poorly to the shiny surface it will scrape off with a fingernail.

Woodwork Even if the paint is in good condition and you just want to change the colour, it needs lightly rubbing down with fine abrasive paper, otherwise the new paint will part company with the old at the first knock from vacuum cleaner or kick from booted foot. This is called keying, and wet-or-dry paper, used wet, is particularly good for it. Wet it with white spirit to degrease and key in one go. Steel wool (grade 000) is good too but be careful to brush off every particle before painting, particularly if using a water-based paint, or you could end up with rusty flecks in the finish. Or you can use a product called liquid stripper, which washes and prepares the surface in one operation.

If the paint is disfigured by runs, or chipped, more thorough rubbing down starting with coarser paper, is necessary to smooth these out. Scrape off any paint that's actually flaking off. Stripping paint off completely is rarely necessary, and there is absolutely no virtue in doing it unless there are so many layers that the doors no longer close. Well-rubbed down old paintwork, given an undercoat, makes an excellent foundation for new paint. Just strip any sections that are really bad: often window ledges. (See page 137 for a guide to stripping techniques.)

Wherever wood has been scraped or stripped bare, prime before painting to seal the surface.

Walls When these are papered the crunch question is always *must* I face up to stripping it all off before redecorating?

Yes, if it is old, thin or multi-layered, or was badly-hung in the first place, with overlapping or gappy seams. The wetting action of new paint lifts wallpaper up wherever it is not firmly stuck to the wall, and unattractive blisters bloom all over the place. Old wallpaper also drinks up paint and paste, so reducing coverage rates and making new paper difficult to hang as it cannot be slid around on the wall easily.

No, if it is a single layer of good-quality paper, well-hung, firmly in place and reasonably clean. Especially if it has an interesting texture, such paper makes a good foundation for a coat of emulsion. (If blisters appear after painting, prick small ones with a pin; slit larger ones and stick down.) Another consideration here is that in old houses stripping off wallpaper may reveal walls in terrible condition, and even take some of the plaster with it, so that all you achieve is to create more work. Watch out for papers with gold in the pattern — this *always* shows through paint, even if not for a few months; the effect can be attractive or horrible, depending on the pattern. And do not paint directly over a vinyl paper — the surface is too slippery, and in any case they are easy to strip: simply peel off the plastic top layer, leaving the backing paper on the wall as a perfect foundation for the paint. But do it gently — if bits of backing paper come away too the patches are hard to disguise.

To remove other wallpapers easily give them a really good soaking. (Go easy near light switches and sockets. Protect them with a bit of polythene, or wrap in a bit of old towel to soak water up before it creeps in.) Proprietary products to put on the water help but are not essential. If the paper has a washable surface, or has been overpainted, score with a serrated wallpaper scraper or wire brush to let the water penetrate. The paper is ready when the scraper will lift it off easily in quite large strips. If you try to force it off you will get lots of little triangular marks from the stripping blade in the plaster which are very noticeable under emulsion paint.

If old walls are badly pitted, cracked or flaking don't waste time trying to get them smooth enough to paint on. Sand, scrape and fill roughly, then hang some paper before painting (see page 57).

CHOOSING PAINT

Getting the right paint is not just a question of choosing the right colour, but the right type for the job in question. Pick the wrong kind and you can make the job harder than need be, and end up with an unsatisfactory result. Also paint technology advances rapidly, and there may be just the paint for you sitting in the shop, only you've never heard of it. Take your pick from:

Emulsion paints Choose these for walls and ceilings. Being water-based these vinyl paints are easy to apply and dry in a few hours. Matt emulsion is best for concealing defects on less-than-perfect walls, and gives a softer look. Silk emulsion gives a pleasant sheen and looks best on newer plaster or over a lining paper. Both can be washed, vinyl silk more so than matt. Coverage: about 11 sq metres per litre for silk; 12 for matt.

Solid emulsion At the beginning of 1984 ICI Dulux introduced a solid emulsion which comes ready to use in a plastic paint roller tray. Like all new wonder products it is a little more expensive than the standard variety, but is much cleaner and easier to use. It is available in brilliant white and six 'natural white' shades; coverage is about 12 sq metres per $2\frac{1}{2}$ litre tray.

Gloss paints Choose these for woodwork and metal. They are oil-based, the toughest and most washable. Most people prefer the high gloss finish; satin or eggshell finishes are also made but are less hardwearing. Some gloss paints are non-drip (thixotropic); they are very thick and very often enable a one-coat job to be done. Whatever type you choose look for three vital words on the can: Easy Brush Clean. This means that brushes can be washed in hot water and detergent after use, which is far, far easier than messing about with white spirit. (If you do have to use white spirit for brush cleaning leave it in the jar for a week or two, when the paint will have solidified at the bottom. The white spirit can then be poured off and used again.) Gloss paints require overnight drying. Coverage: about 8.5 sq metres per 500 ml for conventional gloss; 6 for non-drip.

Undercoats and primers For a perfect job gloss paint (unless non-drip) should be preceded by a matching undercoat. This is a completely matt paint which covers up the colour beneath and is just the right texture to give the top coat maximum grip. It is easier to paint with than gloss, so it makes good sense to use it, rather than, as people often do, two coats of the gloss finish.

Primer is only needed if the wood or metal, or sections of it, have been stripped bare. Universal primer is economical as it is suitable for wood, metal and plaster; acrylic primer/undercoat is quick as, being water-based, it dries in a few hours, and does both jobs in one (do not use on metal). Coverage: about 7.5 sq metres per 500 ml for undercoat.

All-purpose paint Dulux silthane silk is an oil-based paint that gives a silky finish. It's by way of being a cross between gloss and vinyl silk, so for a quick job you could go right through a room with a big can of it. It's also a good choice for painting walls and ceilings when a very hardwearing finish is needed — say in steamy kitchens or bathrooms. (Never use gloss paint here: it's expensive, hard to do, unattractive and quite unnecessary.) Overnight drying time is required. Coverage rate: 12 sq metres per litre.

Machine-mixed paints For a really huge choice of colours (over 500) choose paint from one of the mix-while-you-wait machines such as Dulux Matchmaker, Berger Colorizer and Crown Colour Cue. The colour cards available for these paints are an invaluable decorating aid, as each one shows a group of co-ordinated shades, and you can take a batch home to study at your leisure. (See page 68 for some advice on choosing colour.) Machine-mixed paints come in gloss and satin finishes; matt and silk emulsions.

Textured paints These are particularly good for elderly ceilings, as they both disguise a poor surface and, because of their elasticity, keep cracks covered. Polytex comes in white and six pastel shades and gives a roughcast finish with a roller, a finer finish if applied with a brush. You can also, if so inclined, comb it into patterns while wet. For use on walls pick a smoother-surfaced product such as Polyripple, which is equally flexible and flaw hiding but less prickly to the touch.

Special paints All kinds of products are available to deal with nasty problems like resin bleeding out of knots in new wood, persistent stains, rust and damp. A big DIY store will have a selection.

Out of doors High-quality emulsion paints can be used on exterior walls, but for a long-lasting job choose a masonry paint or exterior wall finish, which are formulated to resist the onslaughts of wind and rain and cover cracks. High-gloss paint is usually suitable for exterior woodwork and metalwork, but check the can before buying.

Can sizes Think metric: all brands are now packed in metric sizes. Emulsion paint is sold in litres, 2.5 litres and 5 litres. For those of us brought up on imperial: these correspond to the old quart, $\frac{1}{2}$-gallon and gallon cans. In gloss paint the sizes normally needed for doing woodwork are 250 and 500 ml, which correspond to the old $\frac{1}{2}$ and 1 pints. Smaller and larger sizes are available.

Prices Paint prices vary considerably, and it always pays to shop around. The big DIY supermarkets and chain stores, who buy by the paint lake, have the lowest prices, if not all the colours. But if you only want a small quantity of a standard item, the prices at the shop nearest you may prove the best bargain viewed in terms of woman-hours and petrol or bus fares.

On the whole you get what you pay for in paint: higher prices bring better coverage and subtler colours. But DIY supermarkets' own brands are very good value, especially if you only want white. Standard paint ranges have a reasonably good choice of colours and contain all the most popular light and pastel shades, plus the new whites with a hint of colour. But if you want subtle off-beat colours you have to pay more for the machine-mixed ranges. Textured paints are not cheap, but you should get away with one coat.

PAINTING TECHNIQUES

Modern paints are so easy to use that it's almost impossible to do a bad job provided you've prepared the ground reasonably well. Always use a roller for applying emulsion. It's far less messy than a large paintbrush, particularly on ceilings, and big brushes are expensive and heavy to use. Fill in the gap round the edges where the roller won't reach with a small paintbrush or paint pad. Do not over-thin the paint or it will spatter about; roll it on up, down and across to make sure that no bits are missed. However, tiny bits always *do* get missed, and for that reason two coats are always better than one, unless you are simply recoating with the same colour. Also the first coat often looks a bit patchy, and only the second gives perfect smoothness, plus proper depth of colour if you are using anything stronger than a pastel shade. If you start early it's perfectly possible to apply two coats in a day. Should you not be painting the skirting boards, watch out for a fine paint splatter appearing on the top and wipe off with a damp rag as you go along and *before* it dries on. (Splatter also appears on watches and glasses; remove watch and wipe glasses clean before it dries. Also protect your hair from the instant-granny effect of white paint smears.)

When painting woodwork make sure to brush the paint out quite thinly using a criss-cross action so as to get an even coat (unless using non-drip; this is meant to be put on thickly and brushed out less). Watch out for runs and curtains (drips and wavy lines of thick paint) developing and avoid them by always finishing with upward strokes of the brush.

On doors, don't bother with all that business about painting in numbered sections. The main thing is to paint *quickly*, so that you are always painting into a wet edge, and won't get any demarcation lines. On no account stop for more than a minute or two; if the phone rings, ignore it. With a panelled door, don't let paint accumulate on the ledges, or it will run down during drying time and spoil the finish; brush it out of the corners, preferably with a small clean brush. Flush doors are the devil to paint well, and you may find that a big paint pad gives a better finish, or the small roller sold for getting down behind radiators. Divide the door mentally into three horizontal sections, start at the top and paint thinly.

To paint a sash window, pull the top (outer) half down and the bottom (inner) half up as far as they will go. Paint everything you can reach on the lower part of the outer sash, not forgetting the underside, and just the underside of the inner one. Then go up to the top and paint the soffit (the underside of the top of the frame) coming down the side a little on each side where the outer pulley is. Push the inner sash almost fully down and the outer sash almost fully up and continue; do not paint anything not painted before, and never the sash cords.

Whatever the type, paint a door or window first, frame last.

Do take the trouble to remove items of door and window furniture before starting. It makes painting easier as well as keeping them clean; if they *are* clean, that is. Often some idiot has already painted them, and they will need stripping. Fortunately paint stripper works very well on metal (if possible put them in a bath of it — use a metal or glass container) and you may find some nice brass underneath the gunge. Over-painted plastic door handles (also electrical fittings) can be stripped with chemical stripper but do it quickly before it starts to attack the plastic.

To keep paint off the edge of fitted carpets when painting the skirting board (also window panes) stick on strips of masking tape. Use a small brush (20mm) for fiddly work like glazing bars; a medium one (40mm) for most of the time and a large one (50mm) or paint pads for big areas like door panels or skirting boards.

Two enemies stand between you and that mirror-like gloss shown in the paint advertisements: dust and assorted foreign bodies. Don't sweep or vacuum the room immediately before starting to paint: allow several hours for dust to settle. Wipe over horizontal surfaces with a rag moistened in white spirit immediately before painting. Do not wear woollies; professional decorators always wear cotton coveralls. Make sure that the brush itself isn't full of dust. Always work in daylight; artificial light is never as bright, and you miss seeing the nasties: specks of dust, hairs and little flies are drawn irresistibly to the wet paint and will be stuck fast by morning. Lift them off straight away, ideally with a small dry brush. While the paint is drying keep people and pets out of the room. Gloss paint needs to dry overnight, unless you use a quick-drying lacquer such as Japlac, which can be recoated in 6 hours. And don't shut doors or windows for several days after painting them; just wedge them ajar. Although dry, the paint is still soft, and if the door/window is a tight fit in the frame the two can stick together so that when you open it a nasty mark appears down the edges. (With exterior doors, either wedge and secure with a door chain; or use quick-drying-lacquer, start early and complete next day.)

Tackle redecorating with paint in this order: ceiling first, walls second and woodwork last. (If papering walls do this last, after all painting is finished.)

CHOOSING WALLCOVERINGS

When you sally forth to acquire some wallpaper the whole business can be quite overwhelming because there are so many thousands of different types and designs on offer. It's not just wallpaper anymore, either. Nowadays we buy wallcoverings, which can be paper, plastic on paper, all plastic or a wide variety of other substances: metallic foil, fabric, cork or strands of grass. And most of them are not cheap; papering is almost always more expensive than painting. But if you can manage to find the right one, wallpaper has several advantages: it hides bad walls, gives a more finished, 'clothed' look; and is the only way of getting a pattern on to walls. (If you are the sort of person with the time and inclination to stencil your own you're reading the wrong book.) Keep three factors clearly in mind when browsing through pattern books:

1 Aesthetic: Do I really like this? Will I still like it next year? Will it go with the carpet/sofa/curtains?

2 Practical: Is it the right type of paper for the grotty walls I am lumbered with and the room involved? (See below.)

3 Economic: Can I afford it? Wallpaper prices vary enormously, from around £2 a roll for cheap thin paper printed in one or two colours, to £30 for something heavily embossed or hand printed. High cost does not necessarily mean better quality. Which end of the scale you should be approaching depends on where the paper is to go, and how soon you fancy having to replace it.

Learn to use the pattern books to help you make the right choice. Many now include the international performance symbols on the back of the samples, which are very helpful. They show at a glance whether a paper is washable, light fast, dry strippable, ready-pasted etc., and what the distance between design repeats is.

Another factor is that even a large DIY superstore will only have a certain amount of papers actually in stock. These, naturally will be ones that appeal to popular taste. So if you insist on walking out with it there and then you must restrict your choice to what's on the shelves (which can concentrate the mind wonderfully!). If you want something a little more *recherché* it has to be ordered but this usually only takes a few days. Whatever you choose, check that each roll has the same batch number — if they differ the colour and pattern match may not be quite perfect.

Ready-pasted wallcoverings Whoever invented these did a great service to the beginner decorator. They have dry paste on the back which is activated simply by dipping the length into a cardboard water trough. At one stroke this cuts out the need to buy pasting and smoothing brushes; mix up messy paste; and have a pasting table or other long worktop on which to work. Almost all ready-pasteds are paper-backed vinyls, so see the provisos about vinyl wallcoverings in general.

Vinyl wallcoverings Although quite a bit more expensive than traditional wallpaper, vinyls are well worth the money because as the plastic surface is tough, can be washed hard, even scrubbed, and shrugs off steam and grease spots, they last for many years without becoming shabby. They are easy to hang as they do not stretch and tear like ordinary paper. (But in old houses with bumps in the plaster a certain amount of stretch is an advantage as it enables the paper to accommodate them.) They are also easy to get off again, as they are dry-strippable, or peelable. Instead of having to soak and strip, you simply peel away the vinyl top layer, leaving the backing paper behind on the wall.

Polyethylene foam wallcoverings These are the ones where you paste the wall, not the covering (Novamura was the first and is the best known). They are made completely of plastic foam, with a decorative top surface, and are much lighter in weight than vinyls. Both these properties make them exceptionally easy for a beginner to handle. You mix up the paste in a roller tray, apply it to the wall with the roller, and hang the paper straight from the roll, cutting each length off after smoothing it on with a household sponge.

Polyethylene foam, unlike vinyl, allows walls to breathe. This, together with their warm-to-the-touch surface makes them particularly good in bathrooms or kitchens subject to condensation. (For complete dissertation on this Great British Problem see page 30.) Like vinyls they are completely washable and can be dry-stripped.

Machine-printed papers These are the traditional wallpapers where a design is printed on to a roll of paper. Prices vary depending on the number of colours used and the quality of the paper, but generally they are cheaper than vinyls. Because they are only paper they cannot be washed, only dusted down, so they are best in lightly used areas like bedrooms (unless you are the kind of nut-case who likes to repaper every year!) Hanging some of this is another good way to start your career as a paperhanger, as it is cheap enough to cause no hair-tearing if one or two lengths go awry and are wasted. But don't choose the very cheapest, or lining paper; a thin paper tears and stretches all too easily in inexperienced hands. Choose a medium-priced, medium-weight one, preferably with a small all-over pattern which will hide every mistake except hanging a length upside down. Easiest of all is a paper from Crown's Matchless Collection of patterns designed so that they do not have to be matched.

Washable and spongeable papers A halfway-house between vinyls and paper, these are machine-printed papers with a matt or glossy coating protecting the pattern. They are a good choice if the budget's too tight for vinyl but something more durable than plain paper is called for. By the nature of the beast, washable wallpaper is almost impossible to strip off when the time comes, but dry-strippable ones have now been developed, so look for a peel-off symbol on the sample.

Embossed wallcoverings Here the design is not just printed on top, but stamped into the wallcovering so that it stands out in relief. The embossing may emphasise a floral pattern, or imitate the appearance of leather, fabric, tiling or timber panelling. Duplex embossed papers are made from two separate layers of paper so that the embossing stands out in stronger relief.

White wallpapers Many of these are also embossed, but they differ from the above group in that they are designed for over-painting. They are ideal when you want plain coloured walls but the plaster is in poor condition and needs a cover-up job.

Ordinary lining paper is often recommended for this purpose, but in my experience does little to disguise even the mildly rough surface left where a previous decorator has emulsioned over flaky paint and glued it to the surface. Being thin and completely without texture it just moulds itself round every pimple. Its only virtue is extreme cheapness, but it is best kept for cross-lining (hanging horizontally) before hanging an expensive hand-printed wallpaper.

Much better, and nearly as cheap, is wood chip, the Victorian terrace dweller's best friend. This contains flakes of wood fibre which give it an interesting porridge-like texture. It's a good beginner's choice as although it is soft and tears easily the texture makes mistakes invisible once it is painted over. You can actually live with unpainted woodchip for quite a while, but it yellows eventually.

Slightly more expensive white wallpapers are called relief papers and offer a wide variety of designs ranging from Victorian-style embossed patterns to nubbly fabric effects (linen, hessian etc.) and random patterns meant to resemble rough plaster.

Anaglypta, Supaglypta, Vynaglypta and Lincrusta are the brand names of different types of very solid, hardwearing embossed wallcoverings. The last two are expensive but last virtually for ever.

White embossed papers were once used a lot to cover bad ceilings, but today many people, including myself, would choose a textured paint; less decorative, but far less trouble to get up.

Hand-printed papers Definitely not for the beginner: these are expensive, may have the old-fashioned selvedge down each side which has to be trimmed off before hanging, and are sometimes very susceptible to colours smearing if paste gets on the design side. But they offer the most superb colours and designs — for example, the William Morris papers still being printed by Sanderson's from the original blocks — and can be an excellent choice for a feature wall.

Fabrics, flocks and exotica Although many wallcoverings are printed to look like different sorts of fabric you can also buy the real thing. Hessian is the most widely available, but if you can afford it you can hang felt or silk on your walls. Hessian is said to be for the advanced paperhanger, but I have not found it so, provided that you get the kind with a paper backing, not just furnishing hessian. It can be a bit temperamental about sticking down at the edges, but provided you use a good strong paste mix and soak the lengths until supple all should be well. Ignore instructions to use a rubber roller to smooth it on to the wall — a clean paint roller does perfectly well. Hessian is not cheap, but excellent for covering bad walls and very durable, although I have found that dyed hessian exposed to strong sunlight fades rather quickly.

Flock wallcoverings are not actually fabrics, but look and feel like it, with their velvety pile cut into traditional floral and striped designs like those you see in Victorian pubs and theatres. Both vinyl and paper versions are made.

Should you be in a no-expense-spared mood you can take your pick from Japanese grass-cloth, made from strands of a dried grass-like plant glued on to backing paper; cork-veneered paper; metallic papers that reflect multi-coloured light; photo-murals and heaven knows what else. Yet another group are what the late great Tom Keating called Sexton Blakes, or fakes: papers printed with photographic reproductions of marble, brick-work and timber panelling. These can be very convincing provided you don't let them anywhere near the real thing, and use them in the way that the real thing would have been. A good example of this type of paper is 'tiling on a roll': blown vinyl wallcovering printed with tile-like patterns, with grouting lines indented in. They are expensive, but cheaper than the real thing; a good choice if you fancy large areas of decorative ceramic tiling but haven't the money to pay for it, or the time and skill to put it up.

Co-ordinates Many of the wallcoverings described above are available in co-ordinated collections, teamed up with matching and complementary curtain fabrics, roller blinds and bed linen. The beauty of these is that you can, with one visit to one shop, achieve the perfectly co-ordinated look formerly only open to those rich enough to employ David Hicks or his ilk; or leisured and patient enough to spend hours trekking around with colour swatches, which also requires a very good eye for colour if ghastly mistakes are to be avoided.

Estimating The lazy way to find out how many rolls of wallcovering you need is to measure the height of the room from ceiling to skirting, plus 10cm for trimming. Then measure all the way round, counting in doors and windows. These two measurements enable you to read off the number of rolls from a chart at the shop. But, no surprise, these tend to be on the generous side, so I always do my own calculations.

Measure the height required as before. An average roll of wallcovering measures about 10.5 metres long by 53cm wide (11yd by 21in). So dividing the height into the length reveals how many pieces can be cut off each roll. In most rooms it comes out at four, unless there is a big pattern repeat. To calculate how much extra this is going to need, add half the design repeat figure printed on the back of the paper to the height figure. (This means that you can't complete the calculation until you have chosen the paper.)

Now go round the room with a piece of string 53cm long to find out how many widths you need. It's fairly safe to assume that small areas like above doors and above/below windows can be papered with off-cuts, or unwanted lengths on the final roll. Divide the number of widths counted by the number of lengths to be got from each roll and the answer is the number of rolls to buy. If you don't trust your arithmetic, in modern rooms with ceilings no more than 2.5 metres (8 ft) high we are talking about between four and eight rolls, depending on whether it is a small bathroom or a large living room.

PASTE AND SIZE

Modern pastes are another development which have helped to make paperhanging easier for the average ham-fisted do-it-yourselfer. They are clean and easy to mix and have plenty of 'slip' and 'open time', which means that you can push the pasted length around on the wall easily, to get it into exactly the right position, and take your time about it.

There are many different types of wallpaper paste, designed for different types and weights of paper; take your pick from advertised brands or DIY chains' own brands. Most come in the form of a powder: the contents of a medium-sized sachet, mixed with 8 pints of cold water, should be enough to hang 5–6 rolls of paper. If you only use part of a packet you can weigh it out by the ounce accordingly. If you are going to do a lot of papering a large packet of an all-purpose own-brand paste would be the best buy, and can be used for all common types of paper.

For vinyl wallcoverings the paste must contain a fungicide, to discourage any mould growth that might start up underneath its impermeable surface. Some vinyl pastes are also labeled heavy duty, as the edges of vinyls tend to curl up, and exert a strong pull on the paste. Wallpaper paste will not stick vinyl to itself, so where lengths are overlapped (every time a corner is turned) it is necessary to use a special overlap adhesive, or if you have some Copydex in the house use that.

If using any of the more *recherché* wallcoverings such as hessian or grasscloth enquire when buying as to what paste to get. Some of these are best hung with ready-mixed paste, which has a lower water content, to avoid any risk of shrinkage while it dries.

When mixing up paste, follow the instructions exactly: you *must* sprinkle the powder into the water, and not the other way round; do that and it goes irretrievably lumpy. Contrary to what you may read in many DIY books, a bucket of paste will keep perfectly well overnight if you don't get finished in a day, or even for several days.

Size is used to seal the surface of a wall before paperhanging so that less water is sucked out of the paste. This makes it easier to slide the paper about. It is normally unnecessary with modern wallpaper pastes, but I do recommend it if you are papering over ancient plaster, which is very porous and thirsty, particularly if you are a first-time paperhanger and need plenty of time to position the paper. It doesn't add much to the work: just slosh it on with a big brush and leave for a few hours to dry. Size can be bought as such, or use wallpaper paste, thinned down so that it will brush on easily.

Note New plaster should also be sized; but if you have had to have some walls replastered wait for six months before trying to paper them. The water content is so high that it will spoil ordinary paper, and a vinyl would prevent it from evaporating as it should. Do a temporary job with a cheap emulsion, or just live with it.

PAPERHANGING

Anyone can hang wallpaper badly, and many frequently do. But to hang it well takes care, attention to detail, and knowledge of a few basic rules. The first time I tried I wasted several lengths when I got to the first corner, as I just could not get it to stick on flat. What I didn't know was that you have to cut these lengths down and put one piece each side of the corner, because the two walls never meet at a perfect right angle, and this is what causes the problem.

Paperhanging is a good job for two, as one can paste while the other hangs. But they need to be on good terms. The hanger frequently starts behaving like a prima donna, and blames the poor paster for everything that goes wrong, causing her to flounce off in a huff.

Redecorate or clean the ceiling, also woodwork, *before* hanging the paper. Take down everything hanging on the walls; mark position of wall plugs with pieces of matchstick left sticking out just enough to feel.

Choosing a starting point The traditional place is close to one side of the window. The idea of this was that by working away from the light, any overlaps between lengths of paper would be less noticeable. Given today's factory-trimmed wallpaper (hardly any is still sold untrimmed) and reasonably flat walls you should not get any noticeable overlaps so really it is out of date. But it's as good a place as any, and as the window wall is the least well-lit one, any novice's errors will be less glaring. Also there are less likely to be obstacles like light switches to cope with. But if you are using a bold-patterned paper, and the room has a dominant feature, usually the chimney breast, start in the centre of that and work round in both directions.

Note If the windows are recessed, not flat on the wall, start on the next wall, so that you don't have to start by dealing with the complications of hanging into a recess.

If using paste, start work by mixing it up, as it usually takes between fifteen and twenty minutes to thicken. Tie a string across the bucket on which to balance the pasting brush. With ready-pasted paper assemble the cardboard trough, fill with cold water and place on the floor at the starting point.

Marking a vertical line The first length of paper must be hung against a true vertical line to ensure that it is perfectly upright. Subsequent lengths are hung against the first, but every time you turn a corner you should mark a fresh line. The only way to mark a true vertical is with a plumb-bob and line, which you can improvise if necessary by tying a key or bolt to a length of string. Tape the end of the string high on the wall. When the weight stops swinging hold it in place and mark a line close to the string; or make a series of marks and then join them up with a ruler or length of batten. (The proper, professional way is to chalk the string and twang it against the wall; but I never seem to have any chalk.) Mark plumb-lines even if only hanging lining paper or woodchip; even though there is no pattern to look crooked, the joins between lengths should be upright. Anyway it's good practice.

The position of the first plumb-line will be 15mm less than the width of the paper away from the window frame or wall corner. Or, if starting on a feature wall, half a width to either side of the centre.

Cutting the lengths Cut the first length of paper to the required length, allowing 10cm extra for trimming. If it has a bold pattern do not start at the end of the roll, but trim if necessary so that a complete motif will appear at the top of the wall after the 5cm has been trimmed off. Cut the next and subsequent lengths of a patterned paper so that the pattern matches. If it is one where the distance between points where it matches is large you may find it less wasteful to cut lengths from two rolls at once. If there is any doubt as to which way up the paper should go mark each length TOP in soft pencil on the back.

Soaking Some papers (usually heavyweights and hessian) have to be left for quite while to allow the paste to soak in and make them supple; ordinary papers need only a minute or two and vinyls are hung straight away. This will be indicated on the wrapper. Whatever soaking time is needed keep fairly closely to it for each length. A large disparity could cause a different rate of stretch, and make it impossible to match the pattern. A convenient way of working is to paste lengths in pairs, so that the first is ready to hang by the time the second has been pasted.

Pasting and folding It is vital to get a good coating of paste all over the paper, particularly down each side, so that it will stick to the wall all over.

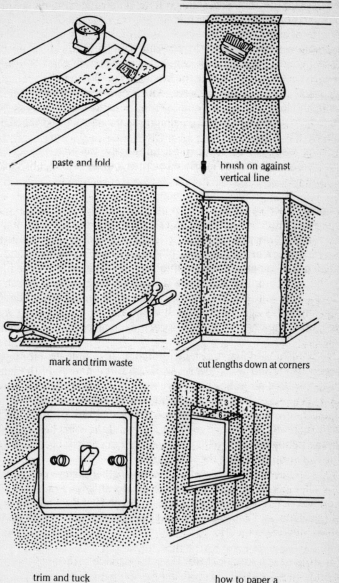

paste and fold

brush on against
vertical line

mark and trim waste

cut lengths down at corners

trim and tuck
behind light switches

how to paper a
recessed window

63

Lay the length on the table, positioning it so that one end and edge are lined up with the table edges; this is to avoid getting paste on the table. Brush paste outwards from the middle, criss-cross fashion. Always brush *outwards* over the sides, to prevent paste from creeping underneath as it might smudge the pattern. To avoid tiring your hand quickly do not hold the pasting brush like a paintbrush, but spread your fingers out over the lower part of the handle where the bristles go in. When half the length is pasted fold it over, paste to paste, with side edges aligned. Continue pasting and fold the opposite end over in the same way. Wipe any stray paste off the work table as you go along. Hang lengths to be soaked over the back of a chair.

If using ready-pasted paper roll it up loosely, top edge outside, and soak in the trough for the time stated on the wrapper before drawing it up on to the wall.

Hanging Once paper is wet with paste it becomes very fragile (vinyl less so) and must be handled with care. To carry it to the wall drape it over your free arm, paste side up, top end nearest you. Have scissors and smoothing brush or sponge ready in apron pocket. Carefully unfold the top half of the paper and slide it into position against the marked line, with the 5cm trimming allowance sticking up at the ceiling. Brush the paper on loosely just to tack it to the wall. Gently unfold the bottom half and position this against the line. If it is wandering away, don't try to force it on to the line but gently unpeel the top piece and reposition the whole thing.

Final brushing down must be thorough to eliminate air trapped between paper and wall. Always work from the middle of the length outwards so that air bubbles are pushed out and escape; be sure not to miss a single spot. Trim top and bottom as described below.

Hang the next and subsequent lengths so that any pattern matches *exactly* (near enough is not good enough) and the joins between each piece are tightly butted together, with neither overlap nor gap. Continue in this way until reaching the first corner.

After trimming run down each join to ensure that each piece is sticking tightly all down each edge. The proper tool for this is a seam roller (but not on embossed papers); a soft cloth or the ends of the hanging brush bristles will do, and if they are recalcitrant a good thump with the side of your fist should do the trick.

Trimming at top and bottom Press the paper into the angle between wall and ceiling or skirting board and mark the line with the back of the scissors. Gently peel back the paper and cut along the line, which will show quite clearly on the back. Do not try to cut the paper with a knife and straight edge, as some DIY books may tell you. The line between wall and ceiling or skirting board is never straight and you will just get into a mess. Finish by wiping off any smears of paste.

Corners When you get too near an internal corner to hang a full width measure the bare bit at both top and bottom in case there is a difference. Add 15mm on to the widest measurement. *After* pasting and accurately folding the next length, cut it down to this width. Make sure to cut the strip off the correct side, so that the machined edge goes against the previous piece and the cut edge laps round the corner. Hang the strip in the normal way, brushing the overlap well into the corner, and trim top and bottom.

Plumb a fresh line on the new wall, the width of the remaining strip away from the corner. Brush some paste on the overlap and hang the strip against the line.

A full width of paper can be taken round an external angle providing that the corner is vertical. If not, cut the paper ensuring that the join is at least 5cm around the corner and hang the remaining strip to match, making sure that it is vertical.

Light switches and socket outlets When you reach a light switch it is much easier to make the effort to find a screwdriver and loosen off the facing plate, so that the paper can be tucked behind it, than try to cut it neatly round. But first switch off at the mains, so that if a blob of wet paste did happen to reach the wiring no harm would be done. Hang the top section of the paper and unfold the rest to hang over the fitting. Feel for its centre, pierce the paper with the scissors and make a diagonal cut out towards each corner. Then cut away the points until there is just enough paper left to tuck behind the face plate. (If using a metallic foil paper make extra sure there are no bits hanging inside the fitting.) Brush the paper down, refit the face plate and carry on as usual.

Use the same technique for recessed socket outlets. If they are surface-mounted make diagonal cuts over the surface, then make more to form a star shape and allow the paper to be pressed down over the fitting. Trim with a very sharp Stanley knife.

Doors, old-style windows and fire surrounds Try the length in position and mark what needs to be removed. Cut this away, leaving a good margin for trimming off on the wall. (Again, be sure to cut the waste out of the correct side of the paper, according to whether it is going round the left- or right-hand side of the obstacle.) Paste, smooth on and trim. If you try to peel back the paper and trim it in the same way as at top and bottom it invariably tears in the corner of the cut-out. It's best to knock it well into the angle with the brush bristles and trim directly with the sharp knife. (Wet paper tears horribly under a blunt one.)

The spaces above doors and above/below windows can be papered with off-cuts from previous rolls. But always work in full widths.

Recessed windows Explaining this is more difficult than doing it! What follows probably won't make sense on reading, but follow it blindly when you actually have to tackle a recess and you will find that it works. The main thing to grasp is that the soffit, or 'ceiling' of the recess is papered separately from the rest. See diagram on page 63.

When you reach the recess, cut a perfectly normal length and paste it to the upper part of the wall. Slit it horizontally where it reaches the front edge of the 'ceiling'. If the recess is shallow and the walls true you may be able to get away with turning the paper below the slit on to the side of the recess. Otherwise cut it down as on any other external corner and paste the cut-off bit on separately. Now paste short lengths on to the wall above the recess, trimming them flush with the front edge. Hang a complete length on the opposite side of the window in the same way as the first one.

Now paper the 'ceiling'. Measure its depth and cut pieces to this measurement plus 4cm, matching the pattern to the short pieces already hung above. Peel these back and tuck the 'ceiling' pieces underneath (don't forget the dab of paste to seal them together). This leaves a little bare patch in each corner; cut pieces to fit, matching pattern and tucking under as before.

Aftercare Until the paste is dry the paper is very vulnerable to damage. So don't move furniture back, or rehang pictures until next day. Keep children away (also cats: I have had one sharpen its claws on a freshly papered wall and ruin it).

Don't rush to clean out the paste bucket immediately after finishing; you may need a little for remedial work. If you were less than efficient with the smoothing brush or sponge, blisters may appear once the paste has dried. These are pockets of air: to release them cut across with a sharp knife, apply a little paste with a small brush and pat down. With tiny ones puncturing them with a pin may be sufficient.

Also look for edges which have failed to stick securely and repaste; wipe off any paste that squeezes out on to the surface straight away.

PAPERING CEILINGS

My advice is: don't. Ceilings are usually papered to hide defects in the surface, usually flaky paint and cracks. It's a hard, neck-aching job, and if that's all you want to do I'd recommend one of the new textured paints every time. But if you insist — some rooms, it's true, do look good papered with a small pattern. And a white embossed pattern gives a very nice effect when light bounces off it. Also if the ceiling is badly damaged, perhaps where a partition wall has been removed, no amount of textured paint will hide the fact (but you could go for ceiling tiles — see page 167).

First you will need still more equipment: a second pair of steps or a pair of trestles, and a scaffold plank to span between them. Also have ready a short length of broomstick or leftover part-roll of wallpaper. Strip off old paper, clean and prepare the ceiling as described above.

Work across the width of the room so that the paper lengths are as short as possible. If there is a window in one short wall start at this end, but work facing away from it so that you are not dazzled by glare. Mark a chalk line on the ceiling 2.5cm less than the width of the paper away from the wall. Cut some lengths of paper to the width of the room plus the usual 10cm for trimming. Paste in the normal way but fold differently: concertina fashion, paste side inside, so that it can be unfolded bit by bit (see diagram). Allow soaking time if so instructed on the wrapper.

Standing on the board at a comfortable height, support the concertina of paper, paste side up, on the broomstick or paper roll. (If you have a helper she can support the paper on a broom — see diagram.) Unfold a little, lining it up with the chalk line, remembering to leave the trimming allowance hanging at the starting point. Brush on, unfold some more and continue. If it starts to wander away from the line correct this sooner rather than later, as it will get progressively worse. When the opposite

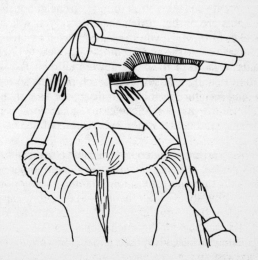

wall is reached knock the trimming allowance into the angle with the ends of the brush. Mark, peel back and trim as usual. Return to the starting point and trim that end; similarly trim the long side edge (you may find it easier to do this last with a sharp knife).

Butt the next length of paper firmly up against the first; do not overlap edges, and match pattern if any. If it is an embossed paper do not be too brutal with the brush or you can flatten it. Have frequent rests to keep neck-ache at bay.

At the ceiling rose, switch electricity off at the mains, remove bulb and shade and partly unscrew the rose cover. Paste the paper on up to the fitting, then pierce it to pull the lampholder through. Make star cuts over the rose, brush the paper round it and trim. Unless you have three hands you will need a second person to support the remaining paper while you fiddle about doing all this.

Note If the room still has an old-fashioned pear-drop ceiling rose now's the time to replace it with a modern one (see page 90).

HOW TO SUCCEED WITH COLOUR AND PATTERN

The colours and patterns that appeal to you are your own affair; far be it from me to offer advice on aesthetic grounds. But from a purely practical point of view, here are a few guidelines, as colour and pattern have a direct effect on how pleasant a room is to be in. For example, I once painted a small kitchen in what I thought was a beautiful shade of nutmeg brown. The effect was to plunge it into deep gloom and make it feel like a prison. If you take a stroll round your neighbourhood as dusk falls, when lights are on but curtains still open, you will see plenty of ghastly mistakes from which you can learn, as well as a few good ideas.

Common disasters are the small rooms that appear to be closing in on the occupants because of the huge flowers all over the walls; heavy stripes all round giving a prison bars effect; patterns so overpowering that people and furniture in the room disappear as if in a jungle. But mostly you'll see the play-it-safe choices: vaguely floral papers, bland, beige and boring; and white, white, everywhere white.

Paint It's not surprising that people find using colours difficult, and opt for these safe neutral schemes, or white (well over 50 per cent of paint sold is white or near-white). After all, professional interior decorators spend years learning about colour theory, and even they can clang. But if you keep to a few basic ground rules it's not too hard to arrive at a solution which is suitable for the small rooms most of us live in, sets off existing furnishings to best advantage, and expresses your personality or the mood you wish to convey.

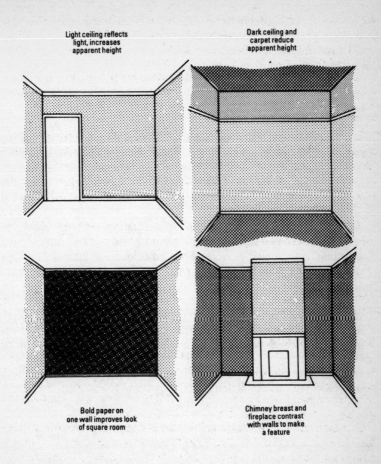

Light ceiling reflects light, increases apparent height

Dark ceiling and carpet reduce apparent height

Bold paper on one wall improves look of square room

Chimney breast and fireplace contrast with walls to make a feature

Although a paint-mixing machine can produce over 500 different shades there are only three basic pigment colours: primary red, yellow and blue. All the rest are produced by mixing these together and adding different amounts of black or white. Every colour has its own 'personality'. The primaries are bright, cheerful and unsophisticated — good for young childrens' rooms. Those at the red side of the colour spectrum — reds, oranges and yellows — are seen as warm and welcoming. Those on the opposite side — greens, blues and

69

purple/violets — are cool and restful. In addition, warm colours seem to *advance*, while cool colours *recede*, visually. So in a big Victorian house the rooms will take bamboo/russet/brown colours very well — they will bring the walls in and make the house feel more cosy. But in a tiny flat the pale and misty blues and aquas will make the most of the space, especially if the scheme uses only one or two colours throughout, preferably including the floor covering.

In decorating, another important aspect of colour is its ability to reflect light. Pale colours bounce light back, dark ones absorb it. As well as the practical effect, this creates a mood. Hence theatres and restaurants are often decorated a rich dark red to create an intimate, exciting feeling; such colours would be out of place in a bank or supermarket, where the mood is businesslike, and plenty of light is needed for people to see what they are doing.

Colours also affect each other. A decorating scheme using co-ordinated shades of a single colour is pleasant and relaxed, but not very interesting. Introducing white and related colours — those next to one another in the colour spectrum — peps it up by accentuating the main colours. And when a colour is introduced from the opposite side of the spectrum the two contrast strongly when used at full strength and can dazzle the eye (these are rather confusingly called complementary colours). Examples of this effect are red flowers against a green background, or yellow stamens in a purple flower. Too much contrast gives a room a restless feeling, so strongly contrasting colours should be used sparingly. Even a certain amount of discord can, as in music, bring vibrancy to your colour scheme.

All the different attributes of colour can be used to advantage by the clever colour schemer.

First set the mood by choosing the main colour. Make a hall cheerful and welcoming with yellow; a hot kitchen cooler with green; a dining room cosy and intimate with brown; a living room relaxing and spacious with warm-toned beige or grey; a bedroom restful with blue. Also consider the direction in which the room faces. North- and east-facing rooms get cold, mostly indirect light, so warm colours are preferable. South- and west-facing rooms, where the sun shines directly in for much of the day, can take cool colours more happily. If the room tends to be dark keep your chosen colour in a pale shade (but this may not matter if it is used mainly at night, in artificial light). If it is very small one of the new nearly-whites, subtly tinted with pink, cream, green or blue could be the answer.

Ceilings are invariably painted white in Britain, but not in other countries — in New Zealand a white ceiling is considered a daring novelty! The high ceilings found in Victorian terrace houses can take quite strong colours, especially if set off by a white cornice (but keep walls pale to compensate for loss of light bouncing off the ceiling). Lower ceilings can safely be painted in pastel shades of any colour, if walls and floors are kept fairly light-toned. In small rooms painting ceiling and walls in the same pale colour is about the most space-making thing you can do.

The floor is an important part of the colour scheme, and often an existing fitted carpet is the starting point. As well as selecting colours to harmonise or contrast with this, bear in mind that if it is very dark, walls need to be compensatingly light, but if it is pale you can afford bolder, deeper-toned walls.

Make colour work for you to enhance decorative features and conceal ugly ones. Emphasise alcoves or attractively proportioned chimney breasts in a contrasting, bold colour; disguise pipes, radiators or other nasties by painting them to match the wall behind. Use white on skirting boards and door frames to make the woodwork stand out as a decorative trim to coloured walls (though pale grey is more practical for doors, to conceal the traces of small grubby paws); or blend them in. With skirting boards, painting them the same colour as the floor covering, rather than the walls, is the best way to make a room look larger. Bright glossy colours are not usually a good idea on strips of woodwork — in factories, pipes brightly painted to identify the contents are visually very distracting, and you will get the same effect with a long run of skirting board.

If you still feel slightly confused about colour pick up a set of colour cards from a paint retailer with a mix-while-you-wait machine. Each card is numbered and shows a co-ordinated colour family; the complete set covers the spectrum, from reds, pinks, oranges, browns, yellows, greens, blues, violet, purple and so back to red. They can be a bit overwhelming at first, but they are very carefully worked out to help people plan successful decorating schemes, and repay close study. Each card shows pale colours, suitable for large areas, at the top; and shades down to strong ones on the bottom row suitable for accenting small areas, say a feature wall or alcoves.

Having said all this about colour a word of praise for white. It's often an excellent choice for decorating the first time around. It's cheap, if you buy a 5-litre can of a DIY supermarket's own brand; quick, as you can get on and do it without spending hours agonising over the exact shade to get; and easy as you can go straight over ceiling and walls without having to be very careful where two colours meet.

Wallcoverings Unless you have Buckingham-Palace-sized rooms, keep well away from anything with a big, bold pattern. If you can't resist one, either restrict it to a feature wall and hang a companion paper on the rest (or paint them); or put it in the bathroom where it doesn't really matter if the design overwhelms all else, and you probably won't spend enough time in there to get bored with it.

If florals are your choice, avoid big splashy William Morris type flower designs and vast cabbage roses and go for one of the many charming mini-prints now available which are specially designed for the small, low-ceilinged rooms of modern houses, and just as at home in old cottages. Similarly, if you like geometric patterns, avoid large scale ones and go for a mini version. Stripes can help make walls look higher, but can also make them advance: either choose a very fine stripe, or limit it to one or two walls.

If a room is very poky, but you need paper to cover bad plaster, pick one that has a plain colour and slight texture rather than a pattern. These are unaccountably hard to find in anything but wishy-washy pastels and I usually end up with a white relief paper and emulsion paint.

Picture rails If there is a picture rail in the room take care how you treat it when decorating, as it has a strong visual effect. The original idea of the picture rail was not only to enable pictures to be hung up without knocking holes in the wall, by using picture hooks, but to balance the proportions of high-ceilinged Victorian and Edwardian rooms. So they should not be removed from such rooms; if you don't want them to be too obtrusive paint them to match the wall. If someone else has had them down either replace them, or paste up one of the very attractive border papers that are now available in their place (about 30cm down from the ceiling). Sometimes a picture rail has been fitted in a room where the ceiling is far too low to warrant it, and it will look much better if the rail is removed. This is surprisingly easy to do, as they are only nailed on.

To accentuate the height of a room with a picture rail carry the paint or paper above it. To minimise height bring the ceiling colour down to the rail.

4   Basic electrics

The electrical maintenance and repair jobs outlined in this chapter are strictly confined to very simple ones. They are all things which I have had to do at various times, and if I can cope, I am sure that you can. The main thing to bear in mind when tackling electrical work is that you must follow the rules exactly, and always reinstate something just the way it was before; not by short cuts or inventions of your own. Being a little frightened of electricity is no bad thing as it makes you careful.

Even if you have no desire to do anything more ambitious than wire up the occasional plug you cannot avoid using electrical appliances every day of your life. So turn to pages 192–4 to brush up on your knowledge of the basic do's and don'ts.

UNDERSTANDING ELECTRICITY

At the simple level of electrical work as covered in this book it is not necessary to understand all the ins and outs of amps, watts and volts, let alone how electricity is generated and arrives at your house. But what you must understand, very clearly indeed, is that electricity at the British mains voltage of 240V is a highly dangerous force, capable of giving the human body a fatal shock.

Electrical installations are carefully designed so that the current can flow only when switched on by you to provide heat, light or power via a fitting or an appliance, and then return to the power station. The amount is registered on the meter, which determines how much you have to pay. The wiring installation is protected by fuses inside the appliance plugs, and then further by fuses in the consumer unit (fuse box in common parlance). Fuses are deliberately weak links which break the electrical circuit and stop the flow of electricity by melting if they are overloaded.

In addition you are protected by a network of 'earth' wires. Electricity has the characteristic of 'going to earth'. If left unchannelled it will flow into the ground by the shortest and easiest route. Earth wires enable it to do this if necessary, as those in the plugs and fittings all connect up to a mains earth which runs from the consumer unit down into the ground under or outside the house.

The main ways you can get an electric shock are by touching a live wire or terminal; touching the metal framework of an appliance which has become live and is not properly earthed; and by cutting through a live flex. In all these cases the electric current returns to earth via your body, giving you an electric shock. This can be anything from a slight tingling sensation to a massive jolt which stops the heart beating. Yet another way to get a shock is by touching a perfectly sound electrical appliance or fitting with wet hands, or even a wet cloth. Water is the best of all conductors of electricity, and being fluid easily finds its way inside a switch or plug, where the current will instantly take the easy route through the water and thence to you. This is why the use of electricity is so tightly controlled in bathrooms.

I don't mean to scare you with all this. The regulations governing electrical installations and appliance manufacture are so strict that accidents are very rare, and usually the result of gross carelessness or ignorance. Just always be aware that you are dealing with a potentially lethal force, make sure that your children are too, and handle anything electrical with corresponding respect, in daily use as well as during maintenance or repair work.

I have assumed throughout this chapter that you have a reasonably modern electrical wiring system with ring mains wiring and flat-pin 13amp plugs. If your system uses round-pin plugs it is some 40 years old or more, and urgently needs replacement.

SAFETY FIRST

Always unplug an electrical appliance before working on it, even if just having a look to see why the beast won't work. Do not reconnect afterwards until fully assembled.

When working on any part of the house wiring, SWITCH OFF AT THE MAINS. Keep this constantly in mind; it's easy to remember when you *start* work, but the danger comes if you have to make some adjustments, and fail to go back and switch off for a second time. The main switch totally cuts of the supply of electricity coming into the house from outside. It is located on the consumer unit and is off when large letters show OFF. The consumer unit usually lurks in the cupboard under the stairs, or in a corner of kitchen or hall. As well as turning off the main switch it's a good idea to take out the relevant circuit fuse and put it in your pocket. This is an insurance against some idiot coming along, switching back on and electrocuting you.

These main fuses will have some sort of cover over them to unscrew, and they should be identified to show what they each control, or at least

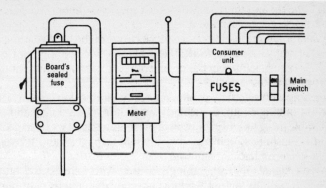

consumer unit controls supply via main switch and fuses.

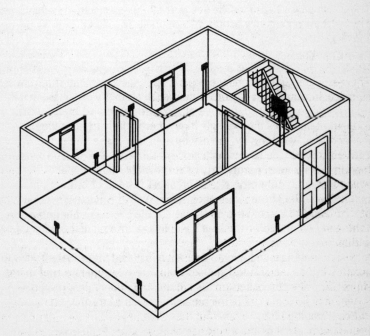

typical ground floor ring main

be colour coded. A white (5amp) fuse controls a lighting circuit; blue (15amp) something like an immersion heater; red (30amp) controls a power circuit; and there may also be a special higher-powered red one controlling an electric cooker.

In addition you should double-check in one of the following ways that an outlet really is dead and safe. Use a mains tester (see opposite) to see if it lights up; turn light switches on and off; plug in an appliance known to be working to test a socket.

Working with electricty requires concentration so don't try to do it with children milling about, particularly when it involves a vital and easily-forgettable thing like switching off at the mains. And if you start a job and get into difficulties, don't try and muddle through; hand it over to a qualified electrician.

Danger signals that something is wrong with an electrical fitting or appliance are intermittent working, overheating, and fishy or burning-rubber smells. Never ignore these; they won't go away, and neglected electrical faults are a major cause of house fires.

See also pages 192–5 for the key points to using electricity safely, and page 212 for emergency action in case of electric shock.

OVERLOADING

There is a limit to how many electrical appliances you can run from an electrical installation at any one time. Usually things work out so that the limit is not exceeded, but as we all acquire more and more electrical gadgetry it becomes increasingly likely, particularly in households with teenagers, all watching TV and drying their hair at the same time. When a circuit is overloaded the main fuse controlling it will blow, and constant mending is no joke, particularly as it inevitably happens after dark. A consumer unit containing circuit breakers instead of ordinary fuses is highly desirable. These switch themselves off in the event of overloading or a fault and all you have to do is switch them back on, after unplugging a thing or two or finding the fault. I would specify a set of these for a new wiring system.

Short of having an additional ring main installed there are two ways to avoid overloading. In most houses there are two separate ring mains, supplying power to sockets on the ground and upper floors respectively. So you may be able to solve the problem by taking an appliance upstairs. But overloading often occurs in the kitchen, and using a food mixer in the bedroom is not really very practical. What you can do here is plug in a 2- or 4-gang extension socket, protected by its own circuit breakers. If you plug in too many things, it simply cuts out and you know you must switch something off before resetting it. These can be bought from electrical retailers and cost about £9.60 for a 4-gang one.

TOOLS FOR ELECTRICAL WORK

Basic tools for working on electrical appliances are the inevitable Stanley knife, and an electrician's screwdriver with a small blade and plastic handle. The proper tool for removing the plastic covering from flex is a pair of wire strippers, which can be adjusted to strip any thickness of flex or cable without touching the wires. But unless you do a lot of electrical work a screwdriver with a flex-stripping blade incorporated is a cheaper alternative; or you can get by with the sharp knife if careful. A pair of long-nosed pliers is also necessary: the blades for cutting flex to length, the jaws for forming loops in exposed wire ends. For appliance repair work you will also need a Posidriv or Phillips screwdriver, to take components apart and re-assemble.

For working on house wiring, if replacing a ceiling rose for example, a mains tester is an invaluable aid. This is a screwdriver which contains a tiny bulb which lights up if electricity is still present; a resistor in the handle protects you from shock. It is a good confidence builder, because although you know perfectly well that as you have just switched off at the mains, everything is totally dead, as electricity is invisible you cannot *see* that this is so. Always test the tester before using: with one finger on the metal bit at the end of the handle, touch the blade to a live terminal *before* switching off at the mains; the bulb should light up. Then switch off and test again.

CABLE AND FLEX

Cable is the stuff that runs around the house unseen (unless your house has surface wiring) carrying electricity from the mains to sockets and light fittings. It comes in various thicknesses for different tasks, and the insulation on the stiff, single-strand wires is colour coded red for Live and black for Neutral; the earth wire may be bare or green. Your only contact with cable will normally be just to connect a fitting on to its ends.

Flex is short for flexible cable. It joins appliances to their plugs, and light fittings to ceiling roses. The wires are multi-stranded and pliable, and the insulation is colour coded brown for Live, blue for Neutral and green/yellow for Earth. (Unless the appliance is pre-1971, when the colours were red, black and green. These colours were changed mainly because a colour-blind electrician could connect things up in reverse and cause havoc.) The thickness of flex increases with the power of the appliance it is suitable for. In the home, these range from very low-rated things like light bulbs (40 to 150 watts) through an iron at 750 watts and a

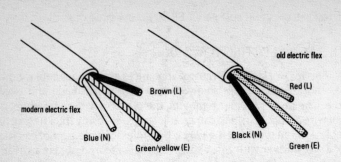

old electric flex

Brown (L)

Red (L)

modern electric flex

Blue (N)

Black (N)

Green/yellow (E)

Green (E)

one-bar fire at 1000 watts (1 kilowatt), to the most power-hungry item of all, the electric cooker, which can be rated at anything from 3 to 7 kilowatts. (Economy note: high-rated appliances are the ones that consume the most electricity and the ones you should use as sparingly as possible to keep bills down.)

The very thinnest flex (3amp), and the only one with no outer layer of insulation (apart from bell-wire) is strictly for ceiling lights, or low-rated appliances (up to 700W) like radios and TV sets. After that all flex has insulation around the wires as well as on them.

If buying some new flex you must be quite sure to get the right kind. Unless it's for a ceiling rose, which takes 2-core (table lamps and wall lights usually have 3-core flex these days) it's not enough to say what it's for. Note down the actual wattage of the appliance, which is always marked on a rating plate located somewhere about its person. Shops selling flex should have a chart from which you can select the appropriate one. If they don't, go elsewhere — Woolworth's is a good place.

Special types of flex are braided ones for use with electric fires, irons and kettles (this is for safety — ordinary PVC sheathing can get cut or melted and the wires exposed); and heavy-duty 2-core flex designed for use with double-insulated appliances such as lawn-mowers and power drills.

WIRING UP A PLUG

Whenever you buy a new electrical appliance remember to get a new plug to go with it. They are often not supplied and it's infuriating to get home and find that you can't try out your new toy without pinching a plug off something else, which always turns out to be the very thing you want to use next day, even if you haven't touched it for months.

First take a look at the flex on the appliance. Inside an outer sheathing of plastic or braided material there will usually be three coloured wires:

78

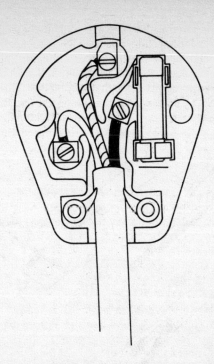

brown (Live), blue (Neutral) and green/yellow (Earth). On an old appliance the equivalent colours are red, black and green. Occasionally there will only be two wires, live and neutral, and no earth. On some table lamps the two wires are the same colour; wire these up as when doing a pendant light fitting — it doesn't matter which goes to the Live pin and which to Neutral.

Whenever there are three wires these *must* all be connected up to a 3-pin plug. This should be marked to show which of the three brass pins (terminals) take which wire. Usually it's L, N and E; sometimes coloured dots. But it's always done the same way: looking at the open plug, flex grip at the bottom, put the blue wire on the Left, brown wire on the Right, and green/yellow earth wire out in front. Every plug I buy seems to have a different design, each more fiddly to connect than the last, but basically they are all the same. Open the plug by unscrewing the large central screw on the back. The two smaller screws secure the flex grip inside. Just loosen these off a bit so that you will be able to thread the flex underneath the flex grip. (Some madly modern plugs no longer have this type of flex grip, but a patent plastic gripper instead; see diagram above.) Inside the plug you will see a clip-in cartridge fuse on the live side; remove this while you work.

The flex must be prepared so that bare wire touches the plug terminals and makes the electrical connection. First remove about 5cm of the outer sheathing; to avoid cutting too far through it and damaging the inner wires, slit it lengthwise, peel back and then cut off. If it's a braided flex bind the cut end with insulating tape so that it won't fray. Thread the flex under the gripper bar or press it into the plastic jaws so that the part gripped is the outer sheathing, *not* the inner wires. Tighten the screws on

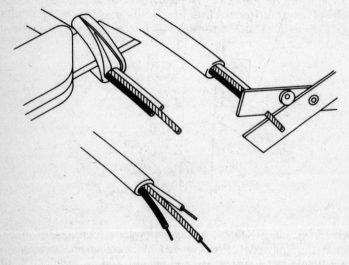

the bar type. (This is very important as the gripper mechanism protects the wires inside from being pulled loose.)

Now shorten the wires so that each one is just long enough to reach the appropriate pin, plus about 12mm for fixing. This bit must be bare wire, so strip off 12mm of the plastic covering. Each wire is made up of several finer wires; twist them together clockwise. If the plug is the sort where the wires fit into holes, double the ends over. If they loop round the terminal, bend them into open loops. Loosen off the tiny screws on each terminal, poke in or loop round the wires and tighten the screws. Check that each one is securely held, with no stray bits of wire sticking out, or any bare wire showing.

Replace the cartridge fuse, checking first that it is the right type for the appliance. A new plug may have a brown (13amp) fuse, which is for appliances rated over 700W. Look at the rating plate on the appliance; something like a lamp or an electric blanket will have a lower rating than this, and should have a red (3amp) fuse. You can use the brown one temporarily; but make a note to replace it. Screw the two halves together again and plug in.

MENDING A FUSE

Instructions for this job feature prominently in every DIY book, but modern electrical installations are very reliable and you may never have to do it (unless you habitually overload it; see above.) I have only had to mend a fuse once in the last five years. Also a modern system may have circuit breakers instead of fuses so that the need never arises. But if it does arise have no fear; there's nothing to it.

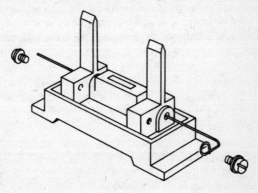

First TURN OFF THE MAIN SWITCH. If it is night-time you are now plunged into darkness, which is why a wise virgin keeps a torch handy by the consumer unit, together with a card of fuse wire. Undo the cover to reveal the row of fuse holders and pull out the one you suspect has blown. You will know when you find it because the wire at the back will have broken. Now you may be able to switch back on if necessary to get some light. Loosen the two screws to remove the old wire. Cut off a new length from the card, which must be of the same rating (thickness) as the original piece. A thinner piece will blow too easily, which is merely irritating; but a thicker one will not blow easily enough, which could be dangerous. The amp rating of each fuse is marked on it; pick wire of the same rating marked on the card. Loop the new wire round one screw, stretch it down the length of the fuse holder and connect it to the opposite screw.

Some fuse holders have cartridge fuses like the ones in plugs. You cannot see when these have blown, and have to test with a new one of the same rating. (Or test with a *metal*-cased torch: place one end of fuse on base of battery, other end on casing and see if torch lights.)

Turn the main switch OFF if you put it back on, replace the fuse holder and test. If it blows again the most likely causes, once overloading is ruled out, are a faulty appliance or wiring, and there is no point in fixing a new fuse until this has been mended. Don't forget to replace the fuse holder cover.

APPLIANCE MAINTENANCE AND REPAIR

The first step in repairing any appliance is a process called fault chasing. Knowing how to do this, even if you don't feel able to tackle the repair yourself, pays big dividends, as it will save you sending for an electrician unnecessarily, or being without an appliance for six weeks or more. At the time of writing electricity boards' call-out charges alone average £16. This is not money you want to shell out for someone to come and change a fuse for you. And with cheaper repair men there is always the question of their probity. If you haven't the faintest idea why your vacuum cleaner has ceased functioning they could reconnect a loose wire and tell you they have replaced the motor.

Initial check for all appliances If something expires in use with a bang and smell of burning it's obvious something is badly wrong. But if it simply refuses to function, first check out all the reasons why electricity may not be getting through to it. Is the plug properly in the socket? Are there any loose wires inside the plug? Has the electricity been cut off because of a power cut, non-payment of bill or lack of coin in meter? Perhaps the plug fuse has blown; check by putting in a spare, or one 'cannibalised' from something else. Also check that the socket is working by plugging in something else.

Another possibility is that the flex has been pulled loose at the appliance end, or has a break in it. Also check for a blown main fuse in the consumer unit; if this has happened nothing on the circuit it controls will work.

Cookers If the oven fails to light on an automatic cooker don't panic; the controls have probably been switched accidentally to the automatic mode when you want manual. Light bulbs in ovens and over hobs fail like any others and can be replaced. A fluorescent hob light may eventually need a new starter — this is a small plug-in cylinder round the back somewhere.

Defunct boiling rings on old cookers can be replaced, but newer ones are made so that you cannot get at them. (It's also wise to replace a ring that shows hot spots, as it is defective and will eventually short circuit. I once had one that did this and not only blew the cooker fuse, but burnt a neat hole in a brand-new saucepan.) But it's not a job to tackle yourself unless you are experienced at electrical work, as if it is not done properly it could be dangerous.

Fires New elements can be obtained for quite ancient-looking fires, whether they are the silica-glass rod or exposed wire type. Bowl fires can also be repaired, but not convectors or storage heaters. Follow the usual procedures: unplug the fire and dismantle carefully, noting how the connections are made. Obtain new element and fit in exactly the same way. Silica-glass elements are extremely fragile, and horribly easy to break while trying to fit them. With the type that fits into spring clips, the trick is to depress one clip while slotting the element carefully into the other. While the element is off give the reflector a good clean and polish to ensure maximum benefit from that expensive electricity.

Irons The major ill of any iron is frayed flex where it rubs on the edge of the ironing board. This is potentially dangerous and should be repaired sooner rather than later. You *can* bind it up with insulating tape, but these temporary repairs have a nasty habit of becoming permanent. With a common-or-garden iron it's simply a question of fitting a new length of braided flex of the right rating. At the iron end, unscrew the pilot light cover to remove the old flex and fit the new in exactly the same way; it can be a very fiddly job if the wires are tightly packed in. A few irons have a flex coupler like the ones on kettles, which makes the job easier; or you can take the easy way out and just buy a complete new coupler and flex.

Other repairs you can make to simple dry irons are to fit a new pilot light bulb, also a temperature control knob if the old one has broken.

Steam irons are much more complicated and not amenable to DIY repair. Look after one by always using distilled water, otherwise the vents in the sole plate rapidly clog with lime scale, and emptying it out after each use. You are supposed to buy specially bottled water, but everyone I know uses melted ice from the refrigerator.

To restore the shine on an iron's sole plate when it becomes dulled with use you are also supposed to buy special products. But I find that a mild abrasive (toothpowder rather than household scourer) or fine (00 grade) steel wool works perfectly well; the thing is not to rub too hard.

Kettles Replacing a dead element in a kettle is something absolutely anyone can do, about on a level with changing a light bulb, and there is no earthly reason you should pay to have it done, *unless* you have got an automatic one that switches itself off and on.

Unplug the kettle and remove the flex coupler from the back. Put your hand inside to hold the element steady and unscrew the cover of the flex coupler plug. Remove the fibre sealing washer from underneath it and pull out the element. Take it shopping with you to make sure that you get the correct replacement. This will come with two new washers: fit the rubber one on to the element. Replace it in the kettle, fit the fibre washer on the outside and replace the cover on the flex coupler plug. Connect and test.

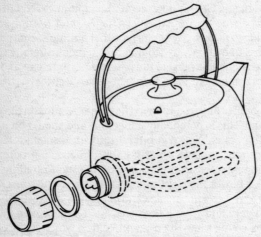

A kettle can also mysteriously cease functioning if allowed to boil dry. This is because it has an auto-safety, spring-loaded cut-out, which has done its job and ejected the flex coupler. It has to be reset before the kettle will work again. Empty the kettle; put it between your knees with the spout down. Inside the flex coupler plug you will see the cut-out sticking up; just push it gently but firmly back with the end of a wooden spoon.

Kettles get very heavy use (how many cups of tea and coffee do *you* make in a day?) and sometimes start functioning intermittently. This is not because they are getting old and tired, but usually because the plug wiring is loose; so mend it. Sometimes it is because the pins inside the flex coupler plug have been pushed out of alignment; these can be bent back, but not before unplugging the kettle, please. The rubber washer on the element will eventually break down; hardware stores have replacement sets designed to fit most kettles.

As with irons, kettle flex eventually gets worn threadbare and should be replaced promptly. For economy buy a new length of braided flex of the correct rating and fit as the old one. For speed (and if the coupler itself is damaged — the plastic collars can break off) buy a complete new flex coupler.

Light fittings When a bulb fails unplug or switch off before removing it. (Don't forget that it will be hot; wait a few minutes or use a dry cloth to handle it.) A simple wall switch is off when the protruding bit is at the bottom. With two-way switches it can be either so if in doubt switch off at the mains. Ordinary bulbs with a bayonet fitting are removed by pressing in and turning anti-clockwise; the Edison screw type just unscrew. Before throwing the bulb away test it in another fitting to make sure that it really is dead. Handle bulbs gently; they sometimes become frozen in place and you can break the glass by gripping too tightly. If it is a difficult one stand high up so that your eyes are above the level of your hands, just in case. Sometimes a bulb pulls out leaving its metal base behind. Removing this means fiddling about with a pair of long-nosed pliers, and you should definitely switch off at the mains.

Fit a new bulb by pressing it in (bayonet type) and twisting clockwise. If you got your switch reading wrong and it lights up when you make contact there's no need to panic and drop it; it won't electrocute you. Just withdraw it and switch off.

Where bulb changing is a problem (with fittings in inaccessible places such as upper landings, or if you are disabled or elderly) fit a long-life bulb to make it less frequent. They are supposed to last twice as long.

With table lamps, bedside lights etc. carry out all the usual fault chasing procedures, then try the switch. Cheap torpedo switches in particular (the type fitted on to the flex rather than the lamp itself) eventually get tired and need replacing. There is no simple way to test that this is the fault; you just have to try one. When attending to any light fittings always check over the flex for any signs of fraying or breaks and replace if necessary (see under Extending flex, page 88).

Fluorescent tubes should last for up to five years but after that become dim and slow to start. Blackened ends and flickering mean that they are on their absolutely last legs. With a few old fittings the tube is released by pressing and twisting, like an ordinary light bulb, but most are released by easing back the end bracket. Obtain a tube of the same length and wattage and fit. If it fails to work properly, and flickers, goes on and off or only produces half the light it should, a new starter is required. The starter unit is a little cylinder usually located on top of the lamp holder which you remove like a light bulb by pressing and twisting. If it is located inside the metal case that forms the body of the fitting you will need to remove the tube in order to remove the cover to reach it.

Light fittings (also wall-mounted fires) in bathrooms are always fitted with pull-cord switches for safety, and these eventually become very grubby. To replace one it is not necessary to get involved with the ceiling rose. I foolishly made this mistake and spent four hours trying to re-assemble the spring-loaded mechanism before stomping out to buy a new one. What I failed to notice was that just below the ceiling rose there is a small plastic fitting; all I had to do was unscrew it, cut the cord free and replace it with a new piece. This is called learning the hard way. (Your fitting may be slightly different — sometimes there is a little eyelet inside the ceiling rose cover — but there will be *something*.)

The average room has a centre light fitting; if you would prefer wall lights, the problem arises, how to fix them without cutting a chase in the plaster? Just ignore the convention that the flex must be concealed, and buy modern-style lights fitted with curly cable, or a flex with a switch in it, which are meant to be exposed.

Plugs Once fitted, the plug on an appliance is usually neglected. A survey once carried out by MK Electric estimated that there could be 70 million faulty plugs in use in Britain. Check yours over and I'll bet you'll find at least one fault to correct.

First look for loose or missing cord grip. The grip is meant to prevent a pull on the flex — as when you try to reach too far with the vacuum cleaner — from reaching the wires inside. If they pull loose the plug will overheat; if they manage to touch they will cause a short circuit; if the earth wire has come out the appliance is no longer safely earthed. Also make sure that the grip was correctly fitted in the first place, so that it grips the outer covering of the flex, not the inner wires. Check that all the wires are firmly held, and connected up to the right terminals. If the live and neutral wires have been connected up in reverse, change them round, because although the appliance works it could be dangerous if controlled by certain types of switch or thermostat.

Throw out any plugs with cracked or broken casings; water could get in or fingers touch live contacts. Vacuum cleaners and electric drills should always have special smash-proof plugs.

Refrigerators The scope for DIY repair here is minimal; fitting new interior light bulbs, and replacing a door seal, if it's the type that unscrews. But if a refrigerator is noisy the reason is usually that it is not standing level, and some bits of cardboard packing under one or two corners should put things right.

If a refrigerator (or freezer) develops an unpleasant smell, either because the electricity has failed and food has gone off, or because you put in something strong-smelling like melon or a tin of pineapple without covering it, wash it down with milk. Leave for about fifteen minutes; if the smell hasn't gone repeat. Then clean in the usual way.

Toasters Limit your efforts to cleansing the beast of accumulated crumbs which, in cases of severe neglect, can cause it to pack up. Unplug, turn upside down, remove the crumb tray and clean it. Shake toaster gently to remove any trapped crumbs; on no account poke about inside it.

TV sets Anything more than twiddling the knobs on the front is strictly *Verboten*.

Vacuum cleaners Did you know that these can go dead simply because the dust bag is full? Blockages are another common ailment. With cylinder and spherical cleaners, if you cannot see the obstruction at the attachment end and fish it out with your fingers, try fitting the hose into the bottom of the cleaner in the hole provided so that it blows instead of sucks, which may dislodge a blockage inside the hose. If this fails poke it out with a long piece of stiff wire; go gently and make a loop in the end to avoid damaging the hose.

With an upright vacuum cleaner, string can become wrapped round the blades of the impeller and stop it dead. Investigate by unplugging the cleaner and pulling off the cover plate on the front of the motor. Here you will also see the fan belt. To fit a new one when the old one is worn out, unplug and unhitch the old one from the drive shaft projecting from the impeller blades. Turn the cleaner over and unscrew the metal shield covering the brush roller. Lift out the roller with the belt; obtain matching new belt. Fit belt round centre slot of roller; refit roller and metal shield. Give the belt a clockwise twist before replacing it on the drive shaft. Refit cover, plug in and test.

When a cleaner is less than efficient look for overfull dust bag, blockages, dirt-clogged felt dust filter; split hose (make temporary repair with strong sticky tape); worn roller or attachment brushes; or poor connections between tubes and/or the attachments.

To avoid future problems empty the dust bag every time you clean. Don't pick up long things like matches, which make bridges for dust to build up on and cause a blockage; string, long threads or rubber bands, or sharp objects.

Washing machines and spin dryers I have not had much personal experience of these, but have heard plenty of horror stories about gross overcharging by repair men, the best being a case where a woman was told that she would require a new motor costing £85, and subsequently made her own repair by fitting the old one with new carbon brushes costing £1.50. But this is no mean feat. All most of us can do is use a reliable repairman, who understands the machine in question and stocks spares for it. The retailer or manufacturer should have a list. But make doubly sure to carry out all the fault chasing procedures before calling for help; and do your best to keep the machine in good order. I am told that this is mainly a question of cleaning the filter religiously after every use, and patting the machine dry inside to keep away rust. A service contract may not be worthwhile if you only use the machine once a week, but will almost certainly pay off if it's regularly used 3–4 times a week.

Spin dryers are a bit more amenable to home maintenance, whether in a twin-tub machine or freestanding. What often goes wrong is that the dryer revolves noisily or erratically. This may just be that clothing has been loaded lopsidedly, or has caught between the drum and its outer casing. But it can also be the result of a faulty brake cable or worn brake lining. Exactly how it's done depends on the make of your machine, but provided that you can get at the part, and have a few spanners, repair should present no difficulty to the mechanically minded.

Extending flex As manufacturers are fairly mean with the length of flex they fit on to their products, a common situation in homes across the land is that an appliance will not reach to a socket, either conveniently or at all. To remedy this what you should *not* do is to join on another bit of flex and bind the join with insulating tape; even as a temporary measure. As I have said before, temporary so easily becomes permanent.

There are three safe ways to lengthen a flex. One is to use a proper flex

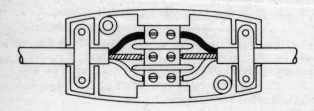

connector. This is a good solution to the problem of bedside lights that are too far away to reach the socket. It consists of a plastic box with terminals inside for each flex end, and cable grips to make sure they stay firmly secured. Make sure to wire it up so that the colours of the flex match from end to end. But do not then let the extended flex trail across

88

the floor or under the carpet. Take it round the wall, securing to the top of the skirting with plastic cable clips. Another type of flex connector consists of two parts: one is a socket, the other has three pins. These are used when the join is not to be permanent, and is most commonly used to connect a long lead to an electric lawn-mower. With these it is *vital* to fit the socket part to the flex ending in the plug, and the pin part to the appliance. If reversed, the exposed pins are live as soon as the flex is plugged in.

This method is not good enough for a portable appliance like a power drill. Here you need a heavy-duty extension lead and trailing rubber socket; you can buy these ready to use with a plug on the other end. The appliance plugs into the trailing socket so that the extension lead can run for some distance before its plug finds a socket. These are very useful things, enabling you to use a power tool out of doors (ideal for messy sanding jobs) and to get other appliances where you want them. But never, never use one to take electrical appliances into the bathroom.

The third method, only suitable for appliances under 500W, is to join two flexes by inserting an in-line type of switch. This would enable you to make an unswitched lamp or wall light reach to the socket; if it already has an in-line switch just replace the flex running from switch to plug with a longer piece. Again, do not let a long flex trail about; pin it safely to wall or skirting board.

In the kitchen it is best to replace a flex, as water could penetrate a flex connector. But do not lengthen the flexes on portable appliances by more than a few inches or they will trail about and cause accidents. Plugging an extension socket (see page 76) into the only convenient socket outlet is probably a better way to solve the problem. With a floor-standing item like a refrigerator, clip the flex safely to the wall. Whether or not you can actually replace a flex depends on how the item was manufactured; some are deliberately made so that no-one can get inside them. Find out by unplugging it and having a good look, if necessary unscrewing a few things, making the usual note of how they went. If it can be done buy a new length of flex of the right rating for the wattage marked on the appliance's rating plate and fit exactly as before.

HOUSE WIRING

Installing additional light switches, socket outlets or ceiling roses should be left to an electrician. But there's nothing difficult about replacing ones which are damaged, out of style or unsuitable, provided that you observe the golden rules: switch off at the mains first and wire the new up exactly as the old. Prepare the ends of new flex as when wiring up a plug (see page 80).

Light switches Some of these are mounted on the surface of the wall; others are recessed into a metal box let into the masonry. So when buying the new fitting make sure that it is of the right type; you may or may not have to buy both parts, base and cover plate. Switches can be one-way or two-way; the latter is the type fitted so that a light can be switched on and off from more than one position; typically at the top and bottom of stairs. So check this too; you must fit the same type. A variation is the dimmer switch which enables a light to be set to graduated degrees of brightness; these are easy to fit in place of the common on/off type, but make sure to get one that will fit on to the existing mounting box.

Switch off at the mains. Unscrew the cover plate and pull it slightly away from the wall to expose the insides of the switch. You will see an earth wire (bare or green) connected to the wall bit, and black and red wires connected to the cover plate. Make a note of how all the wires go before undoing their screws; if you are not replacing the back part leave the earth in place. Screw the live and neutral wires firmly to the correct terminals on the new cover plate. Push the cable back and screw on the cover plate.

A two-way switch has more complicated wiring and you should make a colour drawing of the way the wires are fixed to make quite sure of repeating it; a differently colour-coded cable is used which includes a yellow wire.

Ceiling roses and lampholders A standard ceiling light involves two fittings: a ceiling rose, connected by a short length of flex to a lampholder. In a bathroom or kitchen these should be a different type, with a deep skirt protecting the rose terminals and no flex. Roses normally only need replacing if they are the old-fashioned pear-shaped kind; but lampholders get hot in use and eventually become brittle and break. A new piece of lighting flex may be a good idea while you're up there, if it's the old twisted kind, or formerly white PVC now yellowed and fly-blown.

Switch off at the mains. The ceiling rose is in two parts: cover and pattress (the works). Unscrew the cover and see how the pattress is wired up; depending on the system used it can look quite complicated. If it is connected up to a junction box it will just have the usual three terminals, with matching pairs of wires connected to live and neutral, and an earth wire. But if loop-in wiring has been used you will see a positive forest of wires and at least four terminals, as in addition to the lampholder wires it contains those from the switch and those from *two* cables: one feeding this rose and another going to the next light along. Don't worry about exactly how it all works; make a colour drawing.

Only then disconnect the wires, unscrew the pattress and replace it with the new one. Fix the cable wires in their allotted places. If refitting an existing flex and lampholder do not forget to thread the lampholder flex wires through the rose cover before fixing them. Double check that everything is tight and in the right place, then screw on the cover.

Prepare a new lampholder and flex sitting comfortably at a table. Shorten the flex to the required length and prepare bare wires at both ends. Unscrew the top cover from the new lampholder and thread the flex through. Attach the wires at one end to the lampholder terminals; it doesn't matter which goes to which, but make sure that they are supported by the little plastic elbows, which perform a similar function to a cable grip and take strain off the wires. Screw on the top cover. Thread flex through the ceiling rose cover and fix the wires on the other end to the correct terminals in the rose pattress. If using a conventional lampshade with a ring fitting put this on before replacing the bottom cover. Do this carefully as the covers have a very fine thread which crosses easily causing them to stick fast.

Tip: a little petroleum jelly (Vaseline) smeared on the threads helps to stop this happening, and will make the cover easier to get off in future to clean the lampshade.

Socket outlets Like light switches these can be surface mounted, or recessed into a metal mounting box in the wall. The latter type are not likely to need any attention, but surface-mounted ones can get knocked and broken. Often there is only a single power socket and you would dearly like a double one. You can buy adaptors to use in such cases, but they are not ideal because they tend to come loose as plugs are pulled out resulting in an intermittent supply of electricity to the appliances, which is highly undesirable. Switch off at the mains and take a look to see if a double socket can be fitted; you may find that there are two cables coming into it, which can be wired into a double one. If it is the recessed type this will mean enlarging the hole in the wall to take the bigger mounting box.

Yet another possibility is changing an existing socket for one of a different type. Both single and double ones can be switched or unswitched; or switched with a red light to show when power is on. A switched socket is always preferable to an unswitched one; a neon light is handy to show when, say, an immersion heater is switched on. If you are installing a freezer it's a good idea to wire it into a special type of sealed socket, called a fused connector unit, so that it cannot be inadvertently unplugged. All modern sockets are shuttered: that means power does not flow unless metal pins — i.e. a plug — are inserted into all three holes. In the good old days a curious child who poked a large nail into the right hole could be electrocuted.

Having switched off at the mains, double check with a mains tester, or by plugging in a known-to-be-working appliance, to set your mind at rest that it's absolutely safe to touch the cable. The new socket will have circular weak points in the back of the metal box or pattress; knock out the most convenient one through which to thread the cable. Then screw the fitting to the wall. Leave the cable wires as they are, twisted together in matching pairs. Connect up the wires (all the terminals are labelled so there is no cause for doubt) following the colour code: the wires will probably be the old colours: red for Live, black for Neutral, and a bare wire for Earth. (You are supposed to sheath this in a bit of green sleeving to conform with current wiring regulations.)

Double check that everything is securely fixed to the correct terminal and screw on the cover plate. Switch on and test.

REWIRING

If you buy an old house and rewiring is essential — quite possibly one of the conditions upon which the mortgage has been granted — doing it yourself is perfectly possible. It will save a lot of money; but will take a great deal of time. If the house is empty it may be possible to get an agreement from the vendors to start work once the 10 per cent deposit has been paid but before contracts are exchanged. It is much easier to work in an empty house, without furniture, because a lot of floorboard lifting is involved.

Surprisingly, you don't have to work without a supply of mains electricity until the very last stage. This is because most of the work is non-electrical; laying the network of cables and fixing sockets, ceiling roses and switches. The old mains switch and fuse units do not have to be taken out until you are ready to fix the new consumer unit.

I have not yet tackled any rewiring jobs myself, but my neighbour and keen handywoman Jacqueline has, together with her husband. Electrical wiring is work that many women find congenial, as it calls for patience and dexterity and is not heavy or dirty (except for cutting chases in plaster for conduit, and holes in brickwork for fitting recessed socket outlets). They worked with a copy of the current Institute of Electrical Engineers' Wiring Regulations, which is the professional's guide to what you can and cannot do. This is very technical and you might prefer to work with a book on house rewiring. (But you should still consult the Regulations, because they are constantly being up-dated, and a book might well be behind the times on several points. Every reference library has a copy.) Once they had worked out a layout to suit their house and requirements, Jacqueline calculated the lengths of cable and number of sockets, switches etc. required, went to an electrical wholesaler and bought the lot. This exercise she described as being the worst part of the whole undertaking, because the counter staff treated her like an idiot.

Jacqueline had one advantage in that as the house was to be replastered throughout, she didn't have to do any chase cutting. But she did have to cut a lot of holes in brickwork for the sockets. Doing the actual wiring was a question of sticking exactly to the laid-down plan, and being careful, just as when doing no more than wiring up a plug, to connect well-prepared wires firmly to the correct terminals.

In a curious way a complete rewiring job is safer than doing electrical repairs, for there a mistake can lurk undetected, but with house wiring the Electricity Board will not connect you up to the mains supply until they have inspected your work and pronounced it up to scratch.

When they came to inspect Jacqueline's installion they were most impressed, as she had done everything by the book, and taken none of the short-cuts they expect to see perpetrated by pressed-for-time professional electricians.

Caution to any Australian or New Zealand readers: only licensed electricians are allowed to work on permanent wiring, or equipment permanently connected to the supply. In New Zealand you can work on flex and appliances which just plug into a socket; in Australia you can do so unless you live in Queensland or Western Australia.

5 Working with wood

Many women become quite expert in other fields of DIY, yet hesitate when it comes to woodwork. They feel that it is something essentially masculine and technical which they can't get to grips with. I think the main reason for this is that even today so few girls get the chance to do woodwork at school. And it's a great pity, because woodwork is the most creative of all areas of DIY. Given the time and the inclination you can make practically anything for the home, even aspiring to making furniture as you become more skilled — but that is beyond the scope of this book.

Really women are very suited to woodwork, which is mainly a matter of very accurate measuring and cutting. Great strength is *not* required. Using woodworking tools skilfully soon comes with practice, just like anything else; who can sew a straight seam on a sewing machine first time out, or knit for the first time without dropping stitches all over the place? And you can do a great deal of basic woodwork without ever needing the more advanced tools like chisels and planes. With today's super-strong adhesives there's no longer much need for complicated joints. Someone who makes a drawer with the dovetail joints you see on old furniture is doing it to show off their skills, not because it's necessary. The old craftsmen only had animal and fish glues — we have the advantage of polyvinyl acetate, epoxy resin and urea formaldehyde.

WOODWORKING TOOLS

A surprising amount of woodwork can be done with the basic tools listed in Chapter 1: steel tape for measuring up, combination or try square for marking cutting lines, small panel saw for cutting wood to length and drill for boring holes so that pieces can be screwed together.

For cutting small sections and making more advanced joints you will need a tenon saw, which has fine teeth and a rigid spine; sometimes called a back saw because of this feature. To make an enclosed cut — say cutting a hole in a door panel for a cat flap — the proper tool is a padsaw or keyhole saw. This is just a narrow saw blade with one end fitted into a handle. You can buy a pad saw blade to fit a Stanley knife handle. To get the cut started drill a hole large enough to insert the tip of the saw close to each corner of the area to be removed. The narrow blade lets you change direction while cutting, so you can cut from the holes into the marked-out cutting lines. This type of saw can be used to make curved cuts — for a fancy shape for a spice rack top, say, or a round wooden house number plate — but the best all-round saw for curves is the coping saw. This looks rather like a mini hacksaw, with a replaceable blade that fits into a U-shaped metal frame. The screw-up handle tensions the blade and prevents it bending when used, a common fate of keyhole saws. For enclosed cutting the coping saw is limited by the size of its frame. A fretsaw is an elongated type of coping saw, which takes very fine blades and is used for such work as model making.

A plane is not essential for basic woodwork but lacking one restricts you to using wood of standard widths. A small amount of waste can be removed with a Surform tool, and a large amount by cutting down the length of the board with a panel saw, which is hard work on a long board. With a plane the waste can be removed quickly and easily, leaving a smooth edge behind. Large planes are very expensive, but for general DIY use one from Stanley's economy range is perfectly adequate, and the cheapest costs only about £9. A plane with a replaceable blade is quite a bit more expensive (about £22) but does away with the sharpening chore and the need for tools to do it. A small block plane is also useful, for trimming end grain and bevelling edges.

The very simple joints described in this chapter do not necessarily need chisels, but once you want to do anything more advanced you will need one or two. Chisels are also necessary for the kind of job in which you have to cut a small recess in a piece of timber. Suppose you want to rehang a door so that it opens the opposite way — you'll need a chisel to cut new recesses for the hinges. Do not buy a set of chisels. You may never use them all, and sets are expensive. It's best to get single ones as and when you need them. Probably the most useful size is a 12mm one, followed by 6mm and 25mm. Buy the more versatile bevel-edged type rather than the straight-bladed 'firmer' chisels, and look for those labelled 'ready-honed'. Some chisels are sold just ground, and must be honed sharp by the buyer before they are ready for use. Unless you do a lot of chisel work you can get by without a mallet; much of the time it isn't used anyway, and modern chisels with hard plastic handles can be tapped lightly with a hammer without developing the mashed-up ends characteristic of old wooden-handled ones.

Both planes and chisels have to be sharpened regularly for top efficiency, so unless you know somebody who already has the tools required, you will also have to invest in an oil stone and a honing guide.

Bang goes nearly another £10. The oil stone, for sharpening the blades, has a coarse side for starting and a fine one for finishing off. The honing guide holds the blades at the correct angle to the stone during sharpening to ensure that the cutting edge is not altered. Always store chisels carefully to protect their cutting tips.

A simple and useful traditional tool is the marking gauge. This consists of a wooden rod with a sharp steel pin at one end — at right angles to the rod — and a moveable block that slides along the rod and can be set at any point on it. The pin scores a fine line parallel with the edge of a piece of wood, and at a distance from the edge determined by the setting of the block, which is held against the wood during the stroke. In other words if you want to mark a line 25mm from the edge you carefully set the block with its face 25mm from the tip of the pin. The line scribed into the wood can be a guide for sawing. Once a distance is set on the gauge you can repeat the marking *ad infinitum* and it will always be accurate. A marking gauge is invaluable with materials such as plywood and veneered chipboard which should be scored along the cutting line on *both* sides before sawing to avoid splintering the veneer. The gauge ensures that both score lines are equidistant from the edge.

You may need some larger drill bits than those in your basic set, for jobs such as making finger holes in drawers, or large holes in a sliding door in which to fit plastic finger plates. There are various types of large woodworking drill bits. The cheap ones called flat bits are suitable for general-purpose large hole boring. Make sure that whatever you buy has a round shank that will fit into a hand or electric drill. Some have a four-sided tapered shank which makes them useless unless you happen to have one of the large cranked-handled types of carpenter's brace. For drilling really large holes fast you can get a drill attachment called a hole saw.

Holding and cramping As well as tools you will need various devices for holding wood while you work on it. Absolutely basic is the bench hook, a gadget so simple that you can make it yourself (hooray! no expenditure!). Take a piece of timber, preferably hardwood, about 19mm × 25cm × 15cm. Screw a strip of narrower wood flush along each of its edges and on opposite sides, the strips stopping about 5cm short at one end (see diagram). The bench hook is an aid to sawing without the wood slipping away. Place it on the workbench with its lower strip against the bench's edge and hold the wood to be sawn on the hook against its top strip. The stopped-short end of the top strip can be used as a guide for starting your cut properly 'square', and for this reason it must itself be cut square (see later). Obviously the bench hook can be used whichever way you pick it up. The stopped-short ends of the strips

BASIC WOODWORKING TOOLS

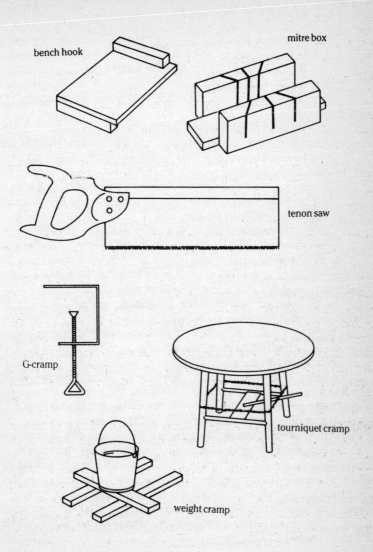

bench hook

mitre box

tenon saw

G-cramp

tourniquet cramp

weight cramp

should be on the right if you are right-handed, on the left if you are a southpaw.

For cutting mitres or as an aid to 'square' cutting you need a mitre box or block. Though these, too, are quite simple you should buy one as it must be 100 per cent accurate. Use only the tenon saw with the mitre box, and if the work is small place a piece of waste wood in the bottom of the box to raise it. Of course the waste wood must be flat and even so that the work remains at right angles to the cutting slots. Hold the mitre box or block steady by placing it on the bench hook (some can be screwed to the workbench).

Though quite a lot of work can be done without a vice, sooner or later you will need one, especially for holding work while cutting joints. If you have a proper workbench you can buy a vice that screws on as a permanent fixture. But if you want to move it about, or have to work on the kitchen table, get a clamp-on type. Also get a couple of cramps with at least 10cm jaws, for holding joints tightly together while the adhesive dries. Cheap ones are perfectly adequate.

Cramping up large or awkwardly shaped items while adhesive dries is beyond the scope of a bench vice or small cramps alone, and you may need to use your ingenuity and improvise. Large flat items can be cramped up by nailing a batten to the workbench or floor, pushing the work tightly against it and holding it in place with another batten, ideally used in conjunction with a pair of folding wedges. On curved components, use a cord or an old bicycle inner tube as a tourniquet, tightening it with a stick. Weight is often the answer, depending on the item. Use anything from an old flatiron to a stack of big books or a pail of water standing on a board.

Make sure, before you cramp glued components up, that when possible they are lying on a perfectly flat surface and that all corners are at true right angles. (Check them with the try or combination square.) Uneven cramping pressure can force an item into a diamond shape, and if this is not corrected before the adhesive dries it will stay that way.

If you become really interested in woodwork and start making a lot of joints, a Jointmaster is invaluable. This is a multi-purpose sawing jig which enables you to make accurate joints of a far more complicated kind than those dealt with in this chapter. It is also good for making a large number of simple cuts quickly and accurately. It takes timber up to 5.5cm × 10cm and is not very expensive for what it does; R.R.P. is £18, but shop around.

WORKBENCHES

Only rich DIY fiends aspire to a traditional, purpose-made workbench. The closest I ever got to such a luxury was a home-made one constructed from heavy secondhand timbers. Odd jobs can be done on a ricketty old potting bench, but for woodwork you must have something much better, or you will never achieve the necessary accuracy. The basic requirement is a work surface of suitable height which is solid, steady and flat.

The Workmate range of portable workbenches was developed to meet some of these requirements at a reasonable price, with the additional virtue that they fold flat for storage. The basic Workmate consists of a metal frame which stands about 75cm (30in) high for general work, but will fold down lower for use as a saw horse. The top consists of two 60cm long parallel timber jaws which form a large vice that can be opened up to a limit of 10cm to hold timber for sawing, planing, sanding etc. Strategically placed holes in the top take plastic stops in various arrangements to hold round, curved or irregularly shaped work. Although the Workmate is sturdy, it is light enough to be carried in one hand. Basic ones cost about £35 and there are several more advanced models offering more features for more money. The Workmate's one drawback as a workbench is that it is not suitable for hammering, which must always be done on a very solid surface (i.e. over the leg of a workbench or table).

Failing a Workmate, if you have a place to put it a large sturdily built old-fashioned kitchen table, the kind with big turned legs, is a good substitute, though it may be a bit low if you are tall. If the top is made of several separate planks, or badly warped and scarred, it will not be flat enough for accurate work, so cover it with a sheet of 12mm chipboard.

If you have no alternative but to work on the kitchen table protect it from vice marks and saw cuts with a sheet of chipboard and push it against a wall to make it as stable as possible.

USING WOODWORKING TOOLS

Using woodworking tools is something that comes fairly naturally, but for those who, like me, never had the benefit of woodwork lessons here are a few tips.

Sawing Most of the tips and rules about sawing are aimed at ensuring accuracy, because good sawing is simply accurate sawing. When marking your cutting line across the timber continue it (using the square) over the edge that will be away from you during sawing. If your first few strokes (with saw slightly angled forward) cut down along the 'edge line' at the same time as they start cutting along the main cutting line the saw

99

will be greatly steadied and much less likely to wander off. If those first few strokes have gone accurately along both lines you should have no trouble in completing an accurate cut right through the timber.

Always saw lightly, almost without pushing; 'letting the saw do the work', as old hands say. Wandering off the cutting line usually comes from too strenuous sawing and too much pressure on the tool. Undue pressure may also tilt the saw blade to right or left, so that the cut through the wood will not be properly vertical. Nor can you saw accurately if you don't stand right behind the cutting line.

Use a panel saw at a slight downward angle, a tenon saw at an even slighter one. A tenon saw used with mitre box or Jointmaster is automatically steadied and guided and is used quite horizontally.

Always begin sawing by making a few backward strokes until you have got a start, steadying the blade against the bent knuckle of your other hand. Saw on the 'waste' side of the cutting line with the blade just skimming it. Remember: the line represents the outer limit of the piece you want to use, so you want no extra taken off it or left on.

Of course, when you prepare for sawing you will bear in mind whether the waste side of the cutting line is to be on the right or left, according to whether you are right- or left-handed. A right-handed person sawing the waste side on the left cannot see the cutting line properly and so cannot check the accuracy of the sawing. Towards the end of the cut support the waste piece with your free hand and make the last few strokes very gently; otherwise the waste will break away under its own weight, usually splintering the wood for your job. If whiskers of wood are left sticking out cut them off with a sharp Stanley knife on a flat piece of scrap wood.

Planing Hold the wood in a vice or Workmate. Find out by trial and error from which end to plane. According to the direction of the grain of that particular piece of wood it will plane more smoothly one way than the other. Test for this with the plane blade set fine. Plane in one long stroke from end to end, adjusting the blade if necessary until the shavings produced are ribbon like. To plane end grains without splitting bits off you must work towards the centre from all sides. Always put a plane down on its side after use unless the blade is fully retracted. This is to avoid damaging the blade's edge.

Using chisels Generally speaking, chisels are for cutting away wood that is not accessible to a saw. They are the fine precision 'scalpels' of the woodworker. Suppose you want to cut a recess in the edge of a board or batten, a sort of neat square notch. Having marked it out, make two saw cuts in from the edge to the proper depth, then remove the wood

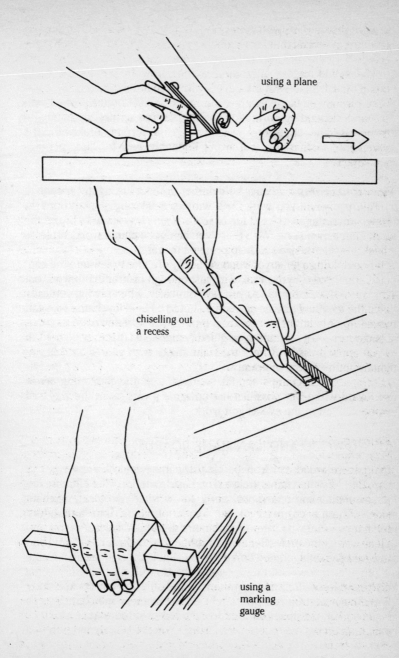

using a plane

chiselling out
a recess

using a
marking
gauge

between the saw cuts with your chisel. Don't try to take it all out at once; remove it in several thin layers, and when you get near the bottom of the recess take great care not to go beyond the right depth. Your final chisel strokes should remove only fine shavings. In work like this the chisel should be used flat, with the bevel away from the work.

Chisels may be tapped with a hammer or mallet or just pushed with the hand, depending on the job. When pushing a chisel by hand you should use the other one sensitively as a sort of 'brake' on the movement, so that the tool won't suddenly jerk forward, perhaps damaging the work.

Vices and cramps Always hold timber in a vice just tightly enough to keep it firm while you work on it without squeezing or marking it. A proper carpenter's vice is made of wood and is less likely to bruise the work than a metal one. With these you can put a pair of wooden pieces (cheeks) inside the jaws to help protect the work.

When holding a length of wood vertically in a vice to saw into the end, place it low down in the vice, with just enough protruding to work on. This is to reduce vibration as you saw. Similarly, when sawing vertically down the length of a piece of wood it should be held low in the vice and moved up only an inch or two at a time as you saw down.

Make sure when cramping up glued components that they do not slip as you apply pressure. Check the right angles with your square as you tighten up the cramp or cramps.

Cramps like G-cramps should be used with the tightening screw downward whenever possible; left upwards it can get in the way and even poke you in the eye as you work.

BUYING WOOD AND MAN-MADE BOARDS

Materials for woodwork can be obtained in several different types of shop. Builders' merchants are good on basic material of the kind used in house-building and renovation; get to know what your local merchant stocks. There's no need to be scared of going into a builders' merchant's — they do cater for amateurs wanting a few feet of this and that as well as the professional chaps buying by the truck load, and you may even see some other women. On the whole the staff are an amiable lot, provided that you know what you want. Go with clear measurements and quantities written down and a tape measure in your pocket; don't expect to get anything cut accurately to size. Builders' merchant's yards are good places to shop for many other things, from a few nails to a new bath. An average merchant stocks some 20,000 lines, far more than a

DIY shop or even a superstore. But they don't deal in tiny quantities. It's paint by the litre, timber by the metre and nails weighed out by the quarter kilo in blue sugar bags — nice old-fashioned touch! Builders' merchant's prices are often much lower than other people's, and they always deliver, usually free. Be prepared for some waiting around — pass the time by getting acquainted with the stock — and choose a weekday afternoon rather than a busy Saturday morning to go.

The timber at a builders' merchant's will be almost exlusively widely-used sizes of softwood, plus some basic types of man-made boards. For a bigger choice of softwoods and boards, plus hardwoods and mouldings, you need a specialist timber merchant. Find your nearest one in the Yellow Pages. They too will deliver, but check whether you have to spend over a certain amount or live within a certain radius to get delivery free.

DIY shops and superstores vary greatly in what timber they stock. Many carry only a limited range of small softwood sections and sell it by the length; no cutting even to the nearest metre. On the other hand a small corner shop may, for example, sell hardboard cut into small pieces which are just what you want.

Sawn and planed timber To buy wood without becoming confused you must understand the seemingly perverse way in which it is not actually the size indicated on the bill. This is because there are two kinds of softwood: sawn and planed. Sawn timber is rough-surfaced, sold just as it comes from the saw mill, and you will need it only for jobs where it is not visible, such as supporting tongued and grooved panelling, or making a frame for behind a bath panel. What you will mostly buy is planed timber, sometimes called PAR (planed all round). This has been through a planing machine, which removes the rough surface, leaving the wood fairly smooth. The amount taken off is about 5mm all round, but as it is by no means exact, the wood is still referred to by its original, unplaned dimensions. So when ordering timber you always have to specify whether this nominal measurement is near enough, or whether the measurements you give are the actual ones you hope to get. Hardwoods are actually the size they claim to be.

It is best to think metric in a timber yard, as the building industry went metric some time ago. For some curious reason everything is measured in millimetres, so you need to keep knocking off noughts to get measurements you can understand. (See page 207 for the idiot's guide to metric conversions.) Having said that, many of their older customers still think in imperial measure and always will, so the merchants are well used to thinking in both. Indeed catalogues of building materials for sale to the general public are still printed with dual measurements, and there seems no sign of this situation changing-in Britain in the near future. As in cookery, what you mustn't do is to mix up the two, or both you and the timber yard staff will end up worse than confused.

Selecting softwood Being a natural material, softwood suffers from quite a few defects, so always pick it out yourself — never order by 'phone — and inspect all sides and edges. Man-made boards can safely be ordered by 'phone, usually with C.O.D. delivery.

Knots add character to timber but they should be live knots — brown ones, not the black dead ones that drop out eventually, leaving a hole in your handywork. Hold the length of wood up horizontally and 'sight' along its edges to make sure that it is straight, not bowed like a banana and possibly twisted as well. Other things you do not want are rough patches, muddy boot marks, workmen's calculations in ball-point and splits in the body of the board. Split ends can be cut off but should not be included in the length that you pay for.

Timber yards with woodworking machinery can cut wood to exact length for you, but if you're dealing with a busy man with a handsaw you should order extra and cut it to the required length yourself. In practice it is almost always better to buy extra. Many yards charge by the full metre anyway, and you pay extra for cutting to size. If you then find that you have made a slight mistake in your calculations, or if the yard didn't get it *exactly* right, the wood is perhaps wasted. It is also better to cut the lengths as you go along rather than doing them all together at the start. Slight adjustments may have to be made here and there, particularly if you are following a published design and your wood is not precisely the same width or thickness. By the way, published cutting lists *have* been known to contain errors.

Softwood is often poorly seasoned, or has been stored in open-sided sheds to become damp, so if possible store it for a week before use, *lying flat*, inside the house. It will then be easier to saw and less likely to shrink or warp later on.

TYPES OF SOFTWOOD AND HARDWOOD

Softwood This is what most people mean when they ask for wood without further specification. It is also loosely described as deal or pine. Softwood is any timber obtained from coniferous trees. When bought it is extremely pale, but varnishing and exposure to light slowly turn it a nice honey colour. Planed softwood comes in varying standard thicknesses and widths, ranging from small sections, starting at a nominal 12.5mm by 12.5mm square, to hefty planks, nominally 33mm thick × 25cm wide. It can also be bought tongued and grooved for panelling work, and machined into an enormous variety of mouldings. Mouldings are lengths of wood cut to various fancy shapes in section. Most mouldings are for building work: door architraves, skirting boards and picture rails, which you might need for replacement purposes. (Newson's Timber can supply almost any Victorian or Edwardian mouldings — see Useful Addresses, page 209). Others you may have occasion to use are round ones (dowel), various beadings or cover strips such as quarter round (quadrant), half round, and scotia (quadrant with a concave front); handle- and stair-rail mouldings; replacement beads for sash windows and weatherboard mouldings for exterior doors.

One or two timbers that are technically softwoods are really quite hard and don't have the pale 'pine' appearance at all. One such is parana pine, a superior pink-tinged wood with an interesting bird's eye grain. It comes in wide but thin planks, ideal for making big display shelves.

Hardwood This is any wood from a deciduous tree — teak, mahogany, oak, etc. Hardwoods have become so expensive now that they have been virtually superseded by chipboard veneered with the real thing (see below). The ordinary timber merchant's stock of hardwood will be limited to a few sections and mouldings of ramin, a cheap hardwood, pale-coloured like pine but with a closer grain and no knots; it is sometimes called Japanese oak. These sections are useful for making small fine things, as the available sizes are smaller than softwood. For example you can get an edge lipping for a work top or shelf in much thinner ramin than in any softwood. Picture frame moulding will also be some kind of hardwood, very often ramin.

MAN-MADE BOARDS

There are many different kinds of man-made board but the ones that you are mostly likely to need are chipboard, plain and veneered; plywood, blockboard and hardboard. They are all made in large sheets of varying sizes, but the most common is 122cm × 244cm (4ft × 8ft). Some retailers will sell only complete sheets, but others deal in halves and quarters, or cut to size. Buying full sheets is the most economical way, but cutting to size is not easy, even if you can use up the whole board. Ideally a full sheet should be supported on a pair of saw horses or low trestles, with two long battens to support it in between them and to stop it whipping while being sawn. But it is possible to manage with four chairs. Most man-made boards are for interior use only, though plywood and hardboard are available in exterior grades.

Chipboard This is made of tiny particles of wood highly compressed with a bonding adhesive. Many stockists have it in only the 19mm thickness, but it is also made 12.5mm thick. Plain chipboard is the cheapest of all man-made boards except hardboard. It is very stable and virtually does not warp, but is not particularly strong. (If it is allowed to get wet it can snap in two.) It is mostly used for things like kitchen worktops, where it is well supported and protected by a plastic laminate or other finish, but it can also be used for utility shelving that isn't going to bear too much weight. If the board is going to be stained and varnished or painted the rough cut edges must be filled with cellulose filler or covered with an edge lipping of wood.

Veneered chipboard There are three distinct types of this: chipboard veneered with real wood, with wood-grain plastic laminate, or with white laminate. It is sold under various brand names in the form of planks, usually 2 or 2.5 metres long, in a wide range of widths, from 15cm to 90cm. The thickness is nominally 19mm but is actually a bit less than that, depending on the brand, commonly 15-16mm. The most popular wood veneers are teak and mahogany. Though veneer gives chipboard extra strength it is still not as strong as real wood. It is excellent for making simple cabinets, and for shelves, particularly deep ones which would be unthinkably expensive to build in real hardwood, and pretty pricey even in softwood. The veneer covers the chipboard's long edges as well as both sides. The ends, and cuts made during construction of a unit, can be covered, if they show, with a self-adhesive matching edging strip which is pressed on with a hot iron. Chipboard veneered with real wood is already well finished and needs only very light sanding followed by oiling or varnishing. The plastic-faced boards need no finishing at all.

Veneered chipboard is not really suitable for making anything involving curves, and lends itself only to simple butt or dowel joints. If you go in for making wall units and furniture with it work out designs which will reduce cutting and waste as much as possible. The manufacturers of Contiboard produce a useful booklet which contains both design ideas and practical tips on working with chipboard (see Useful Addresses, page 208).

Plywood This is made of thin layers ('plies') stuck together with the grain of each ply running across that of its neighbour. These alternating grains make plywood very strong for its thickness, while it cannot split along the grain as softwood may. It can be anything from 3mm to 19mm thick. The most common quality (B/B) has one unblemished side and one in which knotholes have been neatly plugged. Though the grains in plywood alternate, those of the two outer sheets always run in the same direction. This means that all plywood consists of an odd number of sheets. Plywood can also be obtained with a decorative hardwood or laminate veneer.

Thick white birch plywood is splendid for shelving, cabinets, toy chests and other furniture, as its multiple layers give an attractive striped finish to all the cut edges. It lends itself to designs involving curved shapes, to slotting together with egg box joints and to having big holes cut in it. Unfortunately it has become so expensive that many timber yards stock only the cheaper Gaboon ply, which has only three layers, the middle one of a rather spongy dark wood. But thin sheets of this are good for medium-sized sliding cupboard doors, false drawer fronts and cabinet backs.

Blockboard This consists of a core of small wood blocks bonded together between two surface veneers which are usually birch. Like chipboard it is most frequently sold in the 19mm thickness, but comes also 12.5mm and 25mm thick. It is used where strength like that of plywood is required but is cheaper; for example for a kitchen worktop that has to span a long distance unsupported. It has a finely sanded surface, ready to paint, but some small gaps in the long edges may need filling.

Hardboard This is made by squeezing softwood pulp into sheets under high pressure. Most timber yards just stock what they call standard hardboard, which is brown, 3.2mm thick, with a shiny face and mesh-textured back. But it is also made in 4.8mm and 6.4mm thicknesses. A large yard may have several other kinds as well, for hardboard is a very versatile material. Common ones are perforated hardboard (pegboard); screening hardboard, cut into decorative openwork patterns; medium hardboard, which is soft enough for making noticeboards; and standard hardboard finished with coloured enamel or a printed woodgrain effect. Standard hardboard is light and easy to cut, not particularly strong, but cheap. It is ideal for small sliding doors, drawer bottoms, cabinet backs, and for levelling floors. It can be clear-varnished, painted or covered with wallpaper.

MAKING WOOD JOINTS

To join wood successfully you must be able to work accurately and to cut 'square'. A square cut is one which forms a perfect right angle (90°) in both vertical and horizontal planes. Achieving a 90° cut across the width of the wood is simply a matter of using your square to mark the cutting

107

line, then sawing carefully. Never assume that the piece of wood you are working with has square ends; it probably hasn't, and you must trim a bit off one end first to make it square, then work from there.

Achieving a square cut down through the thickness of the wood takes skill and practice. If you tilt your hand and therefore the saw blade, a fraction to left or right, the cut will not be properly vertical, i.e. at 90° to the length (see Sawing page 99). The easiest way to make sure this doesn't happen is to use a tenon saw in a mitre box or Jointmaster whenever possible. But this cannot be done with large pieces of wood, so practise your cutting on scrap wood before rushing in and ruining what you have just bought at vast expense.

The standard way of securing joints is to coat one of the 'mating' surfaces with woodworking adhesive, bring them together and fix with screws or nails — called glue and screw, or pin and glue. Wipe off squeezed-out adhesive with a damp rag before it can dry. If the structure is lightweight or non-loadbearing (for example a spice rack or a picture frame) and can be tightly cramped up while the adhesive dries, the adhesive alone is sufficient to hold the pieces together. But for loadbearing structures like bookshelves or cabinets the nails or screws keep the components squarely together while the adhesive dries and gives the structure additional strength. Alternatively, if you want a structure that can be taken apart, use screws and no adhesive.

(For screw and nail driving techniques see pages 8–9.)

Butt joints The butt joint is an absolutely basic joint for making any kind of box or frame. To line the screw holes up perfectly in both pieces of wood drill fine holes through the upper one, line the pieces up together and mark through these holes with a bradawl into the end grain of the lower piece. Now enlarge the holes in the upper piece to allow the screws to pass through. (Countersink *first* if required.) End grain is soft, and the bradawl punctures should be enough to give the screws a start; otherwise drill pilot holes with a fine drill.

Reinforced butt joints For extra strength a butt joint can be reinforced with a bearer, a piece of square section or quadrant wood glued into the angle formed by the two main pieces. This is used in making strong boxes (e.g. a toy chest), drawers, and shelves. When two pairs of screws are used stagger them so that they go into the bearer without meeting.

Half lap joint This involves cutting halfway through the end of each piece to a depth that equals the width of the wood, then cutting through the thickness so that the cuts meet. This joint makes a strong frame in

108

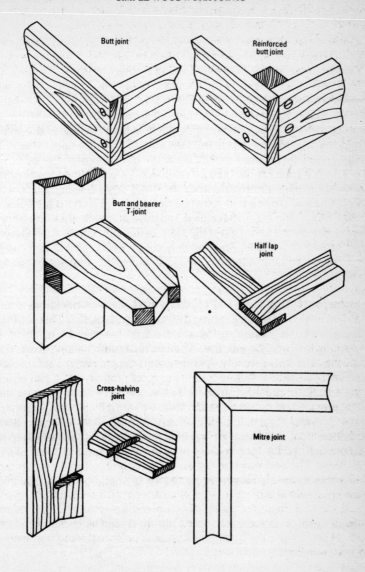

Butt joint

Reinforced butt joint

Butt and bearer T-joint

Half lap joint

Cross-halving joint

Mitre joint

wide, thin wood which cannot be effectively butt jointed. It is also stronger and better looking.

Cross halving joint Often called an egg box joint, this offers a neat way of building a wall unit with lots of internal divisions, and gives a very rigid structure, *provided* that the cutting is done accurately. The width of the slot is exactly equal to the thickness of the wood and is cut halfway across the board. Traditionally, the bottom of the slot is cut out with a chisel. But if you don't have a chisel of an appropriate size there is an easier method. This involves drilling a hole in the middle of the board, *then* making two saw cuts in from the edge to meet the sides of the hole. The drill diameter must exactly equal the thickness of the wood.

A slotted-together unit can be enclosed in a butt-jointed frame or left with short ends protruding from the outer cross halving joints. This works best in plywood; in softwood the short end sections are liable to snap along the grain if handled roughly, although they are secure enough once the unit is glued together. In this joint glue is applied along the insides of the slots. An accurately cut plywood egg box unit can be assembled without adhesive, and dismantled for moving or storage when necessary.

Mitre joint The classic way of joining two battens or mouldings to form a right angle is made by cutting the mating ends at 45°. This cutting is hardly possible without using a mitre box, but may be achieved by marking the two cuts with the 45° angle on a combination square, then sawing extremely carefully. A mitre joint is the only way to get moulded pieces of wood like picture framing to meet properly but it can also be used on flat unmoulded strips for a more attractive-looking corner than that provided by a plain butt joint. Mitre cuts are difficult to cut accurately and the wider the moulding the worse the error will look. Moral: choose small-section moulding for your first attempts at picture framing. Cramping up the four corners of a picture frame is a fairly skillful business. The best way is to use one of the patent picture frame cramps. A simple frame clamp consisting of four plastic jaws and a tightening cord costs about £2.

Dowel joints Dowels are short cylindrical lengths of hardwood and dowel joints are made by drilling opposing holes in the mating pieces of wood components and inserting glued dowels to hold them together. It is easy to do *if* you happen to have a vertical drill stand, which holds a power tool absolutely vertical and enables an exact depth to be drilled. But when done unaided, even with a helper to check that the drill bit is going in upright, both back to front and side to side, it is almost

110

impossible to get both holes absolutely vertical, and coinciding perfectly. However you can buy various dowel jigs which help to solve these problems in various ways. Another cheap and helpful gadget is a dowel locator, which has twin points enabling drill holes to be perfectly aligned. If you can master the art, dowel jointing is an invisible and strong way to make corner joints or T-joints, or to butt narrow boards together to make a larger surface.

Do not try to make the joints with bits of ordinary dowel. Buy the special grooved hardwood dowels which prevent the adhesive from squeezing out; they come in large and small sizes.

Patent joints A variety of patent plastic joints can be bought to join wood components at right angles without cutting joints. They are particularly useful for making strong joints in veneered chipboard, but they add considerably to your costs. They are also rather obtrusive and take up space inside a cabinet. There are various types designed for assembling box-type structures; also one that both hangs a cupboard on a wall and holds the backboard in place, and shelf bearers. Light-weight shelves can be simply rested on plug-in plastic shelf pegs.

Note If you come across some things called corrugated fasteners, don't bother with them. They appear to be the answer to the maiden woodworker's prayer, enabling two pieces of wood to be joined simply by hammering a couple of fasteners across. In practice it's almost impossible to get them in, and even if you do it's a very rough and ready method.

FINISHING

Preparation Although it has been planed, natural timber needs to be sanded smooth before varnishing or painting. Sanding must always be carried out in the right direction: to and fro along the lines of the grain pattern. Sanding across or round and round will scratch the wood. On end grains, the cut ends of the wood, sand in one direction only. Find out which by rubbing a finger along the grain. However rough it feels, one way will be less so than the other, and this is the direction in which to sand. The sanding direction will be the same at both ends of the wood. Because of the need to work with the grain it is best to carry out most of the sanding *before* assembling the piece. Do large pieces with abrasive paper wrapped round a cork block, starting with a medium grade and progressing to fine, or for a super smooth finish, 'flour' grade. To preserve their sharp edges, sand small pieces by rubbing them on a sheet of abrasive paper laid flat.

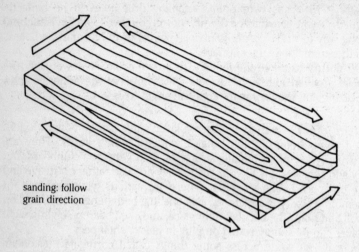

sanding: follow
grain direction

After assembling fill any holes and, if necessary, cover screw or nail heads with matching plastic wood (Polyfilla will do if the finish is to be paint). If it shrinks while drying add a little more; sand flat when dry. Give the piece a final light sanding and remove any pencil marks left visible with a hard pencil rubber or white spirit. Leave it for dust to settle before applying the finish.

Veneered chipboard needs little or no sanding. Countersunk screw heads can be covered with brown or white screw caps.

Clear finishes The quickest, easiest finish of all to apply is teak oil, which, despite its name, can be applied to any wood. It is an improved version of good old-fashioned linseed oil which dries far more quickly. It gives a low sheen and light protection to the wood: fine for display shelving or bookcases, but not for table tops.

Probably the most popular finish of all is polyurethane varnish. It can give a gloss, satin or matt finish, and stands up to practically anything: hot cups and plates, water, alcohol and considerable abrasion. Apply it by brush or a cloth pad, following the instructions. Two coats are usually sufficient. Pick off any specks and brush hairs as you go.

Polyurethane is not so good outdoors as it tends to peel off in a relatively short time. For items to be used outside buy Furniglas

Allweather varnish or Blackfriar UV66 exterior varnish.

A more expensive clear finish, but superhard and glossy, is Rustins' plastic coating. It also dries very quickly (in about 2 hours) and does not darken with age. This is a two-part cold cure lacquer; you have to mix two parts together before it is ready, and once mixed it must be used within the stated time, and any left over thrown away.

Transparent colour finishes These can be achieved in several ways. The simplest is to use a coloured polyurethane such as Ronseal Woodshades. They have what is called a hi-build formula, which means that the colour intensifies with each coat applied.

An alternative method is to apply a wood stain first, then varnish over it. This gives you a bigger choice of wood colours, from pale light oak down to near-black Jacobean oak. Some wood stains are water based (Furniglas) some solvent-based (Rustins, Colron, Blackfriar). Water-based stains can raise the grain of the wood, and sanding smooth then removes some of the colour. To avoid this wet the surface first, to raise the grain, and sand when dry. Apply stain with a cloth pad or a brush, in the direction of the grain, trying not to overlap the strips.

If you want to give the wood an artificial colour rather than a natural wood shade find a shop with a Dulux Matchmaker machine. This can produce Dulux interior varnish tinted with a choice of 40 soft colours: greens, blues, oranges, pinks and yellows. These are a great improvement on the harsh primary-coloured stains and varnishes that were around a few years ago.

If you want a really strong-coloured finish that still allows the grain to show through paint the item with gloss paint well thinned with white spirit. Finish with varnish.

Paint finish Use this if you want to hide what is underneath — for example chipboard or blockboard. It's best to stick to gloss paint; a satin finish doesn't wear nearly as well and rubs off sharp corners very quickly (If you want black, Rustins do a special matt black finishing paint.) For small jobs use tinlets of Humbrol. This is guaranteed lead-free and non-toxic, and absolutely safe for use on nursery furniture or toys. (Most paint is lead-free these days, but don't paint anything for children with an old tin from the garage, just in case.)

(See Decorating chapter, page 53, for painting techniques and how to avoid dust spoiling the finish.)

Although paint is great at hiding defects and comes in glorious colours it is poor at resisting abrasion. So don't paint horizontal surfaces that are used a lot, especially tables. Finish these with polyurethane or plastic coating; or use paint and protect it with a sheet of bevelled-edged glass.

6   Practical projects

The projects included in this chapter are all things which I have had to tackle at some time in the various houses I have lived in. They range from very simple projects like fitting curtain rails and building freestanding shelves to more advanced ones that require a basic understanding of working with wood. But even these can be carried out without specialised woodworking tools such as chisels and planes; just the tools from your basic kit. I have gone into putting up shelves in some detail, because that's what everyone wants to do *first*, and there are so many different ways of doing it. Also it is a good lead-in to more advanced projects: a simple shelf can be elaborated into a sophisticated wall storage system; add sides and it becomes a bookcase; doors and it's a cupboard.

CURTAIN RAILS AND ROLLER BLINDS

Provided that the rail can be fixed to a timber window frame this is an easy job and one that can be done with the minimum of tools: bradawl and screwdriver to put up the brackets, and a Woolworth's hack saw if the rail needs cutting to length.

Modern curtain rails are all designed to look good when the curtains are drawn so there is no need to mess about constructing pelmets. I usually use plastic rail which is cheap, perfectly adequate and so flexible that it rolls up, making carrying a long length home much easier. Aluminium curtain rail is more expensive, but looks classier and is stronger and better for heavy curtains such as full-length lined velvets.

Measure the length of rail required to the nearest foot. If the window is the flat-on-the-wall type allow the rail to project a little on each side so that maximum daylight gets in when the curtains are drawn back. Both plastic and metal rail can be bent to curve round a bay window (do not make the bend in the corners of a rectangular bay too sharp or the curtains won't pull round it). Buy the rail complete with fittings: supporting brackets, gliders and hooks (sometimes these are combined), and end stops if required. The shop assistant or display stand will tell you how many are needed for a given length of rail. If you want the curtains

114

to overlap in the centre, buy an overlap bracket too. If they are velvet a
cording set or pull cords are advisable to avoid marking the material in
the places where they are pulled every day.

Cut and bend the rail if necessary. Count the support brackets and
calculate how to position them — one about 25mm from each end and
the rest evenly spaced in between at roughly 30cm intervals. Where a
rail curves round a corner fit a bracket each side of each bend where the
rail straightens out (this may mean buying some extra brackets). It is vital
to get the brackets level with one another; if they are out of whack the rail
won't go on. Line them up with the top of the window frame, or fix one
and measure from it to a convenient point to fix the rest. (Why not use a
spirit level? Because even if you've got one, quite often there is no room
to use it.)

Check that the brackets are the right way up (some have two fixing
holes, one for face fixing and another for ceiling fixing, of which more
later) and mark through the hole with a pencil. Spike the centre of the
pencil mark with a bradawl to make a pilot hole just large enough to
enable you to turn the screw home comfortably, but not too easily. The
screws must get a good grip to carry the weight of the curtains. In old
houses this is where you discover that the timber frame is peppered with
former fixing holes and/or rotten. Options: plug holes with plastic wood
or cellulose filler; move bracket along slightly; fix to the wall instead as
described below.

Fit one end stop to the rail if applicable, then the gliders, then the other
end stop. Then attach the rail to the brackets — it may slide on, clip on or
screw on. Where gliders and hooks are combined fit them to the curtain
first, then hang on the rail.

Problem fixings If there is no timber frame to fix the rail to, screw a
piece of wood to the wall above the window, paint it to match the wall
and then fix the brackets to that. In the long run this is less trouble, particularly on a wide window, as you only have to make two or three fixings
into masonry, and all the brackets are fixed into wood. Also if you try to
fix them direct it can be very difficult to get them lined up precisely
enough, if the wall is uneven or the drill wanders a bit.

Wall fixing may also be necessary with a small alcove window, as
hanging the curtains inside it means that they still block out a lot of light
when drawn aside.

An even worse situation, fortunately rare, is where the rail has to be
fixed to the ceiling. First make sure to pick a type that can be fixed in this
way. Do not just fix it to the plaster or plasterboard; the weight of the
curtains could easily tear it away. You have to find something solid to
screw into; the builder may have inserted a batten for this purpose, but if

not you have to locate a joist or joists. I have read in other DIY books that you can tell the difference between solid timber and the hollow ceiling by tapping; but I certainly can't. I find it's a case of test boring with the finest drill bit you have. (Although if the ceiling is badly in need of redecorating study it closely: the position of the joists may show up as pale bands.) When the drill is only boring into plaster you get white dust and then it shoots into empty space. Once it hits timber you get sawdust and a solid feel. Depending on which side of the room the window is you may be looking for one joist running parallel with the wall, or the ends of several. Joists run in the opposite direction to that of the floorboards in the room above.

Old curtain rails   These are often worth salvaging even if at first they seem set solid. The trouble is usually just the dirt of ages, sometimes helped along by paint and a bit of corrosion. Take down and wash thoroughly, soaking the gliders etc. in hot detergent solution. Scrape paint off plastic rails very gently to avoid roughening the surface. Use fine steel wool on metal. Dry well and refit. (To keep curtains pulling easily, lubricate any rail now and then with silicone furniture polish.)

Curtain poles   These are simply supported on a large bracket at each side, with a centre one if necessary. For the best effect the pole should oversail at each side of the window so that the decorative finials or end pieces can be clearly seen. Getting the brackets level is just as important here as it is with rails, as a large pole that slopes is very eye-catching in quite the wrong way.

Nets and sheers   These are usually hung on expanding curtain wire put through a hem at the top, but if you want them to draw aside you can get special narrow track and lightweight curtain tape. Stretch expanding wire as tightly as possible across the window and cut to length with pliers. Fit a closed screw eye to each end of the wire; fit open screw eyes to the window. If you do it the other way round the open eyes snag in the curtain every time it comes down for washing. Try to get the eyes into the wood without much more than the aid of a puncture mark with a bradawl to start them off. It's easy to make the hole so big that these tiny screws get no grip at all, or one so weak that they pull out under the tension of the wire.

Roller blinds   Fitting DIY roller blinds is quite straightforward and you should get instructions with the kit. They can be hung either *inside* a window recess, which allows access to items on the sill when the blind is down, and also leaves pot plants in the warmth of the room; or *outside*,

116

which is better for draughtproofing purposes, but means fixing the supporting brackets on to the wall rather than the timber window frame. In either case the fabric should roll off the back of the roller, not the front.

To fit new blind fabric first check that it is absolutely square by following the line of the weave or lining it up with the square corner of a large table. Trim if necessary. Stitch a hem in one end into which to slip the bottom slat. Mark a line on the roller and fix the other end against this. Absolute straightness is essential or the blind will hang slightly crooked and annoy you for evermore. Staples are the best fixings, but if you just don't happen to have an industrial stapler about the house use tiny tacks (3mm). Hammer them well in or they will eventually leave little round marks on the fabric. Fit the slat and pull cord and rehang.

A roller blind can be moved to a new window provided that it is the same size or smaller. To cut a roller down prise off the metal end cap with the *round* pin sticking out. Never interfere with the other cap, with the square pin; this is the business end of the roller where the spring is. Saw off enough wood to make the roller the same length as the distance between the brackets (it is as well to fit them first to get this exactly right). Mark the cutting line all round to make sure the end is cut off perfectly straight. Refit the cap and place the blind on the brackets.

If the tension of the spring is not quite right the blind will either creep up very slowly or not at all; or fly up alarmingly. To increase tension pull the blind down halfway, then gently lift it off the brackets. Roll it up by hand, replace and test. If still more tension is needed pull it down quarterway, remove, roll up and replace. To decrease tension reverse the process: take the roll-up blind off the brackets, unwind a little and replace.

SHELVING

However simple or grand your shelving project, it pays to have a vague grasp of some basic engineering principles before whirling into action. Two main things can go wrong: falling down and sagging.

Shelves supported on brackets, being cantilevered out from the supporting wall, exert great stress on the fixing screws, and if they are not up to the job they will tear out of the wall taking the shelf with them. The danger increases in proportion to the depth of the shelf, and those more than 20cm deep are best supported by an upright-and-bracket system, which is very strong as the uprights spread the load over the wall. But whatever type of bracket is used, the secret of success is long, strong screws. Our old friend the 5cm No.8 is usually suitable; the idea is for there to be at least 25mm of screw in the wall, excluding the plaster covering (allow 15mm).

Sagging in the centre is caused by the supports being too far apart in relation to the thickness of the wood and the weight placed upon it. Most veneered chipboard is only 15mm thick, and needs supporting about every 60cm. Timber is stronger and an equivalent thickness should comfortably span 90cm. But much depends on the loading: heavy loads are TV sets and hi-fi equipment, hardback books and sets of crockery. Light loads are paperbacks, bric-a-brac and general clutter.

Increasing the thickness of the shelf is one way to avoid sagging but not very practical given the horrendous price of timber and absence of thicker grades of veneered chipboard in the average DIY store or timber yard. Lengths cut from sheets of plain chipboard can be used for utility shelving; its strength is slightly less than that of the veneered sort but it comes 19mm thick. But generally the answer is extra support, and there are various ways in which this can be done. Where shelves are supported on brackets always set them in from the ends by up to one quarter of the total length. This not only decreases the centre span and strengthens the shelf but looks better.

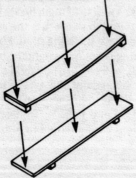

With alcove shelves you can decrease the span length by the simple expedient of fixing an angle bracket underneath in the centre. Other methods: make the shelves more rigid by gluing a batten all along the underside, in the centre; or screw a short batten to the wall to support it at centre back, and glue a long one under the front edge of the shelf; or pin and glue a substantial wooden lipping all along the front edge, extending it to cover the end battens and fixing into them too. If in doubt try end battens only and see what happens. If bowing is very slight, occurring over months, just turn them over periodically (but this won't work if the ends were cut into diamond shapes to fit funny wall angles).

Freestanding shelves Being unable to drill into walls, either because you don't have a drill, or because landlord don't allow, does not mean that you can't make some shelves. A board-and-brick unit can be made using no more than a paintbrush. Buy some lengths of veneered chipboard, or pine ready cut to length, and a few bricks or concrete blocks. The paintbrush is for sealing the bricks or blocks with emulsion paint or polyurethane varnish, otherwise they shed dust for ever. Build the unit according to need, but make it long and low rather than tall and narrow just in case of accidents, and if possible put both the back and one end against a wall. They are actually pretty stable, as the weight of the bricks keeps the lower shelves in place. Arrange to have heaviest items on the top to keep that down.

In an alcove you can use the board-and-board method. It uses up a lot of wood but you can start with just a couple of shelves and add to it gradually. Cut shelves accurately to fit (see page 123). Instead of resting them on battens screwed to the walls rest them on short pieces of the same wood; cut these to the distance required between each shelf and push against each side wall. If the skirting board is thick (12mm) and flat the bottom shelf can rest on that; if not cut another pair of supports. All the upright pieces must be cut perfectly square-cornered or the shelves will wobble (see page 107).

Another alcove method is to build a pair of ladders to support the shelves. Each consists of two upright timber battens and as many rungs as required; 20mm × 25mm timber would be the sort of thing to use. Also cut two extra battens, of timber the same thickness as the skirting board, to space the ladders away from the wall at the top. Make up the ladders, then cut the shelves so that they fit tightly and keep the whole structure rigid. You'll need a helper to measure at least the first shelf, because until braced by this the ladders fall over.

If the room has a picture rail and you have a drill you can make a set of hanging shelves from veneered chipboard and nylon cord. Keep the unit fairly small — say three 90cm shelves — and use it for paperbacks and light ornaments only as picture rails are just nailed on to the wall. Also hang it over a piece of furniture so that it cannot be walked into and shoved sideways. To make, drill pairs of holes in each end of the boards about 15cm in from the ends. Sand the boards and finish as required. At each side, thread a length of cord up one set of holes, through a steel split ring (from stationers'), then down again. Knot firmly at the bottom. To space the shelves apart stick masonry nails through the cord. (It is a bit tricky to get the spacing equidistant; a way of establishing it is to thread lengths of polythene tubing on to the cords.) Hang on picture rail hooks.

Equipment needed: some kind of drill (see page 4), a masonry bit and some wall plugs. There are lots of different types and sizes of wall plug on the market; I invariably use general-purpose (brown) Plasplugs as they accept a range of screw sizes (6–10), and are used with just one size of masonry bit, a No. 12. (Compound filler, the grey powdery stuff formerly sold for mixing with water to make your own plugs, is currently off the market, as it contained asbestos and so presented a slight risk. If and when a substitute appears, it is good for walls in which it is impossible to drill a neat round hole, as a 'sausage' of compound filler can be pushed in to fit whatever shape the hole turns out.)

The diagram shows the procedure, which is exactly the same whether you are putting up brackets, a fitment of some kind, or timber battens. Mark the position of the hole and punch it lightly with a nail punch to give the drill a starting point and to stop it wandering about. Make sure to drill absolutely straight, and withdraw the bit once or twice to shake out masonry dust. Test with the screw to ensure that the hole is long enough to take it comfortably. (Or mark the drill bit with sticky tape to show how far in to drill.) If it is too short, trying to force the screw home twists the plug round and round and you have to start all over again.

Push the plug in and tap it slightly below the surface of the wall. Position the fitment/bracket/batten and drive the screw home.

To ensure that a fitment or batten is straight always use a spirit level, resting it on top while marking the hole positions. With brackets fix one, then rest the shelf plus spirit level on it to find the position for the second.

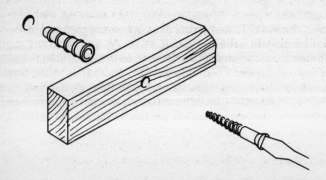

Hollow walls In some houses internal partition walls are not solid, but made from a timber frame covered on each side with plasterboard or lath and plaster. Lightweight fitments can be fixed by using special plasterboard plugs, designed to expand against the back of the plasterboard and grip tight, where an ordinary plug would drop straight through. But for heavy loadings it's best to fix into the timber studs. Find these by the same methods as for locating joists (see page 116). If they turn out to be in inconvenient places span a batten between them and fix along that.

Cellular block walls In many modern houses the inner leaf of the exterior walls is composed of various kinds of cellular concrete block. Their presence is revealed by drilling dust that is grey instead of brick coloured. When making fixings into these it is best to use special cellular block plugs, as these blocks are rather crumbly and ordinary plugs do not get a good grip.

SHELVES ON OPEN WALLS

These can be supported on various sorts of bracket; on an upright-and-bracket system; or by slings.

Brackets range from cheap pressed steel ones to decorative affairs in metal, plastic or wood. Some come complete with plugs and screws. When the two arms of the bracket are of unequal length fix the long one to the wall.

Upright-and-bracket systems These are made by a number of different manufacturers and most consist of slotted metal uprights which are screwed to the wall and carry brackets to support shelves from 10cm to 60cm deep. The shelves can be positioned as required, limited only by the short distance between slots, and subsequently added to or moved around as the mood takes you. A superior system called Click has no slots, which both avoids the slightly industrial look of the others, and allows infinitely variable shelf spacing. As well as being very much stronger than brackets alone, these systems can reduce the amount of drilling into the wall that has to be done. A pair of uprights, fixed with as few as four screws, can support quite a few shelves; with ordinary brackets, every single shelf has to have at least four screws into the wall. To fix one of these systems drill the hole for the top screw of one upright and fix loosely. Swing the upright to a vertical position, checking with a plumb line or weight on a string, and mark the spot for the bottom screw. When the first upright is fully fixed, slot on a bracket, with another one on to the second upright. Balance a shelf and spirit level across them to find the position for the top fixing screw of the second upright; another three-handed job! Finish as before. Arrange brackets to taste and pin shelves in place with short No. 6 roundheaded screws.

Slingshelves This invention consists of slings of tough polyester and polypropylene, in sizes to take shelves from 10cm to 40cm deep. The shelves are simply slipped into the bottom of pairs of slings. As each sling is fixed by just one screw at the top they are ideal for any situation where drilling into walls is difficult. They are also good in old houses with uneven, sloping walls, as the flexible sling adapts to them (upright and bracket systems like nice flat walls). If you cannot find any in your neighbourhood write to Slingshelf, Pewsey, Wiltshire.

SHELVES IN ALCOVES

Nice deep alcoves naturally suggest themselves as a good place to put up shelves and create lots of lovely storage space. But be warned: doing this the conventional way with the shelves resting on a batten each side is not the easy task it may appear. Anyone who so describes it, and talks gaily of having the shelves cut to length in the timber yard, has simply never done it.

What follows is somewhat technical and tedious, and I suggest you skip it unless actually about to tackle the job.

The main reason for all the difficulties is that very few walls meet each other at a perfect right angle, which is what is required if you are to fit a ready-cut, square-ended shelf into the corners of an alcove. In a typical situation the left-hand side wall may meet the back one at *more* than a right angle; while that on the right-hand side meets it at *less* than a right angle. To fit, the shelf must be slightly diamond shaped. And that's not the end of it. The side walls may also lean in or out as they rise, so that a shelf fitted 1 metre up will have to be a slightly different length from one fitted 1.5 metres up. To cap it all, random bumps on side walls will prevent a shelf from fitting in even when theoretically it should. Modern houses seem little better than old ones in respect of right-angled corners, though they may be freer from bumps. But they can present yet another problem: if one side wall is only a timber stud partition, there will be a stud at the side into which you can make the first fixing, but the next one will be too far away.

Do not despair! You can get around all these problems in one fell swoop by proceeding as if the side walls did not exist, and fixing the shelving to the back wall only. Use any of the methods described above for open walls. If cutting the shelves to length yourself, measure across at the exact height where each one is to go and undercut it by about 10mm; with any luck this will enable it to be slid in, and the tiny gap on each side will not be noticed once the shelves are filled. Or if using standard lengths of veneered chipboard, pick ones that will leave a noticeable gap on each side; make a feature of it. (For books, buy screw-on bookend fitments to stop them falling off the ends.)

Having said that, any self-respecting practitioner of DIY should know how to fix batten-supported shelves; it is by far the cheapest method, and essential for utility shelving (inside cupboards for example).

Battens   For most shelving softwood about 20mm × 30mm is suitable. (If using up old bits of wood, thicker, wider stuff will do no harm.) Cut the battens to the same depth as the shelf, or a fraction under. Where appearance matters cut one end of each batten at a 45° angle instead of straight across, so that it slopes back and is less noticeable. (To hide battens completely, cut them straight, exactly to shelf depth, and glue a timber lipping to the front of the shelves.) Drill a pair of clearance holes about one quarter of the total length in from each end and countersink them.

Hold one batten against the side wall at the desired height, check that it is straight with a spirit level and pencil a line along the top on the wall. Mark through the holes in the batten with a soft pencil sharpened to an extra-long point. Remove the batten and immediately ring round the marks before you lose sight of them. Drill and plug the wall as described on page 120 and fix the batten. Cover screw heads with plastic wood. If appearance matters, paint the battens with emulsion paint to match the wall; do not try papering them.

Cutting shelves   Buy the timber or veneered chipboard several inches overlength to allow for trimming to shape. To find out what the angle between the side and back walls actually is use a tool called a sliding bevel. This is similar to a try-square, but adjustable. Put it into the corner above the batten just fixed and open out to fit into the angle, then tighten the locking device to fix it in that position. Mark this angle on one end of the shelf and cut. Similarly find the angle in the opposite corner, at the same height. Mark this on the other end of the shelf, the width of the alcove away from the first end, and cut.

Try the shelf in position and rasp a bit off the ends if it is too tight. Balance it on the first batten, with the spirit level on top, and mark the position for fixing the second with a pencil line on the side wall *underneath* it. Fix batten as before.

Alcove shelves are not normally fixed to the battens; close fitting and the weight put on them keeps them safely in place.

If you don't have a sliding bevel, which I daresay is the case, there are several ways to wriggle round the problem:

1) Use a try-square, large set square or book. Measure the alcove width at the back and mark this on the shelf, leaving an equal amount of waste at each end. Lightly pencil right-angled lines from the marks to the front edge of the shelf. Mark the side walls to show where the front edge of the shelf will come. Place the try-square in the corner and push it against the back wall. Measure the size of the gap which appears at the front (side wall sloping *out*) against the pencil mark; if the side wall slopes *in* it will appear at the back. Add this amount on to the tentative pencil line on the shelf, at back or front as appropriate. Mark a cutting line from that point tapering back to the tentative line.

2) For utility work measure the alcove at shelf height at both back and front, to establish how much difference there is between the two. Cut the shelf in between the two measurements and rest it on extra-thick battens to make sure that it is well supported despite gaps.

3) In a deep alcove or inside a cupboard, instead of using solid board, make the shelving out of separate battens, as in an airing cupboard. Cut each one separately to fit the spot where it is to go. Use a couple of slips of wood to ensure that the battens are evenly spaced. Secure them with woodworking adhesive and weight down until it dries. (This method is also economical, and can be used for display as well as utility shelving.)

Some other DIY books may tell you to scribe the back of your shelves and cut them out in a wavy shape so that they fit exactly against the back wall. This is a complete waste of time, as well as being difficult and hard work. Gaps are soon hidden when shelves are filled. If you are the sort of person who can't stand the knowledge that there *is* a gap, cover it, and those at the sides, with moulding. Quadrant (quarter-round) is traditional but I prefer scotia which has a concave face.

BASIC BOOKCASES

If you want a piece of furniture rather than just shelving it's quite easy to learn how to build bookcases, which can also be used for general storage by adding sliding doors as described below. As well as looking more important, a freestanding unit gets you out of drilling into walls and is easier to take along when you move, especially if you design it to be demounted and packed flat.

A basic bookcase consists of two uprights with a set of shelves fitted in between them. Use whatever jointing techniques you feel most at home with: butt joints, cross-halving or dowel joints (see pages 108–111). Dowel joints need gluing, but with the other two you can omit the adhesive and make the structure demountable.

Shelves in between the top and bottom ones, which must be fixed to

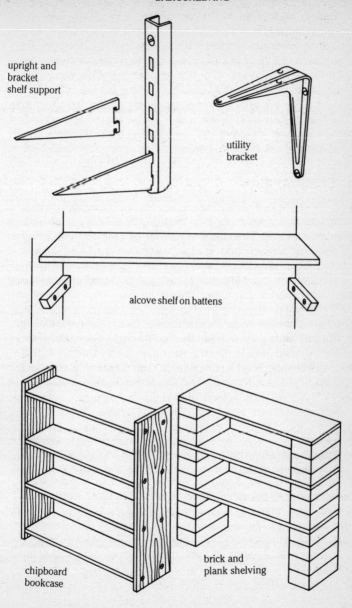

upright and
bracket
shelf support

utility
bracket

alcove shelf on battens

chipboard
bookcase

brick and
plank shelving

125

keep the structure rigid, can simply be laid on plastic shelf pegs. Drill holes at intervals down the side pieces and you can move the shelves up and down as required.

Design the bookcase to suit the items to be stored and the space available, but remember that long and low or tall and narrow always looks more interesting than square. (For perfect safety a tall bookcase should be pinned to the wall with a glass plate fixed to the top shelf.) Similarly it looks better if the uprights project slightly beyond the top shelf. Also allow them to project quite a few inches below the bottom one. This makes for a stronger structure, and by allowing air to circulate underneath reduces the risk of damp books.

SMALL CUPBOARDS

Having mastered the art of making shelves and/or bookcases it's child's play to convert them into cupboards by gluing on sliding track for hardboard doors to run in. The doors can either be painted (both sides to prevent warping, please) or covered with left-over vinyl wallpaper.

Hardboard doors should not be too big: over 50cm square or so they look flimsy and tend to warp eventually. Use plywood instead; more expensive, but more rigid. Other possibilities are translucent plastic sheet, if you can find somewhere to buy less than a full, door-sized piece; or mirror tiles, the large ones, 30cm square or more. As mirror tiles cannot be trimmed make sure to build the box the right size to fit them in.

To make a small wall-hung cupboard (say for use as a bathroom cabinet; much cheaper than buying one) cut four pieces of board to make an open box of the size required, and pin and glue, or screw and glue together. A backboard is not essential but helps keep the box square and rigid; use hardboard or plywood. When the glue securing the box together has dried fit any shelves required inside, set back to leave room for the sliding plastic track. This is available in white or black; just glue it on with contact adhesive, the deeper one at the top. Cut the doors so that they overlap slightly in the centre; height will be the distance from the base of the bottom track to halfway up the top one. Drill finger holes for handles; for a food cupboard close them with plastic finger plates to keep out flies. Fix glass plates at each side or on the top through which to screw the cupboard to the wall.

To make a small cupboard to fit at floor level, say to hide a gas meter, use a length of softwood or veneered chipboard glued and screwed on to a pair of matching uprights (or in some cases one upright and one wall batten). Use timber sliding track, which is less easily dislodged by floorboard movement than plastic, and doors as above. Cut the upright piece(s) to fit over the skirting board. If it is a fancy shape find the outline

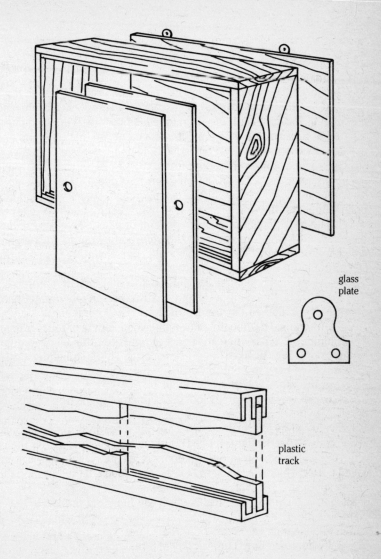

glass
plate

plastic
track

with fuse wire and cut the timber with a keyhole saw. For complete stability pin the cupboard to the wall with glass plates or metal angle brackets.

LARGER CUPBOARDS

Once cupboards get to a fair size it is uneconomic to make them from solid timber or chipboard. Veneered chipboard can be used to make medium-sized ones that look more like pieces of furniture. But for large utility cupboards, such as those built to conceal an immersion heater and make an airing cupboard, the technique is to use the frame-and-panel method of construction, and build it into a corner so that back and one side are provided free by the walls. The diagram shows a typical construction; with some modifications (extra cross rails) this could be made to any size and shape. The front would consist of doors to taste; the top, if the cupboard does not continue to ceiling height, something solid like plain chipboard; the side just a panel of plasterboard, hardboard or plywood. The rough edges of plain chipboard, or joins between panelling material and frame, are covered with softwood or ramin edging strip glued and pinned on. The bottom should have a skirting to match the rest of the room.

A really large unit such as a wall-to-wall, ceiling height wardrobe is best made by buying a kit. Assembly is a two-person job, but not hard once you've fathomed out the instructions. They come in all sorts of styles, with framed hardboard, pine, whitewood, louvre or mirror doors. The 'sliding wall' type, where the doors go right up to the ceiling, require sliding door gear to be fixed to the ceiling joists. This is straightforward *if* they run from back to front in the spot where the wardrobe is to go. If they run the other way there may not be one in a convenient place. Check which way joists run by looking in the roof space; or if that is not possible, by test boring (see page 116).

To avoid ceiling fixing choose what are called wardrobe or door fronts. These consist of sets of large hinged doors with smaller ones above them. The vertical framing around these doors is left sticking up in what are called horns, which are cut off so that they just touch the ceiling, and the empty space covered with a fascia panel.

Kitchen cabinets are not really worth the time and trouble to make yourself unless the standard sizes available just won't fit into your particular kitchen, as mass-produced ones are relatively cheap, especially if bought in KD (knock down) form for assembly back home. But you can save money by buying ones that come without tops, and making your own from chipboard covered with laminated plastic (see page 131). This is usually necessary anyway if you want a completely

SIMPLE FRAMED CUPBOARD

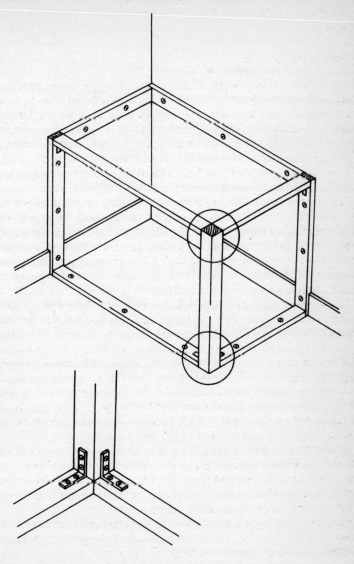

built-in worktop, in order to fit it into the average kitchen's diamond-shaped corners. The thickness of chipboard usually recommended is 19mm, but for short runs, or long ones with plenty of support below, I find 12.5mm quite satisfactory.

Doors and door furniture Although sliding doors can be used on larger cupboards, and frequently are, hinged doors are often preferable. They look more solid; also sliding doors are inconvenient on a cupboard of tall narrow shape, as you have a very restricted view of what is inside. (But you can buy doors that both slide and fold.) Hinged doors are fairly easy to make using either veneered chipboard or tongued and grooved boards, or you can buy a variety of ready-made ones.

Such doors can either fit inside the frame on which they are hung, or close on to it. The first method calls for the most skill, as both parts must be perfectly square and exactly the right size. A door made of boards can be trimmed to fit the opening, but if using veneered chipboard or a factory-made door I would choose the second method, which allows for a little latitude. But there is another consideration: the first method allows face-fixing hinges to be used, which are the easiest of all to fit as they just screw on flat. If using the second method always buy flush hinges, which are fixed directly on to the frame and door with no need to cut a recess as for a conventional butt hinge. Another type of hinge which is fixed straight on to the wood is piano hinge, which is bought by length and fitted all the way along the door. It is very strong and suitable for things like heavy chest lids.

With chipboard doors it is best to use a completely different type of hinge as conventional ones tend to pull out of this crumbly material in time. This is called a pivot hinge and is fixed by drilling holes into the thickness of the door and frame. Drilling the holes accurately is the problem, and a drilling guide should be supplied to help. Such doors can be lifted off, which can come in handy for cleaning.

As well as a knob or handle of some kind to open the door you will need a catch to keep it closed. Both nylon roller and magnetic catches are easy to fit.

Small tongued-and-grooved doors can be made from the thin stuff normally used for panelling walls; but for anything large use something thicker. In both cases the boards are fixed together and strengthened by three cross battens glued on to the inside. Run these right across and place them so that all the door furniture will screw into them, if using thin boards, otherwise there will be problems with screws sticking right through. Buy or cut the boards slightly overlength and butt tightly together. Cut the tongue neatly off the board at one side with a Stanley knife and glue it into the empty groove on the opposite side. If necessary plane down on the hinge side to fit the frame. Glue on the cross battens, one by one. When dry, saw off the waste wood at top and bottom to make the door exactly the required height. Veneered chipboard doors are even easier to make as all you need to do is cut off a piece of a board of appropriate width and finish the cut ends with edging strip. But the width of the door can only be that of the standard sizes on sale, and as you can't adjust the size you must make the frame to fit the door and not *vice versa*.

Traditional-style doors consisting of a thin panel with a frame round it require routing tools and the skill to use them, as the panel is set in grooves cut in the frame. But if you can use a stock size there are plenty of factory-made ones on the market, often with matching drawer fronts. There are also plenty of different-sized louvre doors to be had, with either open louvres (for wardrobes) or closed ones (for kitchen cupboards); quite cheap if made of pine, more expensive if in hardwood.

KITCHEN WORKTOPS

Because these have to withstand constant use and such different kinds of wear, no one material is ideal for all purposes: a large luxury kitchen might have areas of ceramic mosaic for putting down hot pans, marble for pastry making, end-grain sycamore as used on butchers' blocks for chopping, and oiled teak for general purposes. Catering establishments use a lot of stainless steel, the ultimate in hygiene and hard wear. Us common folk usually settle for laminated plastic, which is a good all-round material and relatively cheap compared to the above. But there are some other possibilities.

Laminated plastic (melamine) This is sold under various brand names (Formica, Decamel, Warerite etc.). It is rigid and 1.5mm thick, with a brown underside and decorative topside. The colour and pattern range is wide in the more expensive brands, much less so in cheaper ones. Take a tip from one who has done it wrong twice: *do not choose white*. It shows up every last crumb and tea stain. Also a slight pattern, such as a linen weave, is better for concealing both crumbs and the inevitable slight scratches that appear in time.

The reason that melamine is so popular for kitchen worktops is that it is easy to clean and very hardwearing for the price; stands up well to heat (but not pans straight from burner or oven, or cigarettes); and is cool enough for pastry making. Its main weakness is scratching: never use knives directly on it (this also blunts the knives) but interpose a timber chopping board.

Laminated plastic is not the easiest material to handle. If you can, get it cut to size; but shops will only cut squares or rectangles, not diamond shapes. If you do have to cut it yourself, try and arrange things so that the machined edge is on the front, and your efforts at back and sides. The problem is that the stuff chips if you so much as look at it. So it is best not to try to cut it exactly to size, but a bit bigger (about 3mm), so that rough edges can be trimmed off afterwards.

If you have to cut the piece at odd angles to fit into corners a sliding bevel is essential to measure these accurately (see page 123). Cut either with a sharp tenon saw, or a jig saw fitted with a laminate-cutting blade. (Some DIY books say that you can also score it deeply with a laminate cutting blade in a Stanley knife, held against a straight edge, and then snap it *upwards* along the line. But I have never had the nerve to try.) If using a hand saw, have the decorative side facing *up*, and support it close to the cutting line. If using a power saw have it face *down*, and clamp to the workbench.

Roughen the surface of the chipboard with coarse abrasive paper to give a key for contact adhesive. Brush clean and spread the adhesive thinly over both chipboard and laminate. Leave for the time stated on the tin; it will look too dry to stick, but it's not. Starting at one corner, bring the two materials carefully together; modern contact adhesives give you a little time to manoeuvre, but not much. Placing a sheet of greaseproof paper over the chipboard and slowly withdrawing it can help. Putting a row of drawing pins into one edge gives you something to butt the laminate up against, but is not much use when the edge is one which has been cut oversize. Press the laminate down firmly all over, starting from the centre; it is essential that it bonds at every point, or it will not wear well. Leave for about 30 minutes before trimming the edges.

Trim with a file or block plane, working along the edge, not up or down, to prevent chipping. Finish the raw edges with ready-cut edging strip, if available, bevelling to a 45° angle on all edges and also at any corners. A Plasplugs laminate beveller will create the right angle automatically. If edging strip is not available you *could* cut your own; but I would go for a timber lipping instead; much easier and I think it gives a better appearance. This can be deeper than the actual chipboard; support it with a small batten glued along the underside.

To finish off the worktop and hide any cutting disasters and gaps between worktop and wall, screw a narrow timber upstand to the back and side walls.

Note plastic veneered chipboard is finished with a thinner grade of melamine and is not suitable for the hard life of a kitchen worktop. But you can buy ready-veneered worktops: the most commonly available have the fashionable post-formed front edge (curved) but square-edged ones are made.

Another note however it is surfaced, any kitchen worktop should

132

overhang its base slightly, or spilled liquids drip all down the front of units below and stain them, instead of falling straight to the floor.

Clapped-out laminated plastic Worktops where the laminate is scorched, stained, scratched and chipped can be transformed by gluing on a sparkling new sheet. It is best to remove the old stuff first, because it is too smooth to give a good key for the adhesive, and also may have come unstuck in some spots. This may lever off quite easily; if bits stick fast apply some acetone (nail varnish remover) to try and soften the glue underneath. Acetone will also help in cleaning the surface of old glue.

Sticky-backed plastic Do not confuse this with laminated plastic. This is the kind sold by the metre or in small rolls (Fablon and Contact). It is very thin and best kept for covering shelves. But it can be used as a temporary measure for covering worktops. Constant cleaning eventually wears away the pattern, but somebody usually damages it with a hot pan first. The surface underneath must be flat, or it's hell to get on, and completely smooth — every pimple shows through the thin plastic, even the so-called heavier grade.

Tiles and mosaic Tiled worktops look very luxurious. They are expensive, but should last indefinitely without showing any signs of wear. But you must use ceramic tiles of suitable thickness, not the thin ones designed for walls, which would become cracked pretty quickly. (See Chapter 8 for details.)

Timber and man-made boards Old pine tables are nice to have in the kitchen, but are usually in a pretty unhygenic state. The tops generally consist of several separate planks, and on a cheap table these are probably not jointed together, and so over the years have separated and become clogged with dirt. Take them off, clean thoroughly and if possible plane flat the meeting edges. Refix and sand smooth. Fill holes and cover any screws with plastic wood, but do not try to fill cracks between boards; they only open up again.

Ordinary polyurethane varnish will not stand up too long to worktop wear, but Rustins plastic coating will. The commonly available type gives a mirror-like shine that you may not want, but a matt version is available. For a really authentic look leave the wood bare and scrub it as great-grandmama did.

Chipboard and plywood are a disaster in the kitchen as water makes chipboard swell up, and delaminates ordinary plywood. They are excellent as cheap, flat surfaces, but must always be covered.

ROOM DIVIDERS

Once you have gained confidence by doing some of the previous projects there is no reason not to tackle a large structure like a room divider, should you happen to need one, as it is only an overgrown bookcase with cupboards in it.

There is not a lot of point in carrying a room divider right up to the ceiling. Storage at high level is of little use and it will probably block out too much light. But if you really want a wall-like appearance just carry the uprights up to the ceiling and fix to a ceiling joist or joists with angle brackets (see page 116 for how to locate joists). A giant-sized unit is probably not a good idea upstairs as it might overstrain the floor joists and end up as a downstairs unit.

Veneered chipboard is probably the best material as you can design the unit to use standard lengths and widths and minimise the amount of cutting and waste. As a room divider consists of a series of squares and rectangles construction is a simple matter of glued and screwed butt joints. Design the unit so that heavy items are carried in the lower part, and leave the top fairly open to let light through. For maximum stability screw the unit to both the floor and a side wall. A freestanding unit should be at least 40cm deep and no more than about 1.5 metres high.

Design the unit so that it is attractive from both sides. Fit cupboards with two lots of doors, or pin a decorative panel to one side. Put a hardboard divider (support with shelf pegs) down the centre of shelves meant for small books so that they can be stacked in two rows, both facing out.

BOXING IN PIPES

Painting pipes to match the wall does something to conceal them; but not a lot. A much better way is to box them in, and it's remarkably easy.

Whatever the size of the pipe or pipes, make the box just deep enough to cover them, but wider than necessary so that the box looks like a projecting bit of wall. If the pipes only project an inch or so from the wall all you need are two battens *wide* enough to clear them, and about 25mm thick. (Measure the distance from front of pipe to wall at both top and bottom as it may vary.) Make the front of the box with a length of standard hardboard. Screw the battens to the wall with No. 8 countersunk screws and pin the hardboard on with hardboard pins. As the screws are to be put through the *width* of the battens, and not through the thickness in the normal way as when putting up shelf supports, *and* should penetrate the wall by at least 25mm, they will need to be very long. A trick you can play to enable shorter ones to be used is to counterbore the batten instead of countersinking in the usual way, so that the screw dis-

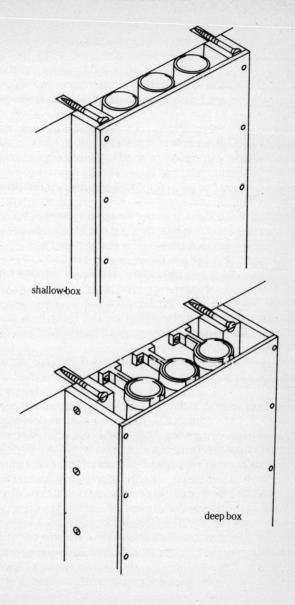

shallow box

deep box

appears down a hole for up to one third of the distance. Depending on the height to be covered, a screw near top and bottom and one or two evenly spaced in between should suffice. Try the hardboard in place before nailing it on; it may need a little shaping with a Surform tool to give a flush fit at the ceiling.

Unless walls are uncommonly flat there will be a few gaps here and there behind the batten, so it's best to finish by covering your masterpiece with lining paper or matching wallpaper, lapping it well over the gap.

If the pipes are big old-fashioned ones you will need a more elaborate structure to get enough depth to conceal them. Screw battens to the wall as before, but first pin a thin piece of wood to their sides to give the depth required. A typical one would use 25 × 50mm battens, and side pieces of as thin wood as you can get in the width required. Finish with a hardboard cover as before.

Sometimes there is a stop tap on the pipes, and you must leave access to this. If it is at low level and inconspicuous, just cut a hole in the hardboard cover with a keyhole saw before fixing. Alternatively make a removable box which clips on to the pipes with Terry clips (these are the round, adjustable clips often used to try and secure a garden hose to a tap). Make this with a hardboard front and sides, pinned on to 25mm-sq corner posts. Glue small cross battens inside the cover at intervals on to which you can fit Terry clips of appropriate size. This type of box never looks as structurally sound as the fixed ones as you cannot paper them to the wall and so gaps show.

When pipes are in a corner you can use a much simpler method. Buy the widest type of polystyrene coving used to finish the angle between ceiling and wall. Position it back to front in the corner, cut to length and hold in place with several thickness of wallpaper. This sounds flimsy, but is surprisingly sturdy in practice. And in any case it is not liable to get knocked about much in a corner. Alternatively use a combination of the first two methods, or the Terry clip method.

What happens at the skirting board? I would settle for stopping the box short immediately above it as the spot is quite often hidden by furniture anyway. Perfectionists will carry the hardboard/timber covers down to floor level and glue on false skirting boards. But be warned: if skirtings have moulded tops you are in for some fancy cutting.

Occasionally pipes disappear into the wall after a few feet or so. In such cases cut the battens at a 45° angle at the bottom and pin a separate piece of hardboard over the opening.

STRIPPING FURNITURE

Nobody gets involved in DIY without at some time or another having to strip off dilapidated paint or varnish; usually from some interesting item of junk furniture that you bought cheap or that Auntie gave you; sometimes during decorating. Even though there are plenty of different ways of doing it, stripping is still a horrible task; the kind of job where halfway through you wish that you had never started. So if you can possibly avoid it, do so. If you can't, make sure to pick the best method for the job in question. You don't have to stick to one, either, but can make good use of different ones for different parts of a piece of furniture. Also it is not always necessary to strip the whole piece, just the worst and/or most visible bits.

Stripping is accomplished in three basic ways: by abrasion, chemicals and heat.

Abrasion This sub-divides into sanding and scraping. Hand sanding, using a cork block and various grades of abrasive paper, is very gentle: use just for getting a smooth finish. Always sand in the direction of the grain; on end grain sand in one direction only (see Woodwork chapter). If you sand round and round or across the grain ineradicable scratches will be your reward. Especially when sanding by machine, be careful not to work over edges or corners of furniture or woodwork or the timber will lose its shape. To sand curves and mouldings use abrasive paper in your fingers, folded or cut into strips; or wrapped round a length of dowel. On

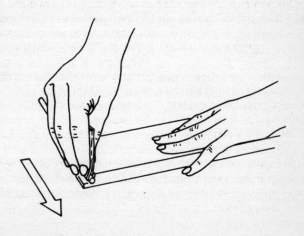

carving use fine (00 grade) steel wool. You can also buy various patent sanding tools consisting of plastic handles with heads designed for different sanding situations — tight corners, curves etc. The abrasive paper on them is self-adhesive so that you just peel off a tired piece and stick on a new one. Abrasive-covered foam blocks (Quiksand) are also useful; and can be washed when clogged with sanding dust.

Standard sheets of abrasive paper for use on a cork sanding block come in a whole range of grades, and you should start with a fairly coarse one and progress to fine. Use an extra-fine grade called flour paper for a really superior finish. The more expensive abrasive papers labelled silicon carbide cost more than ordinary glass papers, but last longer. Another type is known as wet-or-dry. Use it dry for a fine finish on furniture to be given a clear finish; wet on old paintwork to give a good key for new paint. For use on power tool attachments and finishing sanders, abrasive paper is sold ready cut into discs, rectangles or loops to fit; some has a self-adhesive backing which makes changing paper much faster.

Machine sanding can be done with a number of different drill attachments: the rubber disc that usually comes with the drill; a foam rubber drum sander; an abrasive flap wheel; or an orbital or finishing sander (this can be a drill attachement or a separate tool in its own right). All except the flap wheels are then fitted with abrasive paper of the required degree of coarseness or fineness.

The disc sander is a very coarse method: good for removing deep blemishes such as burns or ink stains, or thick layers of paint (but be prepared to use a great many coarse abrasive discs, as paint quickly clogs them up). But do not try and use one for fine finishing work, as because of its rotary action it tends to leave circular marks on the wood. To use, hold the disc at a slight angle and work it over the surface with a sweeping action.

The drum sander's action is gentler, and better than that of the disc because, correctly used, it revolves in the direction of the grain and so obeys the basic rule of good sanding. It is best on gently curving surfaces, such as the back of a chair, but can be used on the flat *if* you are very careful to keep it moving; hold it in one place and your flat surface will develop hills and valleys.

Abrasive flap wheels consist of lots of small flaps of abrasive paper mounted so that they form a small wheel. Their action is slightly gentler than that of the drum sander, but they can be used on any surface. The small ones are excellent for getting into tight corners where no other machine sanding equipment can reach.

An orbital sanding attachment is very gentle, which is why it is also called a finishing sander, as all it is really good for is getting a fine finish on large flat surfaces. Although it does not work in the direction of the grain, but with tiny circular movements, the marks left are invisible to the naked eye. A separate orbital sanding tool is more efficient and can be used to strip paint off flat surfaces, also gently contoured ones if it has a soft base. Some have a bag to catch the dust, and dual action for fine or coarse work. But they cost about £35.

Scrapers are usually used in conjunction with chemical stripper, but can also be used dry if the finish is old and flaky. Hardwood furniture is also best scraped rather than sanded. The proper tool that craftsmen use is a bare blade called a cabinet scraper, but for you and me something with a handle and a replaceable blade is more suitable. Look for the red-handled Skarsten range, which contains many different types and sizes. The smallest one is ideal for getting at the sides of timber slats in a chair back, or into fretwork designs.

Chemicals   These work by dissolving paint or varnish so that it can be scraped or peeled off. The old-established liquid strippers such as Nitromors and Strypit are cheapest and work fast, but only attack one or two layers at a time. The new paste strippers such as Ronstrip are more expensive, need many hours to work, but enable up to ten coats of paint to be peeled off without scraping.

All these products are strong stuff. By definition, something that melts paint isn't going to do your hands or carpet any good. So follow the instructions to the letter, and always wear work gloves (some strippers attack rubber or plastic gloves; ditto plastic containers).

Some liquid strippers are washed off with water; some with white spirit or methylated spirit. The former is more convenient, but tends to raise the grain of the wood, which the latter do not. Also you can go ahead more quickly with the finishing if you use spirit, without having to leave the piece to dry completely. Washing off with spirit is also preferable on a veneered item, as water seeping underneath can lift it off. Liquid stripper softens the wood slightly, so go very carefully when scraping it off or you can do a lot of damage. Don't be impatient; wait until the stuff has worked well enough for the dissolved paint or varnish to be lifted off with a stripping knife, or a shavehook gently applied. Use fine steel wool on twiddly bits.

Liquid strippers are best when a piece is not too thickly painted; or if just varnished. They can also be used on metal, and are excellent for cleaning up brass knobs and handles.

Paste strippers need to be applied carefully, so that there is a thick even layer over the entire piece. If parts are too thin, or get missed altogether, paint will remain in those areas. Although they can then be sanded or scraped clean, the wood underneath may be a different colour from the rest. On pine, particularly, paste stripper has a very slight yellowing effect. As the stuff only works while it is moist it is important to follow the instructions for keeping the item damp until it has penetrated all the layers of paint.

Paste strippers are for use on wood *only*; nothing else. Protect any metal bits such as keyholes with masking tape, or the paste will turn them black. Paste stripper can also turn some hardwoods black, so test before using — on chairs, particularly, test *all* sections, as they are sometimes of different woods. Given these slight drawbacks paste strippers are marvellous for choice pieces of furniture that you don't want to damage by scraping, and unsurpassed for cleaning paint off carving or barley sugar legs.

Heat The good old-fashioned blowlamp has its uses, but to my mind not for furniture. It's almost impossible not to slightly singe parts of the wood, or if inattentive char it, which ruins it for a clear finish. But for house woodwork, provided you intend repainting afterwards, they are fine, provided that you keep well away from window frames, because the heat can crack the glass without warning.

A safer, gentler version of the blowlamp is Black and Decker's hot air blower (see page 46 for details), which is good for both furniture and house woodwork.

An even gentler way of applying heat is to use an electric iron. Set it on high and place it on the painted or varnished wood protected by a piece of kitchen foil. Leave for a few seconds to melt the finish and move it to a new spot. Quickly scrape off the paint. Obviously this method is only efficient on flat, horizontal surfaces.

7 How to lay floor coverings

Laying a new floor covering is one of the most satisfying of all DIY jobs because as the floor comprises such a large area of the room the transformation is startling. Most floor coverings are fairly easy to lay, modern technology having provided self-stick tiles, non-shrink sheet vinyl and carpet that can be cut without fraying. Of course anything in tile form is easier to handle than a large roll, especially if you have to work alone. But a large roll, be it cheap vinyl or expensive carpet, is quicker to get down, provided the room is a simple rectangular shape. Laying your own fitted carpet needs careful calculation as to whether it is actually going to save any money. Many shops make such generous fitting offers that there is no point in going to all that trouble. I myself have only laid carpet acquired secondhand or moved from a previous house. It's not just that no "free" fitting service is then available; working with old material gives you much more confidence, because it doesn't matter too much if you make a few mistakes (and if you feel confident you probably won't make any anyway). But the thought of cutting into a brand-new roll of heavy Wilton bought for £20 a square yard makes me turn pale!

PREPARATION — TIMBER FLOORS

As usual thorough preparation is the key to success, whatever type of floor covering is to go on top. Unless the boards are fairly new they are likely to have any or all of these faults: gaps, unevenness, looseness and a peppering of nail heads.

Start by vacuuming the floor thoroughly to remove dust, grit and debris. There is no particular need to wash it unless there is polish or greasy dirt on the surface which would stop tile adhesive or carpet tape from sticking properly. Next remove all superfluous nails: wear work gloves or your hands will get ripped by unseen sharpies, and work on a charlady's rubber pad to spare your knees as much as possible. I find I usually end up needing three different tools to cope with the different sorts of nails and tacks encountered: pincers, a tack lifter and a hammer, which also comes in handy if in the last resort I have to admit defeat and bash down ones that simply refuse to come out. (It's not a good idea to take the easy way out and hammer all them down; they can work loose again, and particularly under vinyl tiles or thin sheet it's amazing how conspicuous they are — like pimples on the chin.) Fix loose or unnailed boards as described on page 23. All this will raise more dust, so vacuum again.

Very big gaps (6mm or more) should be filled with slips of wood, smeared with woodworking adhesive and hammered into place. If you don't have a plane to reduce them to the size required, have them under-size and fill the remaining spaces with filler. Also use this to fill smaller gaps, and holes of any size. As timber expands and contracts depending on temperature and humidity, a flexible filler such as Woodflex Polyfilla is best; but rather expensive if there is a lot to do. In cases where there are gaps all over, make up some *papier mâché* with finely chopped news-paper, boiling water and plenty of wallpaper paste. (This is also good in cases where gap-filling is going to show, as you can dye it with wood stain.)

Uneven boards are much more difficult to deal with. It involves a lot of fiddling about, lifting boards and packing them up from underneath with cardboard. Sometimes individual boards have a distinct curve in them and there is no cure for this. Such floors are best covered with a hard-board underlay (see opposite).

PREPARATION — SOLID FLOORS

Concrete or other solid floors generally need much less attention. But if there is any suspicion that it might be slightly damp, test as described on page 30, particularly if laying vinyl. If it fails the test treat with a water-proofing compound. Clean the floor thoroughly so that it is absolutely free of any gritty particles; take special care if laying thin sheet vinyl. Fill any noticeable holes with a small bag of ready-mixed sand and cement. (To make it stick, brush the holes out with thinned woodworking adhesive first.) A concrete floor which has a great many holes, or is uneven overall, can be levelled with a proprietary levelling compound. I have not had to do this myself, but it sounds fairly straightforward: the compound is poured over the whole floor, about 4mm thick, and left to find its own level and harden. Another method is to lay sheets of insulat-ing board down loose and stick hardboard on top.

Some concrete floors remain powdery however often they are cleaned, and if the floor covering is one that is stuck down, a coat of concrete floor sealer is required.

HARDBOARD UNDERLAYS

Deciding whether or not it is necessary to lay a hardboard underlay before the floor covering is always difficult. There's a great temptation not to, because of the apparent extra work, and expense. But on old floorboards it cuts out a lot of the dreary preparation work, and is also a good investment in the long term. It's more important with vinyl and cork tiles, which being stuck down, respond to movement of the boards underneath by breaking up; less so with vinyl sheet, carpet or carpet tiles, which are laid loose and taped in places. But even these can, unless very thick, develop a pattern of parallel 'wear' lines after a year or two, faithfully mirroring the joins between each board and its neighbours.

Another way to approach the problem is to lay hardboard as a floor covering in its own right, to be covered with carpet later if and when funds permit. I once had a chequerboard floor of foot squares of light-and dark-coloured hardboard, sealed with polyurethane, which was much admired and often taken for cork at first glance. Viewed as a floor covering hardboard is very cheap, and when laid on a ground floor it also improves insulation by preventing draughts coming through cracks between floorboards.

Standard hardboard 3 2mm ($\frac{1}{8}$ in) thick is the stuff to use. It is smooth on one side and textured on the other; opinions differ as to which way up it should be laid. Generally you are advised to lay it rough side up; but if you want it as a floor covering obviously you need the smooth side, and in fact several vinyl flooring manufacturers recommend this way too. If possible check the instructions for the type of floor covering you buy. But if you've already put it down, and it's not as recommended, don't panic; it really isn't all that critical in a domestic environment. But if you are going to lay carpet on top using double sided tape it must be smooth side up or the tape won't stick.

A full sheet of hardboard used to be neatly described as an 8' by 4'; now it is an incomprehensible 2440mm × 1220mm. For use as an underlay quarter-size pieces are convenient to handle; buy it ready cut for convenience, or cut up full sheets, for economy, if you have the space and equipment to do so.

Ignore instructions you may find in other DIY books to condition the hardboard with water; unless your house has been empty or is freezing cold and damp to boot this is usually unnecessary. The idea of all the palaver is to make sure that the board does not buckle after fixing. All you need to do is stack the boards in the room where they are to go for four or five days before fixing them, which in my case is quite likely to happen in the normal course of events. But to do it properly, lay each board against the wall separately on its long edge, mesh side out. This allows the boards to acclimatise to the right moisture content.

As an underlay put the pieces of board down however it is most convenient — if you can find a nice square corner start there — staggering the joints between pieces, and avoiding joints coinciding with those in the boards below. Fix with 20mm hardboard pins or losthead nails, whacking them down really hard so that the heads are lost below the surface. (Ring shank nails are sometimes recommended but are difficult to find, and not essential for a floor only subjected to ordinary domestic traffic.) Place the pins at 15cm intervals, starting at one corner of the board and fanning out; if you pin down each corner and move inwards you can build in a central bulge. Butt the pieces lightly together.

As a floor covering lay 30 or 60cm squares of hardboard, starting in the centre of the room as when laying vinyl tiles. Fix with flooring adhesive to avoid the 'pocky' look of nails. Finish with 2–3 coats of clear polyurethane or floor sealer.

VINYL, CORK AND CARPET TILES

All these are easy to lay, being small and light to handle. Vinyl and cork tiles are usually 30cm square, carpet tiles 40cm or bigger. Carpet tiles are the easiest of all, as they are loose laid; self-adhesive vinyl tiles next and those requiring separate adhesive (some vinyl and most cork) last. Carpet tiles are a good alternative to roll carpet as they can be moved around to redistribute wear and hide any stained ones. Cork is superb for warmth and resilience underfoot, combined with easy cleaning, and ideal for kitchens and bathrooms. Cork can be pre-sealed, or sealed after laying. The plain ones are best for uneven floors as they can be sanded after laying to remove any irregularities. Sealing after laying is also best if a totally waterproof surface is required. Vinyl tiles are the cheapest, available in a wide range of colours and patterns. They are the coldest and hardest underfoot; but a small range of cushioned vinyl tiles (Dunlop Debonair) is now available; these have a similar thickness and feel to cushioned vinyl sheet.

Maintenance More expensive vinyl tiles have a built-in shine, but ordinary cheap ones have to be polished if you want a shine. To remove black scuff marks rub gently with steel wool.

Estimating If the room is a plain rectangle and the tiling is to be all one colour/pattern, simply measure length and width and multiply them together to get the area in square metres. Buy enough tiles to cover plus a few extras for any mistakes. (The same applies with carpet tiles, to have spares to put down later if necessary to replace stained or worn ones.) Most tiles are sold in packs sufficient to cover a square metre or yard, and you can often get loose ones as well.

If the room is a complicated shape, or if you are going to lay a design of different coloured tiles, it's best to work it all out on squared paper first. Some manufacturers' leaflets include useful diagrams scaled to the size of their tiles.

Laying The basic principle of laying all these types of floor tile is that you start in the centre of the room and work outwards. This is done for two reasons: 1) as few rooms are perfectly rectangular, starting against one wall would make the rows of tiles run noticeably askew; and 2) so that the border of cut tiles is roughly the same size all round. Tools required are: steel tape, plenty of string, a piece of chalk, a hammer and some small nails for setting out; Stanley knife and steel rule for straight cuts; a large pair of scissors, or better a pair of multi-purpose snips, for curved cuts.

Check before starting that the thickness of the floor tile, especially if laid over hardboard, is not going to prevent the door(s) closing. If this is going to happen you must *first* either plane a bit off its bottom; or fit rising butt hinges to lift the door clear. (Or try fitting a coarse sanding disc into a power tool upside down so you can sand a bit off the underside of the door.)

The instructions that follow relate to laying floor tiles in the conventional way, at right angles to the walls. But suppose you want to lay a chequerboard floor to look like the ones in old Dutch paintings, running diagonally across the room? Follow the same general principles, but start by laying the first tile with its centre where the chalk lines cross, corners pointing down the lines, and use that as a basis for laying a double row all down the room. I wouldn't try this until you have already had some practice at plain tiling: all the border tiles will be triangular, and need some pretty skilled cutting.

Setting out Chalk a length of string and stretch it down the centre of the room, parallel to the most visible long wall. Secure at each end with a nail in the floor or skirting. Stretch another chalked line across it at right angles to divide the floor into quarters. Starting in the centre lay an experimental line of tiles out against each string. If on reaching each wall, the bit to be filled with a cut tile is very small, move the rows back a little to make it at least half a tile wide. Cutting very narrow strips is wasteful, they are difficult to stick down satisfactorily and look ugly. If you have to do this adjusting, it's safest to dry-lay rows of tiles in all four directions so that you can be quite sure what's going to happen at each side. (Don't be tempted to have any of the border tiles an exact fit, because unless the room is a perfect rectangle small wedge-shaped gaps will start to appear as you go along; always leave about 5cm for trimming

145

off.) If there are fixed projections like a bath tub also check the layout to avoid cutting narrow strips when you get to the front of this. Once the layout is established reposition the strings, remove the tiles and ping the strings against the floor to leave chalk marks.

Laying Start in the centre of the room and tile one quarter section. Then do the remaining quarters; finish with the border tiles. Be careful to butt tiles tightly together, and align corners accurately. If they start to get out of true correct this straight away, as it only gets worse. Lay the tiles according to the pattern, or the arrows printed on the back (ordinary marbled vinyl tiles are laid with the grain running opposite ways on each tile; if you run them the same way they look very odd.)

With self-adhesive vinyl tiles all you have to do is peel off the backing paper, position the tile and smooth it down with a duster. With cork ones, or unglued vinyl, spread just enough of the recommended adhesive on to the floor to lay two or three tiles, using a notched trowel or spreader to make a ridged bed.

Carpet tiles are normally laid loose; pin the first one in place with double-sided tape or temporary tacks so that it stays there as an anchor for the rest. Before starting, make sure there are no gaps under the skirting boards into which border tiles could slip; if so fill with cellulose filler. Butt the tiles tightly together following the arrows on the back. In a large room it's a good idea to stick every third row with double-sided tape to forestall any tendency for the tiles to drift apart.

Border tiles In most rooms the pieces of tile which have to be cut to fill in gaps round the edge are very slightly wedge-shaped, not perfectly rectangular, so each one has to be cut individually. They must always be cut so that the machined edge lies against the last full tile, and the cut edge against the skirting, where any slight roughness will not be noticed. Place the tile to be trimmed to size on top of the last complete one (*make sure it is the right colour with grain or pattern running the right way*). Place a spare tile on top, pressed tightly against the skirting, with edges aligned exactly with the one below. Pencil a line across and cut. The exposed bit is the bit that will fit the space.

Use the same technique to cut an L-shaped tile to fit round an external corner, except that you have to mark and cut the tile in both directions. To be perfectly honest I find this confusing, and make a paper pattern, but you may have a better brain than me. A pattern is also required for internal corners; see below.

If the tiles are being laid with adhesive it's best to cut all the border pieces to size first, and then stick them down. But make sure to number them, and their position on the floor, before they get hopelessly mixed up.

146

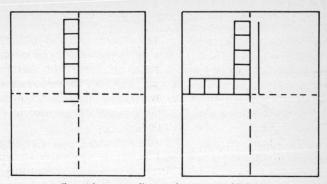

try tiles against centre lines each way to establish layout

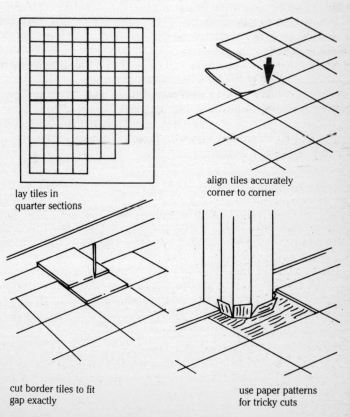

lay tiles in
quarter sections

align tiles accurately
corner to corner

cut border tiles to fit
gap exactly

use paper patterns
for tricky cuts

To cut internal corner pieces, and complicated shapes to fit round moulded door frames, pipes, wash basins and lavatory pans, cut out some pieces of newspaper to the same size as the tiles. (Use the corners of the sheets so that you have one guaranteed right angle.) Put one of these patterns into the space to be filled and roughly cut off the waste. Then cut the edge to be trimmed into a fringe; this makes it easy to mould the paper exactly to the shape required. Pencil on a cutting line and cut out. Try the pattern in place; if it isn't quite right have another go, or mark arrows on it to indicate where a bit more or less is needed. Cut the tile according to the pattern (again, watch for colour/pattern/grain) using scissors or preferably snips to get curves accurate.

Where a tile has to go right round a small obstacle, usually a pipe, slit it at the back in order to get it in place.

Finishing off Where the tiling comes to an end at a doorway (the finishing line should run under the centre of the closed door) protect the raw edge with a metal edging strip. These come in various styles according to the type of tiles, and what happens on the other side of them. You just cut them to length and screw down tightly.

Self-adhesive and carpet tiles can be walked on straight away, but leave others for 24 hours for adhesive to harden.

Finish unsealed cork tiles with two or three coats of a quick-drying floor sealer such as Bourn Seal. This should dry in about three hours so that the job can be done in a day. Or use clear polyurethane and put it on at night so that it can dry overnight. Protect the floor with newspaper next day and re-coat next night.

SHEET VINYL

A large roll of vinyl floor covering is much more difficult to manoeuvre than individual tiles, and in a large room the sheer weight of it means that getting it down is a two-person job. But it does have several advantages: a large floor area can be covered very quickly, without joins, as the stuff can be had in 2m, 3m and even 4m widths. For a kitchen sheet vinyl, especially the more expensive extra-thick variety, is warmer and softer underfoot than vinyl tiles (and less likely to break dropped crockery!). Being laid loose, it accommodates itself to the seasonal movement of a timber floor, so is less likely to need a hardboard underlay than cork or vinyl. Look out for ends-of-rolls and off-cuts at floor covering shops; these can be quite large and should be considerably reduced in price.

The ideal room in which to lay sheet vinyl is one of completely rectangular shape, without alcoves, chimney breasts, or built-in obstructions like sink units. The worst possible room is a bathroom with a pedestal washbasin, lavatory pan and bidet; all of them not only fixed obstructions, but curved ones. I wouldn't attempt it, but you can if you wish, by making a giant paper pattern (see later). Standard sheet vinyl is easier to lay than the extra-thick sort.

If the skirting boards are being renewed, do this *after* laying vinyl sheet and you can conceal a multitude of cutting errors.

Maintenance all vinyl sheet has a built-in shine. You may find that your vacuum cleaner tries to swallow it, despite the double-sided tape round the edges. Mine has a simple mechanism for reducing the suction, but I'm not sure if all do. When pulling out a heavy appliance such as a cooker for repair or to clean behind it, protect a standard sheet vinyl floor with whatever sturdy sheet material comes to hand. Being loose-laid it is vulnerable to tearing, and also dents quite easily.

Estimating Calculate which width will suit the room in question and buy enough to cover the floor area plus about 7cm all round for trimming. When you get it home unroll it and loosely reroll the other way, to curb its tendency to fight back when you try to lay it flat. Leave it in a warm room for a couple of days; this makes it supple and easier to handle, and gives it time to do any stretching it may have in mind.

Laying Tools required for laying sheet vinyl are few: steel tape, Stanley knife and steel rule, and a felt-tipped marker pen.

With any luck you will be able to line one edge of the vinyl up against the longest unobstructed wall and not have to do any trimming there. Lay it out like this and see how it looks. If the pattern appears to run down the room crookedly, pull it up against that wall at one one end until it looks right, which will mean trimming after all.

Immediately before starting give the floor a last vacuum or sweep to make quite sure there is no grit to get stuck under the sheet, unnoticed until it is all in place, and also make a final check for protruding nail heads.

First trim the sheet roughly to fit. Cut off any large amount of excess, and cut roughly round obstructions such as a fireplace, always leaving at least a 7cm margin for final trimming. The usual method of trimming to fit is to press the overlapping piece hard into the angle between skirting board and floor with the steel rule, then cut against the rule with a sharp knife. Keep checking that the cut is in the right place. If you find that your first attempt is not very good, pull the sheet up a bit (but always leaving enough for trimming on the opposition side) and have another go. At corners, slit the trimming allowances down first, then cut at each side. To get round curves or complicated moulded door architraves, make a series of downward cuts and then press the sheet well in and trim with knife alone. (Sometimes you get lucky and find that the builder has cut an architrave a little short, which means the floor covering can be poked underneath and will look perfect however rough your cutting.)

Neither this method, nor simply butting the machined edge of the sheet up against a skirting board, produces a perfect result, because of the inevitable slight undulations in its surface. For a perfect fit you need to use a method called scribing. This is not difficult in itself, but becomes very complicated if you try to do it all round, as you have to move the sheet up and down to do it, and could land up with a perfectly scribed sheet, slightly too short or narrow for the room. I would only bother if a very noticeable skirting was particularly wavy, and keep it to just one edge, no more.

To scribe, tape a felt tip pen on to a block of wood. Lay the sheet of vinyl out parallel to the wall but slightly away from it. Make a bold locating mark on the skirting and carry it well out on to the vinyl. Run the block of wood along the skirting board so that the pen marks a line on the vinyl: this will exactly reflect every bump and dip in the skirting board. Cut along the line with scissors or snips and push the sheet against the skirting, lining up the marks.

If the room is large and you have to join two pieces of sheet vinyl, match any pattern, and overlap them slightly. Then cut through both layers with knife and straightedge for a perfect join.

To lay sheet vinyl in a small room much encumbered with obstructions (i.e. a bathroom) the easiest way in the long run is to make a room-sized paper pattern. Get enough sheets of brown paper or left-over wallpaper to cover the floor when taped together, stopping 5cm short of the walls all round. Carry the paper behind fittings like the lavatory pan by slitting it. Now use the scribing technique described above to mark the exact outline of the floor area, going all round the bath and other fitments.

Lay the vinyl out flat in a larger room and tape the pattern to it, making sure that any pattern runs parallel with an unobstructed wall, if there is one; usually it's the front of the bath. Use the scribing block again to copy the outline marked on the pattern on to the vinyl. To make sure of a good fit cut the vinyl according to this outline but just a bit larger to allow for exact trimming when in position.

Finishing off Unless the vinyl is so thick it seems quite happy to lie down unaided, secure it all round the edges with double-sided tape. This used to be essential to stop it curling up at the edges after a while; the manufacturers claim that this no longer happens, but it is still needed to keep it in place when vacuuming. Always use tape to stick the floor

150

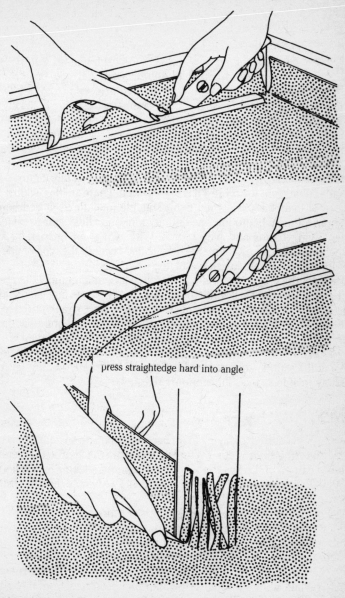

press straightedge hard into angle

make a series of vertical cuts to fit sheet round curves

covering down at doorways, and under any joins.

FITTED CARPET

Laying traditional woven carpets is a job for the professional, and in any case free fitting is sometimes included in the asking price. But modern tufted and foam backed carpet is another story. If you buy from a specialist carpet shop you should get it fitted professionally, but if you buy from a mail order or cash and carry company the fitting is usually up to you. Although it is fairly straightforward in a simply shaped room, I would be inclined to practise first by relaying some existing or second-hand carpet. Handling a large roll of carpet is definitely a two-person job.

Buying and estimating Whatever type of carpet you buy it must be of a grade suitable for the room if it is to wear well. There are three domestic grades of foam-backed carpet: light, suitable for little-used bedrooms; medium for main bedrooms and dining rooms; and heavy for circulation areas, living rooms and play rooms. With woven or hessian-backed carpet things become a bit more complicated because the type of under-lay used affects wear, so ask for advice when buying.

Measure the length and width of all *four* walls, and multiply the greatest length by the greatest width to calculate how much to buy, allowing at least 25mm all round for trimming. Don't forget any extra required to go into alcoves or bays, and that a little extra will also be required at door-ways; the carpet should finish under the centre of the closed door. Even if you have a very wide room, broadloom carpet can be obtained in up to 4.5m (15ft) widths, so you should not have to do any joining, except possibly in side alcoves for economy reasons.

LAYING FOAM BACKED CARPET

Accessories required for laying foam backed carpet are an equal quantity of paperfelt (this both keeps dirt from underneath the floorboards getting into the carpet, and stops the foam backing from sticking to the floor), enough double-sided tape to go all round, and a suitable threshold strip to cover the raw edge at the door(s).

The main tools needed are carpet shears or a modern pair of scissors; a Stanley knife with a packet of heavy duty blades; 10cm piece of hard-board; long straight edge or rule; and a hammer.

Have the room warm (this makes the carpet flexible and easier to handle). Unroll the carpet a bit to find out which way the pile runs. It should be laid so that it roughs up when brushed *away* from the main window. Stick double-sided tape to the floor all round close up to the skirting boards. Get the roll to the right end of the room and slowly unroll it so that the exposed end laps up against the end wall, and the sides lap up equally against the side walls. If it starts unrolling crookedly this will only get worse; reroll and start again. Tread it flat as you go, inspect it carefully for any flaws, and make sure that it is the size ordered. Once you have cut into it you can't send it back. Slit it partway down at the corners so that you can get it flat. If there is a large amount of excess at any point cut this off, leaving 25mm for final trimming.

Only now do you lay the paperfelt. Roll the carpet halfway back. Lay the paperfelt so that it stops 5cm short of the skirting boards to allow for the double-sided tape, and overlap the pieces to make sure that no gaps appear while the carpet is being laid. Roll the carpet back and paper the other half of the floor.

Roll the carpet out again and double check that it is in the right position with a trimming allowance all round, and quite flat. (Note: it is not necessary to cut carpet into the first wall *if* the wall and the carpet edge are absolutely straight and parallel. Just lay it in position and stick down.) Starting on the longest, least-obstructed wall peel the release paper off the top of the double-sided tape and stick carpet down on the sticky surface. Smooth out any wrinkles that may have appeared in the carpet and repeat the sticking process at the opposite wall. Repeat on the other two walls. Now the carpet is secured, push it *hard* into the angle between skirting and floor with the piece of hardboard. The best way to trim it is to hold the knife at a 45° angle against the rule, and cut into the crease between skirting and floor.

At the door fit the threshold strip, tuck the carpet under it and tap the strip down firmly with a hammer, protecting the strip with a block of wood.

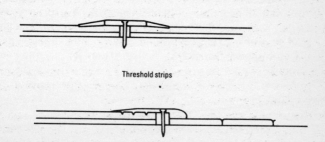

Threshold strips

Traditional carpet The way a professional carpet fitter lays this is to fix gripper strip all round the perimeter of the room, fractionally away from the skirting board. On concrete both gripper strips and underlay are stuck down. On wooden floors the underlay is stapled in place inside the gripper strips, and the carpet laid out on top with a trimming allowance lapping up on all sides. He then stretches the carpet with a tool called a knee kicker, trims it from the back so that there is enough to tuck into the gap between the gripper and the wall and forces it into place with a bolster (similar to a bricklayer's bolster chisel).

But if fitting a secondhand carpet you can use more casual methods. Have the room warm, lay the carpet out and leave it for several hours, even a day or two, to relax and unwrinkle. If it is thin and supple enough, turn it under at the edges and tack in place. If it is very thick, or long-haired, cut it from the back (the weaving lines enable you to cut straight) and treat the edges to stop them fraying. Use a self-adhesive carpet tape and some Copydex adhesive. Seal the edges with the adhesive to anchor any loose tufts, then put the tape on so that about 5mm lips up on to the pile from the underside of the carpet edge. (On some carpets sealing the strands with Copydex alone can be sufficient.) But always protect the exposed edge at a doorway with a proper threshold strip.

If joins have to be made, make sure the meeting pieces have the pile running the same way. For a near-invisible join use carpet seaming tape and Copydex adhesive. Lay the tape underneath the two edges. Roll the carpet back and brush the adhesive in a 25mm band down each edge, also carrying it halfway up the pile. Prop the carpet up and brush adhesive on to the seaming tape. Leave for a few minutes until the adhesive becomes dry and tacky, then press the carpet edges firmly on to the tape, pushing them together. Tap the join with a hammer to firm it. Using self-adhesive tape is quicker, but more expensive and does not make quite such a good join.

Relaying foam backed carpet Once fixed with double-sided tape these carpets cannot be lifted without damage; you have to cut away the taped area all round. Also if the carpet was originally laid without paper-felt underneath the foam may have stuck to the floor in places. So always try to sell such carpets when moving house, or plan for relaying them in a smaller room.

STAIR CARPET

Once again, I would not consider laying a new one. But you could well relay an old or secondhand one. If the stairs are a modern straight flight it is not particularly difficult, just tedious, but old-fashioned winding staircases with triangular treads on the bend are harder.

Stair carpet must be securely fixed because if it comes adrift it could cause a serious accident. Foam backed carpet must be of a suitably thick, heavy grade. Stair rods are the traditional way, but nowadays most people use the invisible spiked strips which grip the carpet from underneath; or with foam backs you can simply tack it firmly. If the stairs are already fitted with gripper strips (Invisigrip or similar), you need a hessian backed or woven carpet to go over them. Unless tacked, foam backed carpet needs special Foamgrip strips. An underlay is essential for unbacked stair carpet otherwise it will quickly start to go bald on the nose (outer edge) of the tread.

Stair carpet will also wear badly on the nosing if it is laid the wrong way, with the pile running up the stairs instead of down. Brushing the pile should roughen it up when done towards the top of the stairs.

If an existing carpet is worn on the nosings, it may be possible to relay it so that this is moved up a few inches. A professional carpet layer should have left an extra length of carpet tucked underneath at the top or bottom for this purpose.

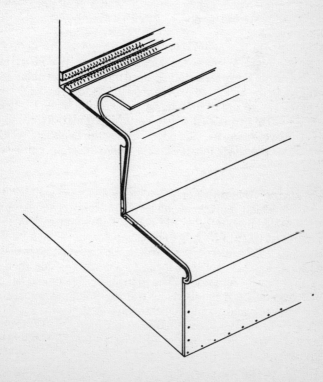

Clean and prepare the stairs as for floorboards (see page 141). Also thoroughly clean any existing stair pads and check that existing gripper strips are firmly in place. To fit new wooden grippers, cut them to length with secateurs or a pair of snips. Nail them in the angles between treads and risers so that the spikes point towards each other and will trap the carpet. (The metal angle type of gripper is nailed *over* the underlay.)

To fit new underlay, start at the top and cover the landing. On the actual stairs, cut it to their width, and into lengths that will run in between the sets of grippers. Fix by tacking or stapling. (But if the carpet is a fraying type that will have to be turned under on cut edges on one or both sides, cut both grippers and underlay short so as to allow for the extra bulk.)

Lay the carpet from the top; check the pile direction before starting. Use a continuous piece for each flight of stairs; if there are any joins they should be in the angle between tread and riser. Cut and trim as when laying in a room. Exactly how you proceed depends on the design of the staircase and landings, but, generally speaking, the landing carpet goes over the nosing and down the top riser. Proceed downwards, securing the top end of the carpet tightly inside the opposing gripper teeth by forcing it in with a piece of hardboard. Stretch it over the nosing on to the next pair of grippers.

When you reach the bottom riser, leave a surplus length so that the carpet can be moved up later when it shows wear on the nosings. Omit the underlay on the bottom tread and instead turn the carpet under at the bottom and over the bottom step. Secure on the bottom riser with tacks, starting in the centre and continuing part-way up the sides.

With the type of carpet that has to be turned under, fix it into the grippers as above. Along the side edges, e.g. by the banisters, secure it with tacks. Also put a tack into the crease where the gripper strip stops short.

Problem stairs   To fit carpet on an old-fashioned stairs with winders, do not attempt folding and tucking under an uncut roll of carpet, as you may see illustrated in some other DIY books. This is very difficult to get right and, unless you just happen to be a carpet-laying genius, ends up looking lumpy. With modern types of carpet and carpet grippers there is no need for it any way. Instead make paper patterns and then cut separate pieces to fit each winder. The triangular piece should be large enough to cover the tread and riser, plus extra for trimming, with the pile running downwards and at right angles to the riser. Cut out a V shape to enable it to fold on the inside corner. Hook it into the grippers at the base of the riser and cut off the waste by running a sharp Stanley knife in between the grippers.

If you want to be really ambitious and completely cover a bull-nose bottom stair — the type with a round end unencumbered by banister posts — treat it as a separate entity, and cut a piece for the tread and another for the riser. Cut the tread piece so that there is a small overlap at the nose edge. Fix it to the grippers at the back and tack the overlap under the top of the riser, and pleat and tack to make the carpet fold round the bullnose. Then cover the bare riser with a separate strip.

ECONOMY CARPETING

If you have a fitted carpet professionally laid, get the fitter to leave you the waste. You may well find that, joined together, the bits will be enough to carpet a small room such as the bathroom, or even a bedroom. In many bedrooms there is only one possible position for the bed, and especially if it is the box divan or under-drawer type, carrying fitted carpet all the way underneath is sheer extravagance. At the very least, keep some of the waste in case disaster overtakes the main carpet and the need for patching arises.

A cheap and easy way to carpet a flight of stairs not already fitted with gripper strips is to cover the treads only, and paint the risers (do this first). It must be the non-fray type of carpet; cord is ideal. As you will only need about half the normal amount of carpet you will be able to take advantage of very short, cheap carpet offcuts or a small secondhand piece. Simply cut a piece to fit each stair tread and tack securely in place with plenty of long tacks, along the back of the tread and underneath the nosing.

When you are in the market for new carpet, always carry the measurements of the room in question with you when out shopping. That way you won't miss a bargain offcut through dithering about whether or not it is quite big enough.

8 Tiling and panelling

Decorating is fun up to a point, but not when it comes round again too often. And there are certain areas or rooms in a house where paint and paper just can't cope with the wear, and something more substantial is needed. So there are times and places where it pays in the long run to invest in more expensive decorating materials which are virtually permanent.

Ceramic tiles are the classic example. They are the only real answer to situations where a lot of water is splashed about. I love putting up tiles. It's light, clean work, and very precise and logical. And you can be as modest or ambitious as you like, starting with a splashback behind sink, washbasin or cooker; progressing to tiling a shower cubicle and then tackling a whole kitchen or bathroom, perhaps using a combination of plain and patterned tiles to create a unique design.

Polystyrene tiles, although quite fragile, will last indefinitely provided that they aren't dented (they are safest on high ceilings.) But they will need repainting from time to time. The more expensive fibre insulating board tiles are really permanent, and a fresh coat of paint brings them up like new.

Putting up pine panelling or decorative wallboards is rather more ambitious than putting up tiles, but once up they are there for good. Pine panelling will just need a very occasional revarnishing, and some decorative wallboards need no maintenance at all.

CERAMIC WALL TILES

Putting up wall tiles is amazingly simple once you master the art of cutting them (take heart, even professional tile cutters allow 5% extra for breakages), and intensely satisfying because once done it looks highly skilled. The secret of success is to plan the layout very carefully before starting. Don't do what I did on my first attempt: miscalculated, no doubt through poor arithmetic, and landed myself with cutting 24 slivers of tile, only 1cm wide, to fit into a corner. Also buy self-spacing tiles or ones with spacer lugs, which are easiest for the beginner to handle. If you really don't feel up to cutting tiles you can still do a washbasin or sink splash-back, or cover a coffee table.

Tiles Ceramic tiles come in two standard square sizes: 10.8cm ($4\frac{1}{4}$in) and 15.2cm (6in). The larger ones are thicker (5.5mm as against 4mm). There are also some 20cm (8in) square tiles and some oblong ones around. The larger the tile the quicker the laying. But being thicker they cost more. Also small ones look better in a small area.

Tiles are available in many plain colours, including ones that exactly match baths and washbasins, and British Standard colours to match B.S. paint; and a riot of patterns. Even a large DIY supermarket will only stock a certain amount of patterned tiles; the more expensive and exotic can be ordered from sample displays. In between plain and patterned tiles there are many mottled and textured ones, which often co-ordinate with a patterned range; also veined tiles, where worms of colour squirm repellently over a white ground.

With the more standard-colour tiles you can get accessories: matching ceramic bathroom fittings such as toilet roll holders, toothbrush racks and hooks; and various types of edging strip to fill in the angle between bath and wall..

Ceramic tiles are not butted together like vinyl floor tiles but laid with a small gap all round, which is then filled with grout to create an imperme-able, waterproof and hygienic surface. Some tiles have spacer lugs or a bevelled edge which creates this spacing automatically. Others (all those from Habitat, for example, and fancy foreign or hand-painted ones) do not have lugs or shaping, and you have to put spacers in to keep a regular joint between them. If spacers are not included in the box of tiles, buy a sheet of plastic ones; unlike the bits of card traditionally used these can be left in place, which saves time.

Basic tiles are called field tiles. For finishing exposed edges (the top row of half-tiling, or the front edge of a window sill) a special rounded-edge (RE) tile is traditionally used, and for corners one with two rounded edges: a REX tile. But tile manufacturers are now going over to what are called universal tiles. These have no lugs, but instead have a bevelled edge all round which makes them self spacing. Every box includes a pro-portion of tiles with two glazed edges for use on top and side rows, and on exposed corners. Such tiles are easier to buy as you don't have to work out in advance how many specials will be needed (or find that the shop is out of stock of them). Just sort out the glazed-edge ones and set them aside before starting.

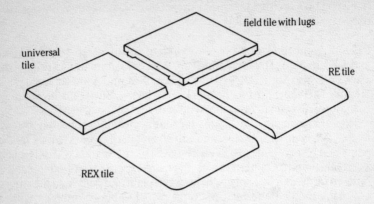

universal tile

field tile with lugs

RE tile

REX tile

Estimating For those with O-level maths and a calculator: figure out the area to be tiled, settle on the tile size and divide the area by the area of one tile. For bears of little brain like me: figure out the area and put yourself in the hands of the shop assistant. Or, having chosen the tile, work it out from the information on the box, which will give the contents and area they cover. In either case add around 5% for breakages (tiles are fragile until on the wall, and it's not impossible there may be a cracked one or two in the box to allow for, as well as the ones you are going to break while learning to cut them). If your final figure means a lot of waste from a whole box, you may be able to buy some singly as well, if it is a popular tile, or to special order.

Tools The main extra tool required for laying ceramic tiles is a tungsten-carbide scriber for scoring lines through the glaze before cutting them. These are cheap and perfectly adequate for thin tiles. If you are using the thicker ones, or doing a large area, you might invest in a patent tile cutter. These come in various forms; a common one consists of a wheel for scribing, and a strong pair of pincers for cutting. (Be careful how you use the pincers; they can viciously nip your fingers.) Other tools required are all from the basic tool kit: steel tape for measuring up, steel rule against which to use the scriber, pincers for removing small bits of unwanted tile; Surform or file for smoothing cut edges, and a large spirit level. (If you don't have one, buy a long piece of polythene tubing and use that instead. How? Fill it with cold tea, tape one end to the wall, and however far away you take the other end, the liquid levels will always be identical.) For small areas of tiling a notched plastic spreader, sometimes supplied free with the adhesive, will suffice for spreading adhesive on the wall, but for a whole room get a notched trowel. All you need for

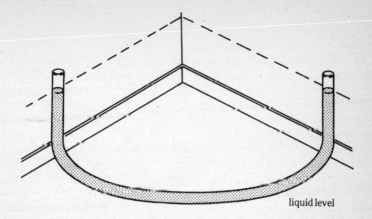

liquid level

applying the grout is a sponge and a round-ended stick, but if you want to spend money you can buy a rubber tile grouter, or one combined with a special sponge.

Apart from the tiles, you need a sufficency of tile adhesive (you can buy this in tubs, ready-mixed, but powder is cheapest) and grouting powder; plus at least two timber battens, say 25mm × 50mm, to the length and height of the tiling.

Preparation Wash down painted walls, removing any flaking material, and fill any major cracks and holes. Level off bumps and fill depressions. If the wall is very uneven the tiles will not go on properly, so you may need to do some preliminary work with Polyskim (ready-mixed plaster), and allow time for this to dry out. Take the shine off old gloss paint with coarse abrasive paper to give a good key for the adhesive. Old wallpaper must come off, but old tiling can be tiled over. Stick back any on the point of falling off, and stick the new ones on with a special thick-bed adhesive. If the tiling only goes half-way up the wall, you get an unsightly view of the double tiles at the top, and must cover this in some way: with beading, shelving or strategically placed wall units.

Tiling the main area Ceramic tiles are laid in rows working from the bottom up. But because the floor or skirting board may not be perfectly level, you actually start one row up, resting the tiles on a temporary batten, and fill in the bottom row at the finish.

Place a tile on the floor/skirting at one corner and mark a line on the wall above the spacer lugs. Repeat at the opposite side of the wall. Fix a batten the whole length of the wall with its upper edge to the marks, making sure that it is perfectly horizontal with a long spirit level or water-filled polythene tube. (Use masonry nails and hammer them only part way in so that the batten can be removed easily when the tiling is complete.) Working from the centre, use a tile to mark off the number of complete tiles required. Just as when floor tiling, if the pieces at each end are very small, adjust the centre tile until they come out at about half a tile wide. Mark the wall against the lugs of the last tile and fix an upright batten in this position; use a couple of tiles to ensure that it is absolutely vertical. You *must* have a perfect right angle between the battens, or the whole tiling will go progressively out of alignment.

Spread adhesive on the wall about a square metre at a time, combing it into horizontal ridges with the notches. Lay all the full tiles, working in horizontal rows. Make sure that all the spacer lugs are touching and corners neatly aligned. Where tiles run over obstructions such as a wash-basin, support the bottom row of full tiles with a batten, leaving a gap below to be filled in later.

If using any accessories such as a soap dish leave a space for it and position after the main tiling has dried. If it is heavy support it temporarily with masking tape.

Leave the main tiling for 24 hours before removing the battens and doing the infilling all round.

Infilling Mark up the tiles to be cut to fit the gaps at each side exactly as for floor or ceiling tiles: place a tile over the last full tile, with another one on top, butted against the wall. Mark a felt tip line down the edge of the bottom tile; the exposed portion, when cut off, will fill the space. If you are tiling the adjacent wall the pieces can be used there, just as when cutting down a length of wallpaper. But much depends on the layout; also it may not be worth bothering with if the tiles are plain, but if they have a pattern, using the off-cuts means that it will match exactly. (Provided that the angle between the walls is reasonably true.)

To cut, put the tile on a board and hold a steel rule firmly on the line. Scribe it hard, several times, so that the line goes well into the glaze, particularly at the edges. Place the tile on top of two headless matchsticks, lined up with the scored line. Close your eyes, breathe deeply and press evenly on each side of the tile. It should snap like a biscuit, neatly along the line. If you have to press very hard you haven't scored deeply enough. Cutting tiles is something that comes with practice, so if possible try it out on a few old or spare tiles. Once you get the knack, I promise you'll be wondering what all the fuss was about. The edge of the tile will be slightly rough and can be filed smooth, but there's no need to do this in corners unless it's too snug a fit. When fixing these small pieces it's more convenient to put the adhesive on the tile, not on the wall.

To cut out awkward shapes and curves to go round obstructions or

FIXING CERAMIC TILES

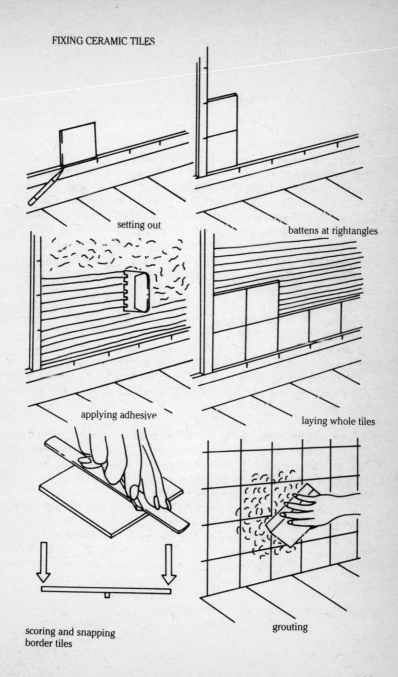

setting out

battens at rightangles

applying adhesive

laying whole tiles

scoring and snapping
border tiles

grouting

163

pipes, mark and score in the usual way, but then gradually nibble away the waste with pincers. When tiles run behind taps or pipes, cut in two, then nibble away the required semi-circle from each piece. The break will be filled with grout.

The bottom row of tiles, below the foundation batten, should mostly go in whole, but you have to nibble a bit off some; sometimes just filing off the lugs will do the trick.

Window recesses If there is a recessed window in the wall, start the tiling centred on it, rather than on the wall. Lay all the full tiles, starting from the bottom, as if the window did not exist, supporting the row above it on a batten. Then do the infilling at all four sides and round the window, filing the cut edges of these last ones to make sure that they are level. Last of all tile the actual recess, starting in the *centre* of the sill, and lining the tiles up with those on the face wall. The cut tiles will come in the corners and against the window where they will be least noticeable. Use rounded or glazed-edge tiles for the outer row, to cover the cut edges on the face wall neatly.

Finishing off Leave the completed tiling for 24 hours for the adhesive to dry. Mix up the grouting powder with water as directed on the packet and work it into the joints between the tiles with a sponge or rubber-edged tile grouter. Leave it for an hour or so until the grout has partly set and then draw a rounded stick (such as the handle of a child's paint brush) along every joint to give a neat finish. Next day polish all over with a dry cloth.

Shower areas When tiling these make sure to use a water-proof adhesive, spread on thickly, without notching and use water-resistant grout. You are supposed to leave it to dry for two weeks after grouting, which is all very well if you also have a bath. I think I sneaked a quick one in mine after a week without ill effect.

If you have a shower fitted over a bath, check that the existing tiling is adhering well, with all the grouting intact, particularly at the top in the case of half-tiling. Also make sure that the gap between bath and wall is tightly sealed; apply new bath sealant if in any doubt, as water seeping behind the bath could cause a lot of trouble in time — i.e. rotting floorboards.

Floor tiles Tiles designed for laying on floors come in two main sorts: the glazed patterned sort that you see in Spanish holiday villas; and the unglazed ones called quarry tiles, which can be red, brown, blue-grey or cream. I don't recommend trying to lay any of them. They are so

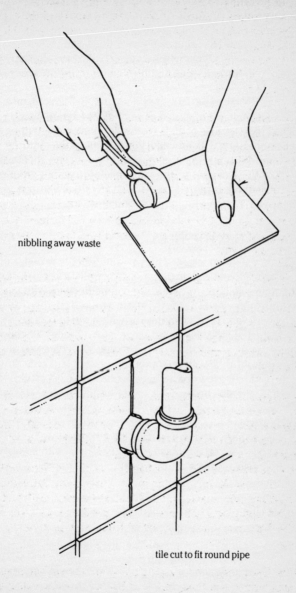

nibbling away waste

tile cut to fit round pipe

thick — up to 15mm — that cutting is virtually impossible. Do not be deceived by what you may read in other DIY books. I have tried in vain to make any impression at all on quarry tiles, and listened to several anguished callers to DIY phone-ins with the same problem. They are also pretty expensive; I reckon that if you can afford to buy them you can afford to have them laid. (But if you must do it, hire a heavy-duty tile cutter.)

If your heart is set on a DIY tiled floor, have a look at mosaic tiles. These are small squares of glazed or semi-glazed ceramic set on a paper or mesh backing. Because of their small size (5cm or less) cutting at edges may not be necessary; with any luck you just cut off the required number of squares and fill the remaining gap with grout. The sheets are quite large (commonly 30cm sq) so they are quick to lay; but grouting takes longer because there is more of it. As with any thick flooring, watch out for the door-won't-close problem before laying.

TABLE AND WORKTOP TILES

For a worktop you need a robust tile; a 4mm wall tile would soon crack. The ones to use are the 15.2cm (large square) wall tiles, which are 5.5mm thick. Some tiles suitable for worktops can be finished with a matching tile trim (Johnson's Cristal); otherwise use a timber edging. The wall can be covered with matching wall tiles, or with a tile upstand.

Table tops get slightly less hard wear, and although it's best to use worktop tiles, you can get away with wall tiles, provided you are not the type of household that will be slamming pewter tankards down on it every night. But buy a few spares in case one or two get cracked in time.

Mosaic tiles can also be used for worktops and tables, and look very classy indeed.

Whichever type of tiles you use, make sure to grout them with epoxy grout, as the ordinary kind will quickly stain. Press it well into the joins and scrape it off flush; do not finish in the usual way with a round-ended stick or you create a dirt-trapping trough.

MIRROR TILES

These are different from ceramic tiles in that they are fixed with self-adhesive pads on the back, and no grouting is required. Tiling a whole wall with mirror tiles would be very expensive, but a few strategically placed to catch the light in a dark hallway can work wonders. They are also good in bathrooms, where an area of tiling can function as both splashback and mirror. Common square sizes available are 10.8cm, 15cm, 22.5cm and 30cm; and 15cm × 30cm rectangles. Large mirror tiles can also be used to make sliding doors for a bathroom cabinet.

POLYSTYRENE CEILING TILES

The feather-light, white tiles made from expanded polystyrene provide a much easier way of hiding a very poor ceiling surface than hanging a thick embossed paper. They also have some sound-reducing and insulating properties, but not a lot.

At one time polystyrene tiles got a bad name because they caught fire rather too readily, but if you get the following points right they are no more dangerous than many other things in the home, such as foam-upholstered furniture; at least no-one can drop a cigarette on to a ceiling tile.

1) When first introduced ceiling tiles were fixed with a thick adhesive applied in blobs; this left air spaces underneath which helped flames to spread. So now you will find the instructions on the packs very emphatic about spreading the recommended adhesive *all over* the tile to eliminate this danger.

2) Check when buying that the tiles are a fire-retardant grade. Even so, do not use them in areas where they might get hot for any length of time (above gas water heaters and cooking stoves, and some heating appliances).

3) Do not paint ceiling tiles with gloss paint. If you have got some, take them down; the paint greatly increases the fire risk. Emulsion paint is all right, and you can safely use it to revive a yellowing ceiling. (New tiles do not need painting, but if you want a colour do it the easy way: *before* putting them up.)

Estimating and buying The common ceiling tile is 30cm square, plain, and delightfully cheap (about £1.40 for a pack of 25, enough to cover 2.25 sq metres). You can also get them with patterns moulded into the surface, ranging from random designs like cracked ice, to formal ones meant to look like old-fashioned moulded plaster ceilings; and in larger sizes — up to 60cm sq. Thicknesses vary, so watch for this when comparing prices. Slightly different, and thicker, are expanded polystyrene panels. These have patterns, usually geometrics or wavy lines, which interlock to give an overall effect once the panels are butted together. Accessories available are covings to cover the join between tiling and wall — mostly plain, but a few patterned ones which match traditional-style ceiling centres. The coving gives a neat finish and hides any badly cut edge tiles; but it can also be used alone, perhaps with a ceiling centre, to restore some of the former glory to a high-ceilinged Victorian room where mad modernisers have removed the original decorative plasterwork.

Buy sufficient tiles or panels to cover your ceiling area, plus a few extras in case of accidents. They are usually sold by the box, but you may be able to buy the common ones loose to make up an awkward number. Complete the purchase with a container of the recommended adhesive and some lengths of coving. (This comes in standard lengths plus ready-cut corner pieces so you don't have to attempt the near-impossible task of cutting a mitre in a curved piece of plastic.)

Preparation Wash or brush down the ceiling. If it is papered this will have to be stripped off. Remove any paint that's flaking off, and any really large lumps. If the ceiling is gloss painted rub it all over with coarse abrasive paper or a wire brush so that the adhesive will get a good grip.

Ceiling tiles are put up just like floor tiles, starting from the centre of the room, and doing it should present no problems at all provided that you work out a good layout before starting. Also make sure, before starting to handle the tiles, that your hands are cleaner than clean, as they pick up dirty fingerprints very easily, which then cannot be removed.

Draw a rough scale plan of the room (a scale of 1 : 20 is convenient; that is, 5cm on the paper represents 1 metre). Divide the area into four and, starting at the centre, calculate how the chosen tile size falls: if the cut tile at each wall is less than half size, move the centre point so that it will be bigger. Very narrow strips, apart from looking unsightly, are hard to stick down satisfactorily, and are wasteful. Another factor to take into account is the light fitting. A ceiling rose should always appear either at the junction of four tile corners, or bang in the middle of one; anything else looks odd. With a fluorescent tube, line the tiles up with one side and cut to fit on the other; or take it down before starting; this is not difficult, but means that as you must then have the electricity switched off you must do at least the middle bit in daylight. You may be able to get away without cutting tiles along one or two walls, as a slight gap can be allowed and covered by coving.

Having worked all this out, transfer the laying lines on to the ceiling with string and pencil. Or, if the room is a regular shape with a perfectly centred ceiling rose, cut a hole in the centre of a tile with the aid of a small glass jar and start straight away from there.

Fixing Otherwise fix the first four tiles where the lines cross and work progressively outwards. Spread plenty of adhesive *all over* the back of each tile with a plastic spreader or old paintbrush. Press them in place very gently with the palm of your hand or a block of wood; pressure from fingertips will dent the surface, especially if you have long nails. Wipe off any adhesive that squeezes out with a clean cloth.

168

Make sure that the tiles are firmly butted together, corner to corner; correct any tendency to go out of alignment at once as it will get worse.

As with floor tiles, border tiles have to be individually cut to fit each space. Get up there with two tiles and place one exactly on top of the last full tile. Push the second one against the wall, sides exactly aligned with the other two. Pencil a line along its edge onto the first one. When cut off, the exposed portion of the first tile should fit the space exactly. To cut, place the tile on a board and use a sharp Stanley knife against a steel rule. They always tend to crumble a bit, which is why coving is a good idea, to hide the cut edges. Use the same method to mark the tiles to fit into the four corners, or make a paper pattern.

To fix the coving, put the corner pieces up first, then fill in with straight lengths as required. If the walls are uneven and gaps appear here and there underneath the coving, a little Polyfilla will put things right.

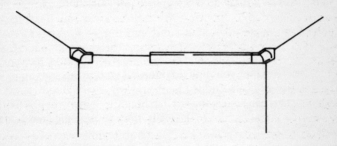

FIBRE INSULATING BOARD TILES

In cases where you not only want to redecorate and conceal a poor ceiling, but provide insulation because it cannot be done via the roof, consider the possibilities of fibre insulating board tiles. They are quite a bit more expensive than polystyrene ones, but you get more for your money.

Fibre insulating board (FIB) tiles are usually 30cm square and 12mm thick, and pre-decorated white. The edges can be bevelled or tongued and grooved, and the surface plain, perforated or fissured. They are light to handle as they contain lots of air, which is why they are good insulators. Fixing can normally be done with blobs of acoustic tile adhesive (yes, blobs are OK with this type of tile). This adhesive has moderate gap-filling properties. But if the ceiling is hopelessly uneven or if plaster is loose it will not be possible to get them level by this method, and they will have to be the tongued and grooved type, stapled to timber battens. These are not widely stocked, but if you can find a supplier he should be able to lend or hire you a staple gun. (I have also used the stapling method and tongued and grooved tiles to cover a decrepit and uneven boarded ceiling, rather than face stripping off umpteen coats of flaking paint.)

It's worth planning the layout of the tiles on squared paper, to arrive at the most economical one, as they are normally sold only in complete cartons. They can either be laid from the centre out, like polystyrene tiles, or lined up with the most prominent wall. Work with ultra-clean hands to avoid marking the pre-decorated surface. Border tiles are easily cut with a sharp knife against a straight edge. The edge of the finished ceiling is best covered with a timber moulding or lengths of fibrous plaster coving. (Paint timber first.)

FIB tiles are not all that widely stocked. In case of difficulty contact FIDOR (Fibre Building Board Development Organisation) see page 209.

PINE PANELLING

Covering a wall with tongued and grooved pine boards is not particularly difficult, *provided* that you only do one wall, and make sure to choose one that is free of obstructions (doors and windows). But it is a major undertaking that will take many woman hours, as it involves first fixing a framework of timber battens to the walls, then pinning the boards to the battens.

For one wall alone, say it is 1.5m (8ft) high by 4m (12 ft) long, you will probably need 6 battens, which means that you could be making 72 fixings into the wall. If you do all four walls you also get involved with doors and windows, which means removing the architraves around them, and framing them with still more battens fixed to the wall.

But to my mind a whole room panelled in timber is rather oppressive, whereas one wall makes an extremely attractive feature, with the bonus of being permanent. Panelling is also good from the practical point of view, as a means of covering a wall that really needs replastering. Patching plaster up, even quite extensively, is one thing, but replastering a whole wall flat and smooth is a highly skilled job. On a more modest scale pine panelling is an attractive way to cover in the side of a bath, in place of some tatty plastic-faced hardboard or a moulded plastic monstrosity. And there should be a timber frame already there to fix into. (I have to confess that to date this is the extent of my personal involvement with pine panelling.)

A builder will probably charge about the same for replastering or panelling a wall, so if you choose panelling which you can do yourself you will save money.

You *could* panel a ceiling, say if you have had the misfortune to have a ceiling get flooded and collapse. It does look most attractive, and you can pin the boards directly on to the joists above, cutting out the batten fixing stage. But before rushing into action bear in mind that you will have to work Michelangelo fashion, flat on your back on some scaffold boards.

Estimating and buying T&G boards (if you want to sound know-ledgeable in the timber yard, they call it matching) come in various widths and lengths, and I would find out first what your local yard stocks so that you can work out the most economical layout. A common size is 10cm wide, which will actually cover 9cm of wall when interlocked with its neighbours.

The boards can be laid either vertically or horizontally: the former emphasises a wall's height, the latter its breadth. Another factor is that horizontal laying may mean that you will have to have more joins, if the wall is longer than it is high. Assuming that you opt for vertical boards, estimate for enough 25cm × 50cm sawn softwood battens (no need to waste money on planed timber) to fix them horizontally right across the wall at intervals of about 40cm up to shoulder height, and about 60cm above that. Pick the T&G boards out yourself (do not order by phone) so that you can discard lengths that are badly twisted, poorly planed, and have damaged tongues and holes where dead knots have dropped out. Order quite a few feet extra to allow for wastage, especially if you are having it all delivered and there is a delivery charge, as you do not want to have to go back for a few extra lengths. Also, if bought some time later, additional lengths may not fit exactly. In addition you will need about 10 masonry nails for every 4 metres of batten (see Fixing); or buy 5cm No. 8 screws by the box, with matching wall plugs; and several pounds of panel pins to fix the boards. Also get some lengths of scotia or quadrant moulding to conceal the join between panelling and the side walls and ceiling.

Store the timber in the room where it is to go, lying flat, for a week if possible, to give it time to shrink and acclimatise.

If there is any danger that the wall might be damp, the battens should be treated with timber preservative, and building paper placed between them and the wall. And if it is an external wall you might want to take the opportunity of improving its insulating properties by placing insulating board or thick sheet polystyrene in between the battens (in this case space battens apart by the width of the insulating material.)

Fixing Getting the battens up is a job for two, but one alone can manage pinning on the boards if necessary. Before starting lever off the skirting board; this will cause some damage but you don't care. If you are

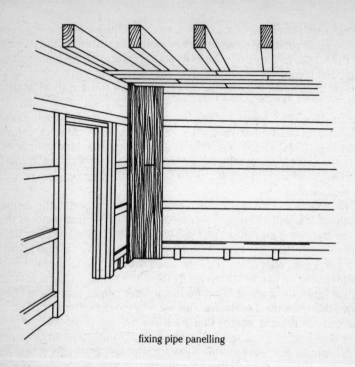

fixing pipe panelling

going to refix a skirting board afterwards (there is no need for one, and you may prefer an unobstructed sweep of panelling) place the first batten just above its top. Otherwise start at floor level.

If using masonry nails to fix the battens to the wall place them at around 40cm intervals. Make sure to get the right length of nail for the batten thickness; read the manufacturer's instructions on the box. The secret of getting the nails to hold fast is to put them *all* into the batten first, then hammer the batten on to the wall. It is also a good idea to wear safety specs when using these nails, as if not hit squarely they can occasionally splinter and fly in your direction.

However . . . you may find that, like me, you are totally incapable of making masonry nails work; or that they just won't penetrate the wall you are working on with the amount of drive that your arm and your hammer are able to provide. For this reason, only buy a few masonry nails at first, to see if you will in fact be able to use them. If you cannot it will have to be screws and plugs. Although this is more trouble, it is the Rolls Royce way of fixing, and you can get away with far fewer — say four in a 4-metre run. (If you have a power tool with variable speed you could get a screwdriver bit to speed things up. I would also invest in a sharp new masonry drill.)

Adjust the spacing of horizontal battens so that the top one comes against the ceiling. With vertical battens, space them evenly at about 40cm centres, adjusting this so that the outermost pair come against the side walls. Level either type by using a big spirit level (for vertical battens you will need the more expensive sort which has a vertical level bubble as well as the horizontal one).

Once horizontal battens are in place, put in some offcuts below the bottom, if necessary, to provide a fixing for the skirting board. With vertical battens, pin off-cuts of the T&G board to the bottom of each one so that any skirting will sit on top of the finished panelling. Mark the floor or make a note of where they are so that you can locate them when covered with boards.

Start at either side and fix the first board with its grooved edge butted up against the wall. Make absolutely sure that it is vertical; as with a length of wallpaper, the first one is the key one. Slight gaps against the wall caused by undulating plaster do not matter as they will be concealed by the moulding (if they are large, fix a wider moulding). Nail the board to the battens through the tongue, driving the panel pins in at an angle. Fix horizontal boards in a similar way, starting with one at the bottom, grooved edge down, and making sure that it is perfectly horizontal.

Continue nailing on boards, butting them up *very tightly*, because they usually shrink slightly in time, and you don't want a lot of unsightly gaps. At the opposite side or top, plane the last board down to fit and nail straight through it, not too close to the edge. Punch the nails below the surface and fill with plastic wood. Finish with beading at sides and top, fixed with small panel pins or contact adhesive.

When lengths of board have to be joined, cut the ends square with the aid of a try square and arrange things so that the two pieces meet on the centre of a batten. Stagger the joints (don't have two next to one another) and place them low down or high up to be least visible.

Electrical fittings If there is a light switch or socket in the wall fit a new metal mounting box so that it will lie flush with a surrounding framework made from offcuts of the battens. (This is not difficult, but see general notes in Chapter 4). Provided that there is enough cable back in the wall, it should be possible to pull the fitting forward far enough to refit it into a framework of battens. Cut the boards surrounding a recessed fitting so that the cover plate will just fit over the cut ends.

Finishing Wait a while before varnishing the boards to see if any of the knots 'bleed' resin; if so seal them with a couple of coats of knotting. (If the boards are in a kitchen it's as well to protect them from grease during this period by covering with paper.) Finish with two or three coats of clear polyurethane: matt for a soft look; glossy for high shine and maximum dirt resistance; satin for a compromise between the two. Varnish has to be applied by brush, not a roller. If you don't already have a big varnishing brush, try one of the new Ting pistol grip ones.

DECORATIVE WALLBOARDS

Various types of decorative wallboards can be used to clad walls instead of natural timber. This can be enamelled hardboard, which is available in many matt or gloss colours, plain or grooved to give a tile effect; or in a wide range of patterns, some with a raised texture. Or it can be wood-grain hardboard, where the effect of many different kinds of woods is achieved either by printing it on, or bonding a wood-grain foil or laminate on to the board (the effect is very similar to a wood-grain laminated plastic). In a more expensive type the hardboard is embossed during manufacture to simulate brick, stone, stucco, deeply fissured woodgrains or traditional fielded timber panels.

Wall panelling is also available made of plywood, finished with real wood veneers given a planked effect by V grooves cut into the face; or with a simulated wood-grain effect printed on to the plywood.

Fitting these large panels is a two-person job, but the work goes much more quickly than with individual T&G boards. Also they can be fixed to the framework of battens with contact adhesive instead of being nailed. If a few nails are used to make quite sure they stay in place they can be hidden in the grooves or lost in the pattern. In theory wallboards can be stuck directly to the wall with lines of contact adhesive, but only if it is absolutely flat; a rare occurrence in the average house. Gun-applied panel adhesives are available but are tricky to handle without experience. Also the use of battens, if it is an exterior wall, automatically improves insulation by providing an air gap.

Most of the decorative boards can be lightly butt jointed without further treatment. Or you can either use a cover strip, or leave a gap, and make a feature of the joins.

The general instructions regarding the use of hardboard apply (see page 143) but you should be able to get specific instructions for handling and fixing wallboards from the supplier, or failing that from FIDOR (Fibre Building Board Organisation) — see Useful addresses, page 209.

INSULATING WALLBOARDS

Solid brick or stone walls cannot by definition be insulated by filling the cavity with foam insulation (which is not in any case a DIY method). But

174

they can have their insulation greatly improved by lining them with some kind of wallboard.

Basic insulating board is a thick, rather spongy member of the family of wood fibre boards commonly known as hardboard. For wall lining it can be obtained in board or plank form. And if you want to insulate and decorate in one go it also comes with a predecorated surface (however, as this board is soft and easily damaged this treatment is only really suitable for bedrooms.) A solid 220mm (9in) brick wall covered only in plaster can have its resistance to the outflow of heat improved by over 100 per cent by lining it with 12mm insulating board fixed to battens.

Decorative wallboards can also be used for insulating purposes. The insulation value of a solid 220mm (9in) brick wall should be improved by over 50 per cent by lining 3.2mm ($\frac{1}{8}$in) enamelled hardboard fixed to 20mm battens. Extra improvement can be obtained by filling the space between the battens with insulating board or thick sheet polystyrene. (Glass fibre quilt is too thick for this job.)

A solid wall can also be insulated by lining it with plaster board, nailed on to a framework of battens with insulating material placed in between. Personally I do not like working with plasterboard. It consists of a core of plaster sandwiched between two sheets of heavy paper, and is extremely heavy, awkward to cut and unpleasant to handle. Finishing the joins between boards involves a lot of fussing about with jointing compound and tape. And after all that it still needs decorating.

9 Keeping out the cold

Although insulating and draughtproofing work may not be the most exciting of DIY tasks, it is one that brings the greatest benefits, in the form of increased comfort and reduced fuel bills. Fortunately, all the work except cavity wall insulation is well within the capabilities of even the complete beginner, and most of it is quite cheap to carry out. A great many excellent products are on the market, and as most of them come complete with instructions I have not gone into any great detail in this chapter on how to do these various jobs, but stuck to pointing you at what's available. And new products appear all the time; so keep your eyes open. (Cautious note: take advertising claims with the usual pinch of salt. Statements like 'this product will reduce heat losses by 50 per cent' tend to mean, when examined closely, 50 per cent (under optimum circumstances) of the heat loss from the particular area to which the product is applied, which is not the same thing at all.)

Heat escapes from a house in every direction. The figures are, roughly: 35 per cent through walls, 25 per cent through the roof, 15 per cent each through floors and gaps round doors and windows and 10 per cent through window panes. Slowing this heat loss down is done in two ways: by insulating — adding warm materials to the structure, just as when putting a cosy on a tea pot or donning a string vest — and by draught-proofing — simply blocking up holes which not only let cold air in, but warm air out.

Insulating the roof is given top priority because it is easy and cheap to do, especially with the aid of a government grant. Although the heat loss through walls is greater in total, dealing with it is both more difficult and more expensive. Draughtproofing is very cost effective. The heat loss here is insidious; you may not even notice all those little gaps, but it is said that if you put them all together, they can amount to the equivalent of a dirty great hole in the front door, which of course you would do something about at once.

As it is perfectly obvious that fuel costs are never going to go down, only up — if someone discovered a new, cheap-as-dirt native fuel tomorrow, any government would immediately slap a tax on it to make it 'competitive' with the other fuels — the more measures you can take *now* to stop that precious heat escaping the better. After that, try to add something every winter. Your ultimate aim should be to keep fuel bills going down a fraction each year, in the face of rising prices.

The cost and energy-saving estimates I have quoted in this chapter are from the Energy Efficiency Office booklet *Make the Most of your Heating*.

INSULATING

HOT WATER CYLINDER

Having an uninsulated hot water cylinder is madness. A jacket should not cost much more than £6, and will cut fuel bills by £15–£40 *every year*. If your cylinder has a jacket which is only 25–50mm thick, replace it with a thicker one, or put it over the top if there is room. These jackets usually consist of a number of padded segments, held together by a collar at the top, and strapped in place round the cylinder. Measure the cylinder to the top of the dome, and round the middle, to get the right-sized jacket. Fit as instructed, taking care not to leave any gaps between segments. If the cylinder has an electric immersion heater inside do not cover the cap sticking out at the top, or the electric cable.

Note some modern hot water cylinders come ready insulated with a bonded-on solid foamed plastic casing, and need no attention. Adding a jacket would lower the temperature of the airing cupboard too much.

ROOF SPACE

Do not rush out and insulate your roof without first applying for a grant from your local council. Because the importance of insulating roof spaces to conserve the nation's energy is now officially recognised, you should be able to get 66 per cent of the cost, or £69, whichever is the smaller; 90 per cent or £95 if you are an old-age pensioner. Normally the only exceptions are if there is some insulation present already; if you start work before getting the council's go-ahead; or if you use materials not recommended by them. If there is no access to the roof space the cost of cutting a temporary hatch should also be eligible for grant.

The current minimum thickness recommended for insulating a loft with glass fibre or mineral wool is 10cm (4in). For an average house this should cost £100–£250, and save £35–£105 thereafter. This is the amount you get a grant for, but there's nothing to stop you putting in more, at the same time or later, and cutting your heat losses still further. But as the joists in most roof spaces are made of 10cm × 5cm timber (4in × 2in), this thickness fills the space between them right up to the top; adding more may cause problems.

Rolls of glass fibre are probably the most popular insulating material. This comes in various thicknesses, so that, if necessary, you can use different ones to build up exactly the degree of insulation you want. Loose-fill materials (vermiculite, particles of mineral wool or polystyrene beads) are preferable if the roof space has an irregular shape, with awkward corners to get into, or if the joists themselves are unevenly spaced.

Flat roofs, or other roof spaces that cannot be reached, can be given some degree of insulation by installing fibre insulating board tiles (see page 169). There is no grant for this.

Once insulated the actual roof space is much colder than it was before. So if it is used to store anything that might be affected, or functions as a spare bedroom, the insulation can be applied to the roof instead of the joists. Use glass fibre enclosed in building paper, which has flanges down the sides enabling it to be stapled to the rafters. This can then be covered with boards or wallboards if desired.

TEN STEPS TO AN INSULATED ROOF

1 Calculate the area of the loft by measuring one short and one long wall on the outside of the house and multiplying the two figures together. Consult chart at the shop to find out how many rolls of glass fibre mat of desired thickness to buy. (A more accurate way to measure up is to check the distance between the ceiling joists (usually 40cm/16in), count the number of spaces and measure their length.) Also buy materials for insulating the cold water tank and any pipes that will not be covered by

178

the main insulation.

2 Assemble tools and materials: some sort of temporary light if there is no light in the loft; sharp knife to cut the glass fibre; and a large board to kneel on while working (the ceiling in between the joists is not strong enough to support your weight). Wear old clothes, rubber or work gloves and ideally a face mask. Remove watch. Take rolls of glass fibre up into the roof space before unwrapping them.

3 Clean the spaces between the joists with dustpan and brush.

4 Start at the eaves and work towards the centre of the loft. Lay one end of a roll in position. Tuck it well into the eaves (use a stick if the roof pitch is low and access difficult) but leave some space for air to get in. If you can see cracks of daylight at the eaves, or if the tiles or slates have no felt or boards underneath them, that will be sufficient. Otherwise cut the ends of the rolls at an angle so a little air can flow over them. Unroll the length, tucking it in lightly but firmly in between the joists, and cut off at the centre.

5 Repeat this process working from the opposite end, butt joining the lengths in the centre. Continue until every space is covered, leaving no gaps anywhere.

6 Where pipes or wiring run above the level of the top of the joists, poke the glass fibre underneath them. Insulate any exposed pipework separately.

7 Do not run the glass fibre underneath the cold water tank. Insulate top and sides of this separately (see page 180).

8 Insulate the top of the trap door by laying a length of glass fibre over it long enough to overlap that between the joists. Draughtproof the trap door frame with foam strip if it is a bad fit.

9 When finished rinse your hands and arms under running water to dislodge any fibres that may have stuck to your skin. (If you do experience any irritation it should soon pass.) Wash clothes used when laying glass fibre separately from other things.

10 If using loose-fill material pour it in and smooth off level with the top of the joists. You may need to block the ends of the spaces with pieces of wood to prevent the material from spilling out. Nail a board to a broomstick to reach into corners. Pour the fill into a large polythene bag to insulate the trap door.

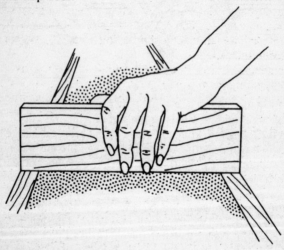

WATER TANKS AND PIPES

As well as the cold water tank, a central heating expansion tank, if present, should also be insulated, together with all exposed pipes. If this is not done while insulating the roof space, freeze-ups are more likely than before, because the insulation makes the actual roof space colder than it was.

Water tanks can be insulated with pre-cut sheets of insulating material, supplied in packs to fit most sizes of tanks; or plastic-enclosed glass fibre mat similar to the jackets used on hot water cylinders. They are simply fitted round and secured with wire or tapes. Or you can simply wrap them up with some of the glass fibre mat used for the main insulation, place a piece of plywood or chipboard on top and cover that with more mat.

Insulate pipes coming in and out of the tank, and any others not already covered, with narrow rolls of glass fibre mat, winding it on diagonally like a bandage, leaving no gaps, and securing with tape or string. Cover everything except the turning wheel or tap of stop cocks. You can also use preformed flexible pipe insulation which is made in various sizes to fit exactly round most common pipe diameters and is taped in place.

WALLS

Modern houses with cavity walls can be insulated by having the cavity filled with expanded polystyrene beads, mineral wool fibres or urea formaldehyde foam. This is not a DIY job; special equipment is required to blow the stuff into the cavities. Cost for a typical semi-detached house is from £250, and the annual fuel bill saving from £50, so it takes some time to recoup the expense.

The insulation of the solid walls found in older houses can be improved by lining them from the inside with various types of board, leaving a gap between wall and board to be filled with insulating material (see page 174). This can be more expensive than having cavity walls insulated; about £10 per square metre. But if the walls need replastering in any case it is well worth considering. A drawback, only noticeable in very small houses, is that the size of the room is fractionally reduced.

Insulating walls from outside can be done, but is not a DIY job, and is expensive; about £25 per sq metre, which could add up to £2,000 for a semi-detached house. The method used is either to fix insulating material to the walls and cover it with a protective rendering; or to apply a thick coat of rendering with insulating material mixed into it. Going to such lengths would probably not be worthwhile except for a house in a very cold, exposed position, as it would also give extra protection against weather.

A less thorough-going method of wall insulation from the inside is to treat just that part of the exterior wall which lies behind a radiator, to reduce the amount of heat flowing directly out. This is an easy and inexpensive DIY job; costing around £6 to do all the radiators in a typical semi-detached house. All you have to do is get some aluminium foil — kitchen foil will do, but a thicker grade is better — and a roll or two of Copydex multi-purpose double-sided tape. (Or you can buy a kit: Dunlop Radflector.) Simply cut the foil into foot-wide strips to make it easier to handle, in lengths equal to the height of the radiator. Stick to the wall at top and bottom; a narrow piece of wood padded with rag will help to press the foil into place behind the radiator. It works by reflecting heat back into the room, in a similar way to a shiny electric fire reflector.

A shelf above a radiator also helps to deflect heat into the room.

DRAUGHTPROOFING

To check for draughts wet the palm of your hand and hold it against the edges of doors and windows. You will probably feel a cold draught coming in; what you can't feel is your expensively heated air zooming out. Other places where warm air escapes are up unused open fireplaces, down gaps between floorboards and under skirting boards, around pipe openings in walls and ceilings, and through ceiling hatches. Curing these faults is easy and cheap: if you have to go round the entire house it should not come to more than £30, and the annual fuel saving should be £15–£40.

Draughtproofing is the only job that I can think of where you can be *too* efficient. If you have any type of heating other than a balanced flue, room-sealed appliance which draws its air from the outside, or electric central heating, some ventilation is essential or all the oxygen will be removed from the room, leaving you feeling distinctly unwell. So don't worry about a few undealt with problems. Never block up air bricks or totally close ventilating grilles, however cold it gets.

Doors First check that the door is not badly fitting for some reason that can be easily rectified (see page 21). Fit a draught excluder across the bottom. Self-adhesive plastic ones are cheap and easy to fit, but don't last for ever, particularly if you have cats, who think that they can open the door by clawing at the draught excluder. Screw-on wooden ones are more durable, better for exterior doors, and can be painted to match the door. Some have a rubber flap, some have a brush, and some a piece of felt, which rides up as the door opens and closes to clear any unevenness in the floor.

Self-adhesive foam strip is the cheapest cure for draughts around the edges of the door, where it closes on to the frame, but it gets very tatty in time, and is very hard to remove and replace. The plastic-faced kind is less prone to yellowing. Also cheap, but much more durable, are rolls of clear hard plastic strip. This is nailed on all round the door frame, and is V-shaped so that when the door closes on it the plastic compresses and fills the draughty gap. One type (Scotch V-seal) glues on, and is said to be particularly good for sliding doors. The old-fashioned metal V-strip is harder to fix than plastic.

If a door is kept closed for the winter (say a sliding patio door, or French windows) a re-usable tubular weather strip can be used to seal any gap down the middle. The tubular bit seals the gap, and is wedged in by a flat bit attached to it.

All exterior doors should have a weatherboard fitted on the outside bottom, to prevent driving rain from penetrating underneath. Patent aluminium and PVC versions of ordinary timber weatherboard moulding often come complete with a draught excluder in the form of a threshold strip which is screwed to the floor.

Another weak point in a front door is the letter box. Draughtproof this too, either with a spring-loaded flap, or the type where bristles cover the opening but allow letters to be pushed through.

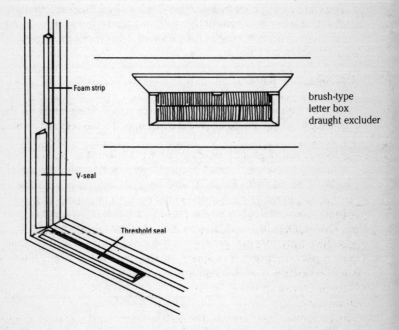

Foam strip

brush-type
letter box
draught excluder

V-seal

Threshold seal

Windows Check windows over to see if they can be made a better fit (see pages 24 and 27). Wooden casement windows (hinged type) can be draughtproofed in much the same way as doors, with foam strip or hard plastic V strip. On metal windows use foam strip, a glue-on plastic strip, or a clip-on aluminium type which snaps over the frame. On sash windows the draught coming up between the meeting rails of the two sashes can be damped down by tacking rubber strip along one rail to cover the join; this allows the window to be opened if required.

Any window that is kept closed for the duration of the winter can be crudely but effectively draughtproofed by sealing round the edges with sticky tape; masking tape is less likely than Sellotape to take the paint off with it when removed. Alternatively you can buy special exterior weather seal tape which is applied from the outside. A much less unsightly way of sealing a window is to use Scotch clear liquid draught seal. This is squeezed on from a tube, and peels of cleanly when no longer required. It is very good for sash windows.

Door and window frames If these have shrunk badly away from the surrounding masonry, and/or mortar has dropped away, draughts or rain may penetrate. Seal these gaps with some kind of flexible sealant. You can buy caulking guns for this job, but I find them as temperamental as ketchup bottles — either the stuff won't come out at all, or a lot comes out all in one place. I prefer the caulking strip type of product which you just press into place.

Fireplaces Block up an unused fireplace as described on page 34. If it is used occasionally, stop draughts rushing up the chimney the rest of the time by fitting some kind of removable panel. Depending on the fireplace design, this could be wedged in, clipped on or secured by magnets.

Floors Although hot air rises, as we all learnt at school, heat also manages to escape through ground floors. Seal small gaps underneath skirting boards with Polyfilla, or if large, fit lengths of a narrow timber moulding in the angle, pinned to the floor and mitred at corners. Cover gappy boarded floors with hardboard, or patch up as described on page 142. A timber floor can also be insulated, by taking the boards up and putting glass fibre mat in between the joists, just as in the roof space. But there should always be a 25mm air space at the top. Thick fitted carpet also will insulate and draughtproof a cold floor.

DOUBLE GLAZING

This comes in a category of its own because it is both insulating and draughtproofing. The air space created between the two leaves of glass or plastic insulates; the tightly sealed inner pane stops draughts getting in. In addition, double glazing makes a room more comfortable by reducing the cold down draught from a large area of glass (the cold radiator effect).

Whether or not double glazing is worth the money has been the subject of considerable controversy, partly because some over-keen sales organisations made exaggerated claims for it in its early days. Certainly it is not cheap. An outlay of between £300 and £1500 for a whole house, with an annual fuel bill reduction of £25–£70, takes a long time to recoup. For most people double glazing is probably something to consider *after* having done all the other things recommended to keep warmth in, cold out. But if you heat your house all day, and have a living room with large ill-fitting Victorian sash windows, or enormous picture windows, facing north or in a very exposed position, double glazing might be well worth considering for that room only.

If you are out all day, thick curtains lined with aluminium-backed lining (Milium) and drawn promptly at dusk are very effective heat conservators. It is also possible to buy special vertically hung blinds which act as night-time double glazing.

Double glazing usually means fitting a second sash inside the existing one. This can be done professionally, or you can buy various DIY kits. It can also mean fitting replacement windows, double glazed and sealed at the factory. Installing these is a professional job, worth considering if you have to have windows replaced anyway because they are falling apart.

As well as conserving heat double glazing also slightly reduces noise coming in from outside. By how much depends on the size of the gap between the two panes. A gap of 25mm is sufficient for thermal insulation purposes. A larger gap does not improve the thermal insulation, but will give improved sound insulation. If sound insulation is your major concern the gap should be at least 10cm, preferably more; up to double that.

Fitting double glazing is a DIY job that I have not yet tackled, but only because a million others have taken precedence. It cannot be considered advanced work by any means. Whatever system you choose, basically what you do is buy a patent PVC or aluminium frame, screw it to the window frame and get panes of glass or plastic cut to fit into it. A popular kit made by Polycell enables most types of window to be double glazed, whether they are the casement or sash type, or fixed. (Metal windows are a bit of a problem as the framing cannot be screwed into it; an additional timber frame has to be fixed around the metal one.) By buying different lengths of framing and cutting them down as required you can provide a suitable arrangement for your particular windows. But it is best not to have a single pane larger than about 2 sq metres (20 sq ft) as large panes of glass are difficult to handle and easy to break.

Double glazing must always be a tight fit, otherwise condensation may appear in between the two panes, and draughtproof seals should be included in the kit.

Glass is traditionally used for double glazing, but plastic is becoming increasingly popular because it is considerably cheaper, light to handle and you can cut it yourself. Some plastics may lose their crystal clarity in time, and plastic also scratches more easily than glass; but on the other hand it is virtually unbreakable.

ICI's Transpex same-day double glazing system consists of acrylic sheets and self-adhesive framing strips for fixing these to the window frame. As acrylic sheet can build up static electricity causing it to attract dust, bottles of anti-static cleaner are also provided, together with all the tools required for fixing. This type of double glazing seals the windows closed during the winter, but quick release rings enable it to be removed come spring and replaced when required. A similar system, Scotch Magnetherm, is secured with flexible magnetic strips.

An even cheaper system of double glazing is Scotch Thermal Seal. This consists of a sheet of plastic film which is secured to the window with double-sided tape, then heated with a hair dryer which shrinks it to a drum-tight, wrinkle-free fit. Although it is super-easy to fit and very effective it is not re-usable. Once you want to open the window again it's had it.

Whatever type of double glazing you fit, make sure that it can be removed in case of fire, and that all members of the household, children included, know how to do it.

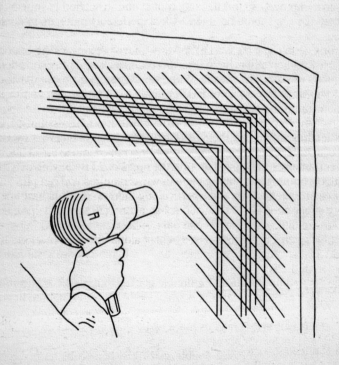

10   Safety first

Some women are put off the whole idea of DIY because they fear it is too dangerous. But it is no more dangerous than everyday life — or taking up a sport, or indulging in aerobics. Thousands of accidents occur in the home every year, and it is just as easy to fall off a stepladder when cleaning the windows as when painting the ceiling. In my own case, by far the worst accident I ever had took place in the kitchen, not when I was building a kitchen cabinet but . . . . trying to open a tin of corned beef. I poured blood, was rushed to hospital and have a scarred thumb to this day. By contrast my worst injuries from DIY work have been mostly aching muscles, protesting after hours of crawling round a floor pulling out nails, dozens of trips up and down a step-ladder, or long sessions bending over a workbench, which right themselves once the job is done.

But you do need to be aware of what the dangers *are*, if you are not to join the fair number of DIY enthusiasts who do silly things and end up in casualty departments. So please read this chapter carefully!

Other women fear that DIY work will ruin their hands. But I have found that washing up is far more damaging to the hands than DIY, gardening makes them dirtier, and sewing inflicts a myriad of needle punctures far more unsightly than the odd callous. Finger nails do sometimes get broken, but when mine are totally destroyed it's because I've been sitting at my typewriter chewing them while thinking how to compose my latest *œuvre*, not wielding a paintbrush or saw. (Builders have dreadful hands, it's true, but only because they are working every day, and rarely bother to wear gloves let alone use cissy products like handcream.)

USING TOOLS

Cutting tools Blunt blades are the *least* safe, as you have to apply excessive pressure to get them to cut, which leads to slipping. So have saws sharpened regularly, or buy replacement blades. Always keep a stock of Stanley knife blades.

Start a saw cut by drawing the saw blade gently backwards, using your free thumb as a guide, until the teeth are safely into the timber. Whenever possible use a bench hook, mitre box or vice to support the wood securely.

When using a Stanley knife to cut a line against a steel rule, hold the rule down firmly, with fingers spread out and clear of the knife, and make several light cuts with the knife rather than one heavy one. Work on a flat, non-slippery surface. In any other situation when using knives or chisels, work *away* from your body so that if the blade should slip no harm is done.

Hammers and pincers Use these as described on page 8 and you should come to no harm. Beware cheap imported claw hammers: they will bend if used to pull out a hefty nail, or far worse, can shatter in use, or the whole head may fly off.

Woodworking tools Hold timber securely with cramps or in a vice whenever possible when cutting joints. Place cramps so that the wing nut used to tighten them up is underneath, not on top where it could stick in your eye as you bend over the work. For many operations a sharp chisel should not need striking with a mallet; use both hands to hold it and work away from your body.

When changing a plane blade, use a large screwdriver and work on a board; do not hold the metal in the palm of your hand. Take care not to drop a plane blade on your leg or foot.

Blowlamps Never leave a lighted blowlamp alone for a second; turn it off if you have to leave the room. And watch which way it is pointing when you put it down. Ideally, work in an empty room; otherwise remove all curtains and soft furnishings nearby which could catch fire. The paint scrapings are very hot, so protect your hands with work gloves, and make sure that they drop on to a metal tray or dampened floorboards — never carpet or newspaper. Keep the flame well away from window panes — they crack very easily in the heat.

Power tools Unless the tool is double insulated (indicated by a square-inside-a-square symbol on the rating plate, and the fact that it has a two-core flex) it *must* be fitted with a 3-pin plug and the green/yellow earth wire *must* be connected to the earth terminal. An unearthed tool could kill you if you happened to strike metal when drilling. Always check before drilling into a wall for the possibility of electric conduit — usually directly above or below sockets and switches.

Do not use a power tool with wet hands or under wet conditions. Hold the tool steady and firm, and with a drill bit at a perfect right angle to the

188

work. Never try to correct its direction while drilling; the bit could snap dangerously. When using a sanding disc, make sure that it has stopped spinning before putting it down or touching it; a fast-spinning disc edge can cut your fingers. Do not use an old drill that makes a lot of noise or produces blue sparks; there is something wrong with the electric motor. If doing a lot of power sanding a disposable mask is a good idea if you are sensitive to dust.

If you hire large power tools that you are not familiar with go to a firm which provides free user instructions compiled by the Hire Association Europe.

Storage Keep sharp tools safely in racks or boxes; don't leave them lying around where they could fall and injure someone, especially a child. Keep sharp cutting edges guarded, and drill bits in a case or stand.

LADDERS AND ACCESS TOWERS

Stepladders Buy a stepladder in proportion to the ceiling heights in your home. You should always be able to work standing low down enough on it to steady yourself on the top with your free hand. Make sure that it has a platform at the top to take the roller tray, paint can or bucket. Check the ladder over now and then for loose screws or any damage. Always use a stepladder fully opened, and standing on a level surface. (If you use it outside on soft earth, stand it on some boards.)

Ladders Never use a ladder at a steep angle, or it may fall back taking you with it. The golden rule is 'One metre out for every four metres up'. Do not stretch out too far to either side or the ladder may slip; get down and move it along. Do not work standing so high up that you have nothing to hold on to.

Always support a ladder in some way at the bottom, depending on ground conditions. On soft earth stand it on a board and nail a batten to the board to stop the ladder from slipping. On paving or hard ground put bags of something heavy (cement or garden refuse bags filled with earth) against its foot. On uneven ground level the legs with pieces of board and secure the ladder to a stake driven into the ground behind it and firmly tied to both side rails. The top of the ladder should never rest against the edge of roofing material, or on glass or guttering, but against the wall.

Do not over-extend an extension ladder: there should always be at least a three-rung overlap. Take the ladder to the wall in the closed position and then extend it. Handling a ladder of any size is a job for two, to avoid it getting out of control and causing damage to you or your windows.

Always paint from a paint kettle hanging on an S-hook, and carry tools up in a bag (or wear a carpenter's apron with large front pocket, from work-wear shops such as Millets), so that you always have a free hand to hold on with.

Check wooden ladders in particular for any deterioration before using. Store big ladders safely locked up or padlocked, so that burglars cannot make use of them to reach your first floor windows.

Access towers For a major operation like exterior decorating an access tower is much safer and easier to work from, although more expensive to hire than a ladder (and you need a ladder as well, to climb to the platform on top of the tower). These towers have castors which enable them to be pushed along; double check that all four are locked before climbing up.

CLOTHING

Wear comfortable old clothes, but nothing loose — trailing sleeves can catch in power tools, and wide-bottomed trousers are dangerous on ladders as you can step on them. If you have long hair tie it up securely. Wear sensible shoes that will not fall off. They should be sturdy enough to give your feet some protection from falling objects and nails on the floor, so sandals, running shoes or plimsolls are all out.

Protect your hands with stout work gloves for rough, heavy work, sanding, handling glass or using a blowlamp; but not for woodwork and other skilled jobs where you need the sensitivity of exposed finger tips. Always wear rubber gloves when handling paint stripper and other chemicals.

Wear plastic goggles to protect your eyes from flying particles when wire brushing metal and hammering in masonry nails. They are also a good idea when machine sanding and using a blowlamp. If laying glass fibre insulating quilt wear gloves and a face mask, as the fibres are irritating to the skin and nasal passages.

If you have to tackle a really filthy job you can buy disposable plastic coveralls; or buy suitable togs at a jumble sale and discard afterwards.

HANDLING AND STORING MATERIALS

Always read the instructions *first*, not in the last resort, however irritatingly small the type in which they are printed. Note whether the product has any toxic properties or is inflammable, and treat accordingly: that is, work with ample ventilation or away from naked lights respectively. (A classic accident is spreading contact adhesive on a kitchen worktop without extinguishing the pilot light of a gas cooker; a sheet of flame can appear in seconds.)

When handling anything heavy and/or large, wear strong shoes, preferably boots, to protect your toes if it drops. To lift a heavy item like a bag of cement, go down on one knee and support the bag on the other before putting it into a barrow to move it. A shopping trolley can be a good way to move heavy items if you have no barrow. Move large heavy wallboards (also furniture) by 'walking' them across the floor from corner to corner.

Store paints, adhesives and chemicals safely away from children. Label anything that is not in a branded container (i.e. petrol or paraffin). Never, ever store liquids in old soft drink bottles; labelling is not enough as even if a child can read it, she still may not know it is not for drinking. Keep containers tightly closed in places where they will not be knocked over.

Do not decant white spirit into plastic cups: they gradually dissolve and the contents leak out. Remove nails from secondhand timber *before* storing it.

WORKSHOP PRACTICE

If you have a garage or shed to work in make sure that it is not a death trap. Use a properly installed socket to run lighting and/or power tools; don't rely on makeshift wiring extensions or adaptors. Make sure that the lighting is good (150W bulb — not 40W!); poor visibility is a sure way to an accident. Clean up shavings after woodwork and dispose of all rubbish, particularly oily rags; they are all fire hazards.

Don't try to work in freezing cold; cold hands fumble and slip (also cold delays the setting time of some adhesives and drying times of paint). The best kind of heater is a wall-mounted electric one; if you have to use something else make sure to place it well away from the work area. And keep some ventilation going, particularly if using toxic chemicals.

If you must smoke in your workshop use a proper ashtray with an indented rim to hold cigarettes safely, not an old tin lid. Never throw butts on the floor to ignite sawdust or shavings.

LAST WORD

One third of all DIY accidents happen to children under five who are onlookers — so tidy up as you go!

For an accident-free DIY career engrave these words on your heart or over your workbench:

DO NOT RUSH

FIRST AID BOX

Every home should have a first aid box or cabinet to cope with general family emergencies as well as any DIY accidents.
This should include:
  Cotton wool
  Roll of gauze
  5cm and 7.5cm wide bandages
  7.5cm crepe bandages
  25mm roll of zinc oxide plaster
  Pack of assorted sticking plasters
  Prepared sterile dressings (consult your pharmacist)
  Safety pins
  Pair of scissors
  Pair of tweezers

SAFE HOUSE

As well as making sure that you develop safe DIY working habits, make sure that your house is a safe house. Here's a check list of some of the most obvious dangers, which cause accidents in homes every day of the year which could all be avoided.

KITCHEN

DO	*DON'T*
Have non-slip floors with no small mats.	Have stove and sink on either side of a door.
Wipe up spilt liquids at once.	Hang tea cloths or washing over cooker.
Keep children away from cooking area.	Have cupboards high up out of reach; if you must, buy a safe solid step-stool.
Keep pan handles, spouts, flexes and sharp knives safely away from children's reach.	Leave a chip pan unattended; or fill it more than $\frac{1}{3}$ full of oil.
Keep boiling hot food and drink out of children's reach.	Fit polystyrene ceiling tiles above a cooker, in case of a pan fire.
Keep cleaning aids such as bleach and disinfectant in high cupboards.	Let electric flexes trail over a cooker hob at any time.
Use up poisons such as caustic soda or oven cleaner in one go (or store with garden chemicals in locked cupboard in shed or garage).	Handle plugs, switches or electrical appliances with wet hands.

HALL, STAIRS AND LANDINGS

DO

Have good lighting and use it; electric lights are cheap to run.

Have at least one hand rail on stairs.

Make sure all carpets are securely fitted and not worn into holes, especially on stairs.

Lay carpet on stairs so that it reaches beyond the top step and continues on to the landing.

Oil heaters: keep out of main circulation route and if children are present fix heaters to wall or floor. (Do not fill or carry when alight.)

DON'T

Cram hall full of furniture, prams, bikes etc; it is your escape route in case of fire.

Leave things lying on floor, especially on stairs.

Store newspaper or inflammable liquids in cupboard under stairs (if they catch fire the stairway funnels flames up through house).

Stack things on storage or convector heaters.

LIVING ROOM

DO

Guard open fires in the presence of children or old people (it's illegal to leave a child under 12 (7 in Scotland) alone with an unguarded fire).

Brush soot off chimney regularly and have it swept annually.

If chimney catches fire, or wall gets hot, call the Fire Brigade — it's free.

Unplug TV and electric fires at night.

DON'T

Keep matches and lighters, sewing equipment, breakable ornaments or any sharp objects where small children can get at them.

Have trailing electric flexes to trip people up.

Run flex under carpets.

Put hot ashes in a plastic dustbin.

Keep fires or TV sets close to curtains. Hang mirrors over fireplaces where they tempt people too close.

Dry washing around an open fire, oil heater or radiant electric fire.

Stack things on storage or convector heaters.

Light a fire with petrol or paraffin (use firelighters); or try to make it draw with newspaper (use an old tin tray or metal sheet).

BEDROOMS

DO

Check that electric blankets have BEAB or B.S. 2345 marks and use strictly according to manufacturer's instructions. If missing, get *Electric Blankets* leaflet from local electricity board. Have serviced every three years.

Switch off all radiant heating appliances at night.

Fit guards to open or radiant fires in children's or old people's rooms.

Buy nursery equipment that shows the British Standard kite mark. This shows it has been made to the highest safety standards.

DON'T

Smoke in bed.

Give children candle nightlights; use low wattage mains or battery lights.

Dim a bedside lamp by covering it; fit a low wattage bulb.

BATHROOMS

DO

Store medicines and pills in child-proof medicine cabinet.

Keep razor blades out of children's reach.

Fit handrails etc. for an old person; but get specialist advice first.

Put cold water in bath first, then hot, for both children and the old.

Have gas water heaters serviced annually. Turn them off before entering bath. (Bathroom water heaters should always be the sealed, balanced-flue type.)

Have a non-slip floor without mats.

Have pullcords for lights and wall heaters.

DON'T

Block up an air brick or any other ventilator fitted.

Leave children alone in bath.

Bring any electrical appliance into bathroom except a shaver, used in a shaver socket.

Let cigarette ends or anything hot touch a plastic bath; apart from possible damage, some can burn.

GENERAL

<table>
<tr><td>DO</td><td>DON'T</td></tr>
</table>

DO	**DON'T**
Check that all cigarettes are out before getting into bed.	Run an iron or any other electrical appliance from a light fitting.
Shut as many doors and windows as possible at night as a safety precaution against fire spreading.	Paint polystyrene ceiling tiles with gloss paint (it causes fire to spread more rapidly).
Fit a smoke detector. This will give very early warning of fire.	Delay between switching on a gas appliance and lighting it.
Unplug all electrical appliances not in use.	Overload electric sockets with lots of appliances plugged into adaptors: one appliance, one socket is safest.
Keep a torch and spare fuse wire or cartridges near consumer unit (fuse box).	Store aerosol containers near heat (even on a sunny windowsill), burn or puncture them; they can explode.
See that all gas fires and radiant electric fires have integral guards and keep well clear of furnishings.	Toss hot cigarette ends or spent matches into waste paper baskets.
Be extra safety conscious at Christmas: cards, decorations and the tree are all fire hazards. Keep cards away from an open fire.	

ADHESIVES

Modern adhesives are marvellous and enable almost anything to be stuck firmly to almost anything else. But it's important to pick the right one for the job, as although the packaging may suggest that each one is the universal wonder product, they are mostly quite specialised.

No adhesive will work properly if the surfaces are dirty or greasy, or if they do not meet properly (a badly cut woodwork joint, or two pieces of a broken plate not properly aligned). Depending on the type of adhesive, bonding strength may be reached in seconds or hours. If you try to rush a slow-setter, failure will be your reward. Most adhesives are easiest to apply, and set more rapidly, in warm conditions.

With many adhesives some form of pressure has to be applied to hold the two surfaces together until an initial bond has been achieved. This can vary from holding the item in your fingers for a few seconds; putting it under a weight; binding or bridging the join with sticky tape; or putting the item in cramps or a vice. In many cases adhesive alone is quite enough to make a very strong joint, but if great stress is expected some reinforcement is needed, often in the form of screws.

Woodwork For joining wood and general household repairs to wood PVA (polyvinyl acetate) adhesives are unrivalled. They consist of a creamy white liquid which is clean and easy to spread on, and bonds firmly enough for the item to be handled in about 20 minutes, if further work has to be done. Alternatively the item can be left for 24 hours, when full bonding strength will have been reached. These adhesives all require light but sustained pressure on the join during the initial drying period.

Some brand names: Evo-Stik Resin 'W', Woodfix, Bostik 8, Humbrol Extra Bond Dunlop Woodworker.

Being water-based, PVA adhesives are not suitable if the joint is likely to get wet. For joining wood out of doors use a synthetic resin adhesive such as Cascamite. This consists of a tin of powder which is mixed with water. Joints have to be kept under pressure for 6 hours.

Decorating For hanging wallpaper use a cellulose paste suitable for the type of paper (see page 60). For sticking vinyl wallcovering to itself (where lengths overlap) use a special overlap adhesive or Copydex latex adhesive.

For putting up ceiling tiles you can use either a strong mix of wallpaper paste, or a special polystyrene adhesive which comes ready mixed in a squeezy bottle. The latter is stronger and has some gap-filling properties which help level the tiles if the ceiling is uneven. Always apply ceiling tile adhesive all over, not in blobs which creates air spaces which help flames to spread in the event of fire.

Adhesives for tiling can be in powder form to mix with water, or ready-mixed. The former are the most economical. Special types are made for areas which get very wet (shower cubicles) or hot (around fires or boilers); and for uneven surfaces or when tiling over old tiles.

Laying floorcoverings Adhesives used for sticking down hard floor-coverings such as cork and vinyl tiles, or a hardboard underlay, are a thick, mastic-type, some based on rubber resin, some on synthetic latex. Mastic-type adhesives are also used for fixing panelling to walls, for which purpose they may be packed in a caulking gun, as the adhesive is applied in lines, not spread on overall in the usual way. Make sure to buy a flooring adhesive recommended for the type of floor covering involved. Some brand names: Evo-Stik and Dunlop flooring adhesives, Dunlop cork adhesive, Evo-Stik Gun-o-prene.

Carpet is most conveniently fixed with double-sided tape. This is also used to secure carpet tiles and sheet vinyl at key points.

Craft work For any light sticking job use one of the clear glues supplied in small tubes, which work quickly and are almost invisible when dry. Some brand names: PAC, Evo-Stik Clear, Uhu, Bostik 1.

For young children a PVA-based white adhesive is preferable, as it will wash off hands and out of clothes, is non-toxic and non-addictive. Some brand names: Childsplay, School glue, Bostik Stik 'n' Fix.

For just sticking paper use a paste or gum such as Lion or Bostik paper paste.

China, glass, metal, hard plastics Joining these hard substances calls for a super strong adhesive: epoxy resin, named by the Guiness Book of Records as the world's strongest. These consist of two parts, resin and hardener, which come in separate tubes. When mixed together they slowly harden — about twelve hours at room temperature, or 30 minutes in a low oven. During this time the join must be held together; sticky tape is usually sufficient. Apply the adhesive thinly, and if any does squeeze out scrape it off when it has solidified a bit but not hardened. Crockery mended with epoxy resin can be safely soaked and washed in hot water and used for boiling liquids. Some brand names: Araldite, Araldite Rapid, Power Pack.

A similar type of adhesive, (Bostik 7), sets more quickly (about five minutes) and is more effective on hard plastics.

Yet another two-part adhesive, Bostik 10 Hyperbond, consists of a tube of adhesive and a bottle of activator. It is very convenient to use as there is no mixing: you brush the activator on to one surface with the brush provided, and squeeze beads of adhesive on to the other one. An initial bond is obtained in three minutes, so it's quite practical to sit and hold the join tightly together without bothering with any sticky tape. This adhesive is unique in that it will bond an oily surface, which must make it ideal for car and bike repair work.

General purposes If you don't go in for woodwork, and want one adhesive that will do everything, use a small pack of contact adhesive. This will stick virtually anything to anything with only hand pressure. But don't try it on polythene or expanded polystyrene (tiles, sheet, and the small round balls used in craft work) as it dissolves them.

However, in DIY contact adhesive is the one used for veneering, whether with real wood, or more likely, laminated plastic. (For this you will need a large tin; coverage rate should be given on it.) Contact adhesives used to be called impact adhesives because they gave an instant bond, which meant that you had to be sure to get the sheet in the right place the first time. But now you get a few minutes to adjust the position, provided that no pressure is applied. These adhesives are applied thinly to both surfaces with a plastic spreader and left for 15 minutes until they are touch dry before the surfaces are brought together.

Contact adhesive is also good for small woodworking jobs, particularly in situations where cramping would be difficult, as when sticking loose bits of moulding or marquetry back on a vertical surface.

Some brand names: Evo-Stik Time Bond, Bostik 3, Superstik, Thixofix.

Also general-purpose are the new Super glues (cyanoacrylates). These work very rapidly (in about 30 seconds) but are so expensive that they are only practical for small-scale jobs. They also have the unfortunate ability to stick your fingers together. Some brand names: Loctite, Bostik (supplied with solvent).

Note contact and other solvent-based adhesives are highly inflammable. Don't smoke, and make sure pilot lights are put out.

Solvents In order to remove adhesive which has got on to fingers, clothes or carpets you need to know what dissolves it. Work quickly; the harder the adhesive becomes the less well the solvent will work.

Adhesive	*Solvent*
Clear craft glues	Acetone (nail varnish remover)
Contact adhesive	Acetone
Double-sided tape	Lighter fluid
Epoxy resin	Acetone or methylated spirit (Nitromors paint stripper if hard)
Flooring mastics:	
synthetic latex	Water
rubber resin	Petroleum solvent
Latex	Lighter fluid
PVA adhesives (woodworking and others)	Water
Super glues	Special solvent from manufacturer
Synthetic resin (outdoor wood glue)	Warm soapy water
Tiling adhesive	Water
Wallpaper adhesives	Water

SECURITY

Check the security of your home by imagining that you went out without the key, and trying to get in without it. If you can do so, by using a 'hidden' spare key, climbing through a back window, using a plastic card to push the front door lock open, or putting your arm through the cat flap and reaching a key, so can the burglar and the vandal.

Someone's home is broken into by thieves about once every 90 seconds. The national annual figure for housebreakings is well into the hundreds of thousands, and rises every year, which means that every year the chances of *your* becoming the victim of thieves rises accordingly.

Police records show that some 90 per cent of housebreakings are facilitated by inadequately secured doors and windows. So good door and window fastenings are your first line of defence. You can fit nearly all of them yourself, so there's no excuse for not being adequately protected.

Every outside door of the home should be fitted with a mortice deadlock, ideally one with a British Standard kite mark. A deadlock is a lock with a bolt that cannot be retracted without using the key. When you move into a new home it is always a good idea fit new outside door locks. An old lock, perhaps the original one fitted by the builder, could be a cheap 2-lever model which any thief can open in seconds. And if subsequent owners have fitted new ones, there's no way of knowing if they have been careless with spare keys, and someone somewhere out there has access to your home in his pocket. Also many front doors have only a springlatch or nightlatch, the kind fitted on the inside face of the door, with a knob that can be used to fix the bolt in the closed position at night. These were originally meant to be used in addition to a mortice lock, for extra protection at night. As many cannot be deadlocked from outside, they are easily opened. If you have one of these, leave it there and fit a mortice deadlock in addition. These are the ones that fit into a recess cut into the edge of the door. Making a recess involves boring a series of holes with a large auger bit, then finishing off with a chisel. If this is not possible, replace the original nightlatch with a modern one which features a mechanism that triggers automatically every time the door is closed, so that the bolt cannot be moved without the key.

In addition, exterior doors should have bolts at top and bottom for extra security when locking up at night. (Double doors, such as French windows, should also have bolts.) Conventional surfaced-mounted bolts (any large sturdy ones, not tiny things with short screws) are easiest to fix, but mortice bolts, fitted into a recess in the edge of the door, are more secure.

Which is the most important, front or back? In one sense whichever door one leaves by is the most vulnerable because it cannot be bolted from the outside and its lock is its only protection while the house is empty. However more than 60% of break-ins are effected from the back, where the thief can work unseen by people in the street. So pay

199

particular attention to all locks, bolts and window fastenings at the back. Also keep any side gate bolted, just to make life that bit more difficult for the would-be thief.

Many people totally neglect to lock or even close windows. But a window, for a thief, is as normal a way into a house as a door, so windows should never be left open while a house is unoccupied. Not even that tiny pantry window that surely only Puss can get through; many thieves are juveniles who will have no trouble at all in wriggling in. And old-fashioned fasteners are highly insecure. Those on sash windows can often be opened by sliding a knife blade between upper and lower sashes — try it for yourself as a test. All windows should be fitted with modern locking fastenings, which cannot be opened even by the prowler who breaks the glass and puts his hand through in an attempt to open the window from the inside. The Copydex Houseguard range of window locks caters for virtually all types of window, and is designed for quick and easy fixing.

Having fitted all these locks, don't let them give you a false sense of security; take care of the keys. Always carry them with you, never leave them under mats, on top of door sills or on strings inside letter-boxes. And *use* the bolts on exterior doors, every night as a routine, not just now and then.

Another good habit to develop is always to lock the garage doors, even if you're only going out for a few minutes. An open garage with no car in it is an open invitation to thieves, many of whom work on a very casual basis, taking opportunities as they present themselves. An open garage not only shrieks 'they're out!' it can also provide a good selection of housebreaking implements, perhaps a ladder to reach that open window.

Another way not to advertise your absence is to leave a light on in at least one room when you go out in the evenings; and draw curtains before you go. If you've read the Electrics chapter you'll know that leaving lights on is *not* going to cost a fortune. Don't make it the hall light, which thieves recognise as a simple-minded ruse.

When going off for longer periods, or on holiday, ask a neighbour to keep an eye on the house, and at least to remove leaflets and free sheets left sticking out of the letter-box, or lying visibly inside a glassed-in porch. If possible get them to draw curtains night and morning (never leave curtains half-drawn as a compromise; it's just a dead give-away.) Or buy a time switch with a long delay period to switch a light on and off at appropriate times.

Always check the credentials of strange callers. Some thieves carry out reconnaissance by pretending to be meter readers or local authority inspectors. Genuine officials and workmen understand and will not mind. If you live alone, fit a door chain and always use it. A spyhole in a solid door is also a good idea. They are very easy to fit; all you have to do is drill a hole.

Finally, if you are not sure about the security of your home, do not hesitate to contact your local Crime Prevention Officer. There is one at every police station and it is his job to help and advise members of the public. He will call at the house, inspect it and make recommendations about locks and other considerations.

EMERGENCY ACTION

Emergency	What to do	What not to do
Bleeding	*Minor cuts*: wash with soap and water. Dry, holding up high if possible to stop bleeding. Cover with sticking plaster. *Deep cuts*: Pinch edges of wound together or press hard on it. If possible raise it above heart level. Maintaining pressure, slip a pad or dressing over the wound and secure firmly with a bandage knotted over the wound. Call ambulance or get medical help. If bleeding continues apply a second dressing over the first.	Do not apply a tourniquet. This is now thought to be unnecessary and possibly damaging in amateur hands.
Burns and scalds (scalding is burning by hot fluid)	Apply cold water: run tap over limb or plunge into sink. Apply water-soaked pad if burn on face; give sips of water for a scalded mouth and throat. Continue for ten minutes to relieve pain. Cover burn with clean bandage or cloth and get expert help if anything more than superficial.	Do not use ice; tests have shown that cold water is best. Do not put person into a cold bath as this is too much of a shock to the system. Do not remove any clothing burnt on to the skin.
Chemical burns	Wash the substance away immediately from skin or eyes with running water. If pain does not subside fairly quickly get medical help.	

EMERGENCY ACTION

Emergency	What to do	What not to do
Chip pan on fire	Turn off heat. Cover pan with saucepan lid, frying pan or damp cloth. Leave covered until cool.	Do not move the pan — air movement will fan the flames, and towards you. Do not throw water or sand on it — burning fat will explode.
Clothing on fire	Wrap person in blanket; rug or overcoat. If your own clothing catches alight fall to the ground and roll over and over to smother flames, preferably on carpet. Treat burns as above.	Do not let the person run around in a panic and fan the flames; use force if necessary to get them to the ground.
Electric shock	If the person is still in contact with the electrical appliance or fitting, unplug it or switch off at the mains before touching them. If this cannot be done stand on a rubber mat or put on wellingtons and push person free with a long broom handle. If they have stopped breathing give artificial respiration. Call doctor in any case.	Do not touch a person until detached from the electric current or it may pass through you. Do not rush into action with wet hands.
Flooded ceiling	If a lot of water accumulates on top of a ceiling its weight eventually causes the whole thing to fall down. So puncture it in several places with a bradawl and let the water flow through into containers (you may need dustbins).	

EMERGENCY ACTION

Emergency	What to do	What not to do
Frozen and burst rising main (the main water pipe entering house, usually in kitchen)	Turn off main stop tap on the pipe. Turn on cold water tap to empty out any water; leave on. Play a hair dryer on the frozen pipe to melt the ice; or wrap it in cloths and pour boiling water over until water flows from the tap. If the greater volume of the frozen water has fractured the pipe bind it up tightly (ideally with pipe repair tape) until the plumber comes.	Do not use a blowlamp to thaw out a pipe; plumbers do but they know just how much heat to apply.
Other frozen and burst pipes	If possible locate and turn off a stop tap which controls the part of the system where the trouble is. Find out by turning off a stop tap then opening taps and flushing loos to see if water stops flowing. (Far-seeing types get to know their stop-taps in advance.) Once water has been drained away from the trouble spot proceed as above: thaw the ice and bind up fractured pipe. If the hotwater system is involved turn off gas or oil central heating; damp down a solid fuel appliance.	When venturing into the roof space to investigate stop taps and cisterns tread only on the timber joists. If you step on the ceiling in between, your foot will go straight through.

If you turn the water back on after making a temporary repair, do not turn it fully on, but keep it to about half the normal flow.

If you go away during the winter do not leave the house stone cold. Programme heating to come on for short spells at midnight and dawn. If there is no automatic heating, turn off all stop taps. |

EMERGENCY ACTION

Emergency	What to do	What not to do
Frozen waste pipe	If a tap drips constantly it can cause a sink, washbasin or bath waste pipe to freeze up overnight. Thaw the pipe out with a hair dryer or hot cloths. Until washer is replaced (see page 38) keep plug in plughole at night.	
Gas escape	Although the natural gas now used throughout Britain is not poisonous, a build-up of gas can still cause an explosion. If you smell gas first look for left-on cooker taps, blown-out pilot lights or accidentally turned-on gas-fire taps. Open window to dissipate gas before relighting. If this is not the cause turn gas off by the mains gas tap (by gas meter), open windows and call the Gas Board's night or day emergency service (free).	Never look for a gas escape with a naked light.
Fires, small	Shut door and windows of room where fire is. Use water for most; especially chimney fires. But if an electrical appliance is involved unplug it or switch off at mains first. Burning oil heater: the burning oil spills out on to the floor. If carpeted use water, but on a hard floor the oil and water do not mix, so use a smothering technique. Earth or sand are good for smothering small fires (say in a waste paper bin) but not ones involving oil or fat.	Do not go away and leave a supposedly extinguished fire, or throw clothing or fabric involved in a fire into a waste

206

EMERGENCY ACTION

Emergency	What to do	What not to do
	Rugs, blankets and overcoats are all good smotherers; effective for TV fires.	bin. Fabric can smoulder for quite a long time and spontaneously re-ignite.
	If your efforts do not succeed within a few minutes *shut the door on the fire* and call the fire brigade; give your address clearly.	
Fire, serious	Get everyone out of the house at once, shutting as many doors and windows as possible. Call fire brigade; give your address clearly. Do not go back inside. If possible fight fire with garden hoses until firemen arrive.	Do not open a door that is hot to the touch to investigate a fire. Flames will only surge out and spread, and it will already be too late for you to rescue anyone trapped inside.
Fire, trapped by	If trapped in an upstairs room because stairs are ablaze, close the door and any fanlight or other opening, and block door bottom with bedding. Go to window and shout for help. If room fills with smoke lean out of window, or lie on floor where it is least concentrated; cover mouth with cloth. While waiting for rescue try to prepare a rope from bedding and sheets and tie it to the bed or other heavy furniture in case you have to make your own escape. If you cannot make a rope, hang by your hands from window sill and drop down.	Never jump from a window; always drop by your hands. If above the first floor wait for rescue until the last possible moment. Do not fit double glazing which would trap you in case of fire: that is a fixed-pane type with hard-to-break panes. Do not have window bars unless they can be removed in case of fire.

USEFUL ADDRESSES

Aaronson Board Centre (Holdings) Ltd.
Aro House
18–19 Long Lane
London EC1
(01 606 8050)
Manufacturers of Contiboard and Contiplas; booklet available.

J.D. Beardmore & Co. Ltd.
3 Percy Street
London W1P OEJ (also at Bristol and Hove)
(01 637 7041)
Vast range of reproduction cabinet fittings.

British Carpet Manufacturers Association
Margam House
26 St. James Square
London SW1Y 4JH
(01 839 2145)

Buck & Ryan Ltd.
101 Tottenham Court Road
London W1
(01 636 7475)
Extensive range of tools

DIY Plastics Ltd.
Suffolk Way
Abingdon
OX14 5NP
(0235 30666)
Specialists in plastic sheet for double glazing and other purposes. Mail
order catalogue available.

The Eaton Bag Co. Ltd.
16 Manette Street
London W1V 5LB
(01 437 9391)
Mail order supply of rattan, bamboo, raffia, cane, grass matting, etc.

Fibre Building Board Organisation Ltd.
1 Hanworth Road
Feltham
Middlesex TW13 5AF
(01 751 6107)
Advice and information on use of fibre building boards.

General Woodwork Supplies
76 Stoke Newington High Street
London N16 5BR
(01 254 4543)
Stockists of hardwood including mouldings, cut to size if required.

Magnet Southerns
(260 branches — see local telephone book).
Doors, windows, kitchen units, wardrobe units, timber and man-made boards. Free all-colour catalogue.

W.H. Newson Group
61 Pimlico Road
London SW1 8NF (also at Battersea, Sunbury-on-Thames, Reigate)
(01 730 6262)
Large range of softwood and hardwood, including mouldings, doors, kitchen units worktops, fencing etc.

Rustins Ltd.
Waterloo Road
London NW2
(01 450 4666)
Comprehensive range of wood treatment and finishing products, and specialist paints.

Sarjents Tools
44–52 Oxford Road
Reading
(0734 586522)
Mail order supply of quality tools; catalogue £1.50.

Woodfit Ltd.
Kem Mill
Whittle-le-Woods
Chorley, Lancs. PR6 7EA
(02572 66421)
Specialists in furniture fittings. Mail order catalogue 50p.

METRIC CONVERSIONS

For those to whom the metric system is still a mystery, the conversion tables below offer a rough and ready guide. They are intended to fix in your mind some of the key measurements which occur frequently. Please note that they are only approximate; imperial and metric measurements do not convert this neatly into one another. To convert linear measures exactly use a metric tape or ruler.

Linear measure
(10mm = 1cm; 100cm = 1 metre)

3mm = $\frac{1}{8}$in
5mm = 3/16in
6mm = $\frac{1}{4}$in
8mm = 5/16in
10mm = $\frac{3}{8}$in
12.5mm = $\frac{1}{2}$in
15mm = $\frac{5}{8}$in
20mm = $\frac{3}{4}$in
22mm = 7/8in
25mm = 1in
5cm = 2in
10cm = 4in
15cm = 6in
20cm = 8in
25cm = 10in
30cm = 12in
35cm = 14in
40cm = 16in
45cm = 18in
50cm = 20in

60cm = 24in
30cm = 1ft
60cm = 2ft
90cm = 3ft
120cm = 4ft
150cm = 5ft
180cm = 6ft

Liquid volume
150ml = $\frac{1}{4}$pt
250ml = $\frac{1}{2}$pt
500ml = 1pt
1 litre = 1 $\frac{3}{4}$pt
2 $\frac{1}{2}$ litres = $\frac{1}{2}$ gallon
5 litres = 1 gallon

Weight
125g = $\frac{1}{4}$lb
250g = $\frac{1}{2}$lb
350g = $\frac{3}{4}$lb
500g = 1lb
1 kilogram = 2lb

GLOSSARY

Although I have tried to avoid using technical terms in this book there had to be some, and you may come across more in other DIY books, or in estate agents' particulars and survey reports if buying a house.

Aggregate Gravelly material mixed with cement to make concrete.

Architrave Moulding that covers the join between a door or window lining and surrounding plaster.

Arris Sharp edge where two surfaces meet.

Arris rail Triangular horizontal member of closeboarded fence.

Astragal Type of ornamental timber moulding.

Balanced flue Special type of flue which enables heating appliance to burn air from outside the house and requires no chimney.

Baluster Vertical member of stair handrail.

Banister Handrail supported by the balusters.

Batten Narrow strip of softwood.

Beading Narrow timber moulding.

Beam Structural timber or steel member which runs horizontally.

Bevel Any angle which is not a right angle; e.g. the decorative shaped edge of a mirror.

Blistering Paint defect — bubbles raised by hot sun.

Blooming — Varnish turning white on surface.

Bond Different ways in which bricks are laid to give strength to a wall (e.g. stretcher bond, English bond).

Breeze block Precast concrete building block.

Cames Lead strips holding glass in lattice windows.

Cantilevered Any structure that extends beyond its vertical support.

Cavity wall Modern wall made from two leaves of masonry with a gap between to improve insulation.

Cement Powdered lime and clay mixed with water, used to make mortar and concrete.

Cess pit Underground storage pit for sewage used in country dwellings not on mains drainage. Has to be emptied regularly.

Cistern Water tank, usually cold water storage tank in roof, or WC cistern.

Close-coupled suite Modern WC where the cistern is close to or integral with the WC pan.

Concrete Building material made by mixing cement, sand and small stones with water. Reinforced concrete also contains metal bars.

Consumer unit Set of fuses or circuit breakers, incorporating switch to turn off mains electricity supply.

Corbel Stone or timber structural support bracket.

Cove Shaped cornice between wall and ceiling, formerly plaster, may now be polystyrene.

Crazing Network of hairline cracks in paint, rendering or plaster; makes material pervious to water.

DPC Damp proof course — waterproof layer built into masonry to prevent damp rising up wall from ground.

Dado Lower part of a wall decorated differently from upper part.

Dormer Window which sticks out of roof line.

Downpipe One carrying rainwater from roof via gutters to ground.

Dry rot Timber decay caused by fungus *Merulius lacrymans*.
Started by high moisture content of wood. So-called because fungus renders wood dry and brittle. Very serious; hard to eradicate as can spread through brickwork to find fresh damp timber.

Eaves Lowest overhanging part of roof.

Embrasure Deep window recess.

Face Front of a wall; or to cover one material with another.

Fascia A flat vertical cover; board to which guttering is fixed.

Feather edge Wedge-shaped boards used in closeboarded fencing.

Ferrous Metal containing iron.

Flue Chimney or pipe allowing smoke, gases and fumes to escape.

Footings Concrete-filled trench that gives support to a wall.

Foundation Concrete raft or piles on which house is built.

Frieze Decorative horizontal band at top of wall.

Frog Hollow in upper surface of some bricks.

Furring Narrow strips of wood (battens) fixed to wall to support panelling.

Gable Triangular upper part of wall enclosed by ends of the roof; gable end — that wall.

Galley kitchen Small kitchen built like a corridor.
Galvanised Coated with zinc to prevent rust.
Glazing Fitting glass into windows.
Glazing bars Wooden or metal bars in a window.
Grain varnish Paint and varnish brushed or combed to imitate the grain of wood.
Grinning Paint fault: when colour of previous coat shows through.

Hardcore Broken masonry compressed to form a solid base on which to pour concrete and form a hardstanding or path.
Headstone Central stone of an arch.
Hipped roof Roof which continues down over top of gable end walls.
Horns Excess pieces of timber left on door stiles so that its corners are not damaged in transit; cut off when door is hung.

Ingle nook Deeply recessed fireplace.
Impermeable Not porous.
Impervious Cannot be penetrated.

Jamb Top and sides of a window or door frame.
Joists Timber used to support floors and ceilings.

Kerf The cut made by a saw.
Keystone Central stone of an arch which prevents it from collapsing.

Lath Thin strip of wood nailed to timber to support plaster, as in lath and plaster ceilings and partitions in old houses.
Light Pane of glass in window, or the space for it.
Lintel Structural support over door or window opening.
Loggia Open-sided covered extension to a house.

Mezzanine Intermediate storey.
Module Standardized unit of size used in building design.
Mortar Mixture of sand and cement used to bond bricks and other masonry.
Mullion Slender vertical division between windows.
Muntin Vertical centre pieces in a panelled door.

Newel Main post supporting stairs and banisters.
Noggings Short horizontal members spanning between the vertical timbers in a stud partition.

Ogee Type of timber moulding.

Out of plumb Not vertical.
Ovolo Type of timber moulding.

Parquet Wood floor made of small blocks, often in herring-bone pattern.
Parting bead Vertical timber separating two parts of sash window.
Partition Any wall dividing up space.
Party wall Wall between two separate dwellings.
Pebble dash Wall finish consisting of gravel embedded in mortar.
Pile Concrete or timber column sunk into ground to form foundation.
Plaster Mixture of lime, cement, sand and water used to cover walls and ceilings.
Pointing Filling or finishing mortar joints in brickwork etc.
Polyvinyl acetate (PVA) Material derived from ethylene gas used as a base for adhesives, floor coverings, paints and fabrics.
Purlin Horizontal roof timber crossing rafters in the centre.

Rafter Sloping timber joists supporting roof tiles or slates.
Rails Horizontal pieces in a panelled door, or components in furniture.
Rebate or rabbet Ledge cut along the edge of a piece of timber.
Rendering Protective coat of cement mortar on external wall.
Reveal Side of a window or door opening.
Ridge board Top, horizontal timber in a roof.
R.S.J. Rolled steel joist; often used to support upper floor when load-bearing wall removed between two rooms.
Rust Reddish powdery surface on iron, formed by oxidisation after exposure to water or damp air.

Screed Thin layer of plaster on wall; or thin layer of concrete used to level a floor.
Septic tank Similar to cess pit, but sewage is slowly destroyed by bacterial action and water drained away underground.
Shellac Coloured resin used to make varnish.
Sherardized (screws) Steel coated with zinc to prevent rusting.
Shingles Wood roof or wall tiles, usually cedar.
Siphonic suite Super-efficient type of WC.
Size Thin solution of glue used to seal walls, usually before hanging paper.
Soakaway Area of rubble laid underground to allow water to drain away.
Soda block Abrasive block, water soluble, used for cleaning and keying paintwork.

Soffit Any horizontal surface overhead; soffit board, one underneath overhanging rafters.

Span Horizontal distance between two supports.

Stiles Vertical members of panelled door; also window frame.

Stopping Proper word for filling deep holes; also material for so doing (Brummer stopping).

String Side member of staircase or ladder.

Stucco Plaster-like material used to coat exterior wall surfaces.

Stud partition Dividing wall made from timber covered both sides with plasterboard or similar.

Swedish putty Filler made by mixing paint with cellulose filler.

Template Cardboard or thin metal pattern.

Trussed rafter Factory made rafters occurring at frequent intervals in roof space; too close to allow space to be converted to room.

Turpentine Solvent obtained from pine tree gum, superseded in decorating work by white spirit obtained from petroleum.

Tyrolean finish Roughcast exterior finish without pebbles, made by applying mortar with a special gun.

Wainscot Timber lining or panelling on lower part of walls

Wall plate Horizontal timber laid on walls to carry joists or rafters.

Wall ties Pieces of galvanised metal used to bind the two leaves of a cavity wall together at intervals.

Waney edge Timber edge with bark still on.

Water hammer Knocking sound which can occur when a tap is turned off quickly, caused by shock waves.

Wet rot Timber decay caused by fungus *Coniophora cerebella*. Present when water content is extremely high; dies off when wood dries out.

Woodworm Common name for larva of common furniture and other woodboring beetles, which feeds on timber eventually weakening it. Serious if not treated early.

Index

THE BOOK OF LISTS
by David Wallechinsky, Irving Wallace and Amy Wallace

A truly unique compendium of offbeat learning and fun!

* The 10 worst films of all time
* 7 famous men who died virgins
* 10 sensational thefts
* 15 famous events that happened in a bathtub
* 23 of the busiest lovers in history
* 9 breeds of dog that bite the most
* 10 doctors who tried to get away with murder
* The 14 worst human fears

Plus much, much more!

Hundreds of lists on every subject imaginable involving people, places, happenings, and things, with biographies, nutshell stories and lively commentary throughout. Includes lists specially prepared for this book by Johnny Cash, Bing Crosby, Charles M. Schultz, Pele, Arnold Palmer and many others.

0 552 10747 6   £2.25

THE COMPLETE BOOK OF SELF-SUFFICIENCY
by John Seymour

The Complete Book of Self-Sufficiency is a book for all seasons. Whether you live in town or country, on a farm or in a cottage, in a house with a garden or a flat with a window-box, this book has something for you.

If you want to bake your own bread, brew your own beer, make your own cheese, pickle your own onions, this book will show you how.

If you want to make hay, milk a cow, smoke a ham, design a dairy, convert to solar energy, this book will show you how.

If you just want to grow your own vegetables, bottle your own fruit, dry your own herbs, this book will demonstrate exactly what to do.

The Complete Book of Self-Sufficiency is an invaluable manual packed with illustrations, and every illustration tells its own story, shows you what you need and how to do it.

John Seymour is everywhere recognised as the expert in self-sufficiency. He has lived the life for twenty years, and here he gathers all the expertise he has acquired into one authoritative volume.

0 552 98051 X   £8.95

THE U.S. ARMED FORCES SURVIVAL MANUAL
edited by John Boswell

For decades the U.S. Armed Forces have provided their men and women with instructions about survival under the most diverse conditions. The manuals, pamphlets, and directives that they have issued cover subjects from food to first aid, shelter and fire building. Because of the thousands of hours that have gone into the preparation and testing of the procedures contained in this book, *The U.S. Armed Forces Survival Manual* is probably the most comprehensive and thoroughly tested survival manual ever published.

This complete guide provides the reader with invaluable life-saving information including:

* The psychology of survival; dealing with fear and panic
* How to cope with hazards from poisonous snakes, lizards, and water animals; danger from mammals
* First-aid instruction including basic life-saving measures
* How to make a fire; basic cooking techniques
* Where to find shelter; the proper clothing for various climates
* Finding food and water in the natural surroundings
* Map reading; topographic signals, colours, grids and coordinates
* Compass reading and its uses
* How to survive under unusual conditions; nuclear attack, natural disaster

For complete information on every conceivable emergency situation, this book is an invaluable companion.

0 552 99105 8   £2.95

THE CASTROL MOTORCYCLE TEST MANUAL
How to Pass Parts 1 and 2
by Gordon Cole

As soon as a motorcyclist gets on his machine he joins a million or so others who are using the roads at any one moment. For your own safety and that of other people it is very important that you should learn the correct way to ride your motorcycle by taking a training course, and that you should be able to demonstrate your competence by passing a test.

Over the years various books have been written to help the learner motorcyclist to pass his proficiency test, but until now none of them has explained the marking procedure in detail. THE CASTROL MOTORCYCLE TEST MANUAL explains very clearly just what the best candidate is expected to do, how many faults he is allowed to make, and, more important, how he can avoid making any faults at all while he carries out Part 1 and Part 2 of the motorcycle test.

THE CASTROL MOTORCYCLE TEST MANUAL has been written with the aim of getting you through both parts of the test at your first attempt. It will also help you afterwards to enjoy the freedom and independence that motorcycling has to offer.

0 552 99100 7   £3.95

OTHER NON-FICTION TITLES AVAILABLE
FROM CORGI BOOKS

While every effort is made to keep prices low, it is sometimes necessary to increase prices at short notice. Corgi Books reserve the right to show new retail prices on covers which may differ from those previously advertised in the text or elsewhere.

The prices shown below were correct at the time of going to press.

☐ 09332 7	GO ASK ALICE		Anonymous	£1.50
☐ 12548 2	KLAUS BARBIE: BUTCHER OF LYON		Tom Bower	£2.50
☐ 11772 2	'H' THE AUTOBIOGRAPHY OF A CHILD PROSTITUTE AND HEROIN ADDICT		Christiane F.	£1.75
☐ 12675 6	MAFIA PRINCESS	Antoinette Giancana & Thomas C. Renner		£2.50
☐ 12466 4	MARTIN ALLEN IS MISSING		Anton Gill	£1.95
☐ 12389 7	INDECENT EXPOSURE		David McLintick	£2.50
☐ 12378 1	CORONER TO THE STARS		Thomas Noguchi	£1.95
☐ 12710 8	BARDOT		Glenys Roberts	£2.95
☐ 99105 8	U.S. ARMED FORCES SURVIVAL MANUAL		John Boswell	£2.95
☐ 99100 7	CASTROL MOTORCYCLE TEST MANUAL		Gordon Cole	£3.95
☐ 12585 7	INDEFENSIBLE TREATMENT		Rebecca Hall	£2.95
☐ 99146 5	THE SKYWATCHER'S HANDBOOK (cover)		Colin A. Ronan	£6.95
☐ 98051 X	THE COMPLETE BOOK OF SELF-SUFFICIENCY		John Seymour	£8.95
☐ 10747 6	THE BOOK OF LISTS	David Wallechinsky, Irving Wallace & Amy Wallace		£2.25
☐ 11681 5	THE BOOK OF LISTS 2	David Wallechinsky, Irving Wallace & Amy Wallace		£2.25

ORDER FORM

All these books are available at your book shop or newsagent, or can be ordered direct from the publisher. Just tick the titles you want and fill in the form below.

CORGI BOOKS, Cash Sales Department, P.O. Box 11, Falmouth, Cornwall.

Please send cheque or postal order, no currency.

Please allow cost of book(s) plus the following for postage and packing:

U.K. Customers—Allow 55p for the first book, 22p for the second book and 14p for each additional book ordered, to a maximum charge of £1.75.

B.F.P.O. and Eire—Allow 55p for the first book, 22p for the second book plus 14p per copy for the next seven books, thereafter 8p per book.

Overseas Customers—Allow £1.00 for the first book and 25p per copy for each additional book.

NAME (Block Letters) ....

ADDRESS ....

....